CANADIAN SOCIAL PROBLEMS SERIES

GENERAL EDITOR
Anne-Marie Ambert
YORK UNIVERSITY

Divorce in Canada

Anne-Marie Ambert

ACADEMIC PRESS CANADA

Printed in Canada
Composition by CompuScreen Typesetting Ltd.

ISBN: 0-7747-3040-4

5   4   3   2   1   84   83   82   81   80

Acknowledgements

I have greatly benefited from the detailed comments and challenging perspectives of my colleagues, Fred Elkin and Evelyn Kallen. I wish to thank them for the enormous amount of time they so generously contributed to the review of an earlier draft of this book. To David Perlman's expert and elegant editing, I owe much in rectifying my French way of writing English. Last, but certainly not least, my gratitude to my secretary, Jean Liebman, who processed the many drafts of this book.

Anne-Marie Ambert
July 1979

Contents

List of Tables

Preface

This book follows the tradition set by other volumes in the series in that it is a "first." Indeed, at the time of publication, there is no sociology or psychology monograph on divorce in Canada, other than government reports and demographic publications.[1] Even Americans, who show much enterprise in the realm of texts, have published very few texts dealing specifically with the sociology and psychology of divorce, although many literary, journalistic and "how-to" books have been brought out. So far, the general approach has been to include in textbooks on marriage and the family a few chapters focusing on marital dissolution and related material, such as remarriage. Unfortunately, these chapters are too brief to even begin to do justice to the scope of the subject.

The topic of divorce has generated a reasonably extensive, but by no means sufficient, amount of research. Furthermore, these research results are scattered in such a wide array of journals that the accumulation of knowledge in this field is extremely difficult. For instance, in order to obtain a fairly complete overview of the topic, one has to survey journals in sociology, family life, psychology, psychiatry, counselling, social work, paediatrics, health and demography, as well as law. For this book, the North American journals and texts in

1. Less than ten articles out of over eighty listed in a 1976 bibliography on the family dealt with divorce in Canada, and the majority appeared in one journal, the *Journal of Comparative Family Studies*: see M.D. Bracher and P. Krishnan, "Family and Demography: A Selected Canadian Bibliography," 7, Summer 1976, pp. 367-372.

all these areas except law were thoroughly reviewed. This review was limited to materials on separation, desertion, divorce and remarriage, and did not extend to an investigation of other forms of family structure such as, for instance, widowhood, single-mother families following unwed pregnancy, and remarriage after widowhood. Moreover, some references have been omitted when the books or articles in question could not be located or obtained, in order to avoid a reliance on bibliographies already drawn up. I found it necessary to read all the material on hand since several errors of reporting or of interpretation of data were detected in some well-known family textbooks.

Since I am based in Toronto, more data were obtained about divorce in Ontario and Toronto than elsewhere in Canada. However, this geographic emphasis is simply a matter of expediency and practicality and does not reflect any regional preference or bias. Above all, I exploited Statistics Canada material as much as was feasible, especially the 1976 Census and 1975 divorce statistics, which were the latest ones available. Graduate schools of social work across Canada have certainly generated much material, however uneven in quality, that could be tapped by subsequent researchers. In view of the scarcity of material in Canada (see bibliography) it is quite obvious that the topic of divorce is an unexploited gold mine for Canadian researchers.

More to the point, our society would benefit much from a research programme concerning marital dissolution, which has shown a dramatic upturn since 1968. As indicated in the chapters of this book, more people than ever divorce, remain divorced, or remarry, and more children than ever are involved in these situations about which practically nothing is known. We can use American material to some extent. Certainly, because of socio-cultural proximity as well as economic and cultural dominance, many of the theories developed in the U.S.A. apply to our situation and much of the American data resemble Canadian data. Nevertheless, numerous differences exist between the two countries in this respect; differences stemming from national uniqueness, ethnic composition, divisive and unifying political factors, and history, and we deserve our own data, research and references.

Much American literature on divorce was developed some ten to twenty years ago when divorce rates had already climbed dramatically, while Canadian rates have climbed only very recently and, because of the socio-historic time element, may never reach the magnitude of the American ones. Events that happened twenty years ago had a meaning then which they no longer have necessarily; the experience of divorce and its consequences in 1979 cannot be the exact replica of that of the 1950's when attitudes and socio-economic conditions were different. For these and many other reasons, the provinces and the federal government should fund research on the topic of marital dissolution more generously. A concerted effort to devise a multi-disciplinary and coordinated programme would be very helpful.

In order to make the task of Canadian researchers and students easier, the bibliography at the end of the book presents a separate section on Canadian material, excluding legal literature and, for the most part, theses.

The intent of this book was to review the literature as thoroughly as possible and to highlight the various problem areas discerned. I also developed several frameworks in order to organize the material and especially to pinpoint those areas which beg for research. Hypotheses and potential research questions are raised throughout the text. In addition, I interviewed twenty divorced, separated, and deserted persons, and eight remarried couples, with the specific intention of gathering case material to illustrate hard data and theoretical propositions. Several of these cases are presented in the text. Some material was also derived from the structured autobiographies which students have been writing in my classes in past years. However, the phenomenon of marital dissolution by legal means is only now reaching the student age group as it affects their own parents. Therefore, I have very little material in this respect compared to what I will have five years from now, since it has only been in the last two years that a large number of the offspring of dissolved marriages have come of age. In other words, divorce trends in the parents of schoolgoers are obvious but they are only beginning to appear in the parents of the university student population.

With this climbing of the age pyramid by the children of divorce, the consequent visibility of divorce among university students will probably result in a shift of contents and ideology in the various courses on marriage and the family offered on campuses. In the past, students showed very little interest in divorce. In fact, in teaching the sociology of the family, I have generally omitted my prepared sections on divorce because I have noticed a decrease in students' attention span and a raising of their defence mechanisms at that point. The message conveyed was "Don't talk to us about it. We don't want to hear about it. We want to get married. Divorce is for the others. It will never happen to me." Yet, within these past few years, some of these same students have already divorced and so have some of their parents, brothers and sisters. Moreover, many divorced women are returning to further their education on campuses. The mood is becoming more realistic. Divorce is no longer something out there, but something that can happen to anyone. At an age when they dream of marital bliss, students are now also considering the possibility of thorns, of slow erosion, and of a quick devastation, like a bush fire. They are no less hopeful generally, but are more open to a reality that their older sisters and brothers desperately wanted to brush aside. And, by the same token, students are also discovering new beginnings ... such as remarriage and rekindled happiness for their elders and perhaps also for themselves.

DIVORCE IN CANADA

1 Divorce—A Social Problem?
An Introduction

More and more, the Canadian public's attention is being drawn to the question of divorce. Divorce occupies an increasing number of pages in the family sections of our dailies, and magazine articles abound on the topic, discussing everything from the legal aspects of divorce, the children in divorce, what precedes and follows divorce in the lives of the individuals concerned, to, finally, future trends in divorce. A large group of psychiatrists, social workers, and family experts, as well as child psychologists, have specialized their practices to serve the emotional needs of those who are divorcing, divorced, or trying to avoid divorce.

As we will see in the next chapter, there are reasons for this upsurge of interest in and concern about divorce; more people than before are divorcing, contemplating divorce, remarrying, or settling down into a single way of life after a marriage (or several) that turned sour. Therefore, divorce is at the very least a social situation and reality. However, until recently it was held to be a social *problem*.[1]

---

1. For definitions of social problems, see P.B. Horton and Gerald R. Leslie, *The Sociology of Social Problems*, New York: Appleton-Century-Crofts, fourth edition, 1970, p. 4; R.L. Henshel and A.-M. Henshel (Ambert), *Perspec-*

Indeed, theologians have generally disapproved of divorce, and, in the past, moralists have all, if not condemned it, at least decried it as dysfunctional and disruptive of the stability of society, the family, the welfare of children and the well-being of adults. Even sociologists imply that divorce is undesirable when they place it in the category of family disorganization. This categorization represents a normative judgement of the desirable family structure,[2] rather than an empirical concept.[3] Psychiatrists, child psychologists, and social workers who treat people suffering from emotional or personal problems, have similarly pointed out the deleterious consequences of divorce in terms of the toll of personal hardship it exacts from people. But, as others point out, for each case of a divorced person or a child from a divorced family treated by a specialist, there are four or more others in the same condition who do not need treatment, because the situation is not causing *them* unmanageable suffering.[4] These same specialists are now recognizing this truth and are pointing out that there is more suffering caused by unhappy marriages, to people who choose to remain in a bad marriage, than by divorce *per se*, and that, moreover, the suffering occasioned by the latter is often of shorter duration than that caused by the former.

It is now widely accepted in specialists' circles, and even among laypersons, that an unhappy marriage can be more detrimental than divorce, both to adults and to children. Similarly, many marriages which end in divorce have been more beneficial to the individuals involved than many legally

tives on Social Problems, Don Mills, Ont.: Longman of Canada, 1973, pp. 2, 3; I. Tallman and R. McGee, "Definition of a Social Problem," in *Handbook on the Study of Social Problems*, edited by E.O. Smigel, Chicago: Rand McNally, 1971, p. 43.

2. J. Sprey, "Family Disorganization: Toward a Conceptual Clarification," *Journal of Marriage and the Family*, 28, November 1966, p. 399.

3. D. Martindale, "Social Disorganization: The Conflict of Normative and Empirical Approaches," in *Modern Sociological Theory*, edited by H. Becker and A. Boskoff, New York: Dryden, 1957, p. 341.

4. As Gardner points out, most children of divorce do not need psychiatric help. See R.A. Gardner, "Psychological Aspects of Divorce," in *American Handbook of Psychiatry*, edited by S. Arieti, second edition, vol. 1: New York: Basic Books, 1974, p. 507.

intact unions are and will ever be.[5] It is also being recognized that divorce can be viewed as a beginning rather than an ending: the beginning of a new life, often a much better life. Divorce can be regarded as the termination of suffering for many people rather than as the beginning of suffering itself. Renne defines unhappy marriages as a social disability, an illness, and divorce as a remedy.[6]

Divorce is, first of all, an *effect*, or a *result;* it is a response to a stimulus. Whatever the terminology used, divorce *follows* something and that something is an unhappy union either for one spouse or, more generally, for both spouses, and the children themselves when children are involved. Divorce *per se* cannot be said to cause everlasting problems for adults. Certainly, it is traumatic, for most people, to separate and then divorce, and many persons would still prefer to be in an unhappy union than to be divorced. Certainly, there are problems that follow directly from the act of divorcing: financial problems, problems of loneliness, of lowered self-esteem, of adjustment to a new life, and so on. But there are also joys that follow: the discovery of new freedom, of one's potential, of new friends, of another relationship, relief at no longer being in a tension-ridden situation. In both the short and the long term, the joys probably outweigh the problems.

There are, however, many vantage points from which one can consider divorce. Divorce should not be romanticized, because it *does* signify a failure: the failure of a marriage. But there are more marriages that have failed and remain legally intact than have ended in divorce.[7] Indeed, "stable marriages are not necessarily happy marriages, since stability may be related as much to a lack of attractive alternatives to marriage as it is to positive gratifications within marriage."[8] Divorce is

5. J. Bernard, *Remarriage*, New York: Russell & Russell, 1971 re-issue, p. 86; C. Kirkpatrick, *The Family as Process and Institution*, New York: Ronald Press, 1953, p. 518.
6. K.S. Renne, "Health and Marital Experience in an Urban Population," *Journal of Marriage and the Family*, 33, May 1971, pp. 338-350.
7. J.N. Edwards, "The Future of the Family Revisited," *Journal of Marriage and the Family*, 29, 1967, pp. 505-511.
8. H.L. Ross and I.V. Sawhill, *Time of Transition: The Growth of Families Headed by Women*, Washington, D.C.: The Urban Institute, 1975, p. 39.

neither a pure blessing nor a pure hell. What we should rather say is that a good marriage is a blessing and a bad one, sheer hell.

The point of view adopted in this book is that divorce can be treated as "a normal process with specific tasks to be mastered, recognizable stresses to be dealt with, and satisfactions and goals to be sought for."[9] Divorce *per se* is not the villain it has been made out to be; it is generally both good and bad. Divorce is a reaction to the problem of an unhappy or bad marriage. Unhappiness is a very subjective state and one cannot quibble too much about what an unhappy marriage "means"; it is a marriage in which one or both spouses are unhappy or *feel* unhappy as a direct result of their union or their interaction.

Unfortunately, social statistics are such that they provide us with knowledge of divorce only. We actually know very little of marriages, good or bad. We have no census of unhappy marriages, but we have court records and statistics of divorces. Therefore we cannot study all the types of marital failure; we can only study the ones that are recorded in official statistics—the ones that ended in divorce. And, oddly enough, *these* marital failures are often of lesser magnitude than many that will never show up in court statistics. We do have some incidental knowledge of unhappy marriages, but it is very sketchy, statistically speaking, for the data thus far accumulated depend largely on a few isolated studies, which are often of people who have come to the attention of various experts, such as marriage counsellors, and are therefore a very select sample. Consequently, we have to study the *statistical* social problem, divorce, rather than the real problem: the unhappy marriages which cause divorce.

In the next chapter, we will delineate divorce trends over the years and will present demographical data on divorce in Canada. In Chapters 3 and 4, we will go on to study the causes of divorce: why so many marriages fail, and, more particularly, why more and more people are resorting to terminating a

9. R. Wiseman, "Crisis Theory and the Process of Divorce," *Social Casework*, 56, 1975, p. 212.

failing union rather than remaining in it. We will be dealing with large-scale or societal causes as well as with personal ones. Then, in Chapter 5, we will try to gain some understanding of the phases involved in the process of divorcing; and in Chapter 6 we will focus on the life of the divorced person. In Chapter 7, we will present the available knowledge on the children of divorce, and will offer a series of questions for future research. Chapter 8 will focus on remarriage and then the book will conclude with some general comments.

There is no one theoretical framework which can be adopted for a study of divorce in this country, for there is a wide array of explanatory propositions. I have chosen to use as many perspectives as possible, since such a format allows for a more complete and thorough presentation of the topic. By contrast, focusing upon particular theoretical models would have imposed stringent limitations upon the scope of this book; a book which attempts to further our understanding of divorce in Canada, and to offer a pragmatic sociological framework within which research questions, as yet unanswered, are raised and presented for future analysis.

2   Divorce: Who, Where, When, Why?

How many people divorce each year in Canada? How have divorce rates changed over the years? Is divorce spread uniformly throughout the provinces? How old are people at divorce and how long have their marriages lasted? How old were they when they first married? Are second divorces also on the increase? These are some of the questions that will be explored in this chapter, along with a consideration of other variables such as the number of children involved, grounds for divorce, and socio-economic status, language, and religion.

We will present the relevant statistics on divorce found in the Canadian Census and other government publications in order to establish the magnitude and the distribution of marital dissolution in the population. We will look into divorce rates over a period of time and will compare the Canadian situation with that of the U.S.A. The latter shows some of the highest divorce rates in the world at the moment and is highly relevant to Canadians since the societies are so closely related culturally and economically.

CHANGE OVER TIME

In comparison to the United States where divorce rates have always been high, Canada has had very low rates. Indeed, until the 1960's, Canada had one of the lowest divorce rates of any westernized country.[1] But with the reform of divorce laws here, on July 11, 1968, divorce rates climbed dramatically and

1.   F. Elkin, *The Family in Canada*, Ottawa: The Vanier Institute of the Family, 1964, p. 142.

have continued to do so nearly each year, as seen in Table 1. Rates doubled within one year of the passage of the new laws, and have nearly doubled again since 1969, that is, within a nine-year period. Rates are now over four times what they were before the passage of the new laws. (Higher divorce rates have also been observed in the U.S.A., with the introduction of more permissive divorce laws in various states.)[2] It is also important to note that before 1968 neither Quebec nor Newfoundland had provincial divorce courts; neither had Prince Edward Island and Ontario before 1945 and 1930 respectively. In these provinces, until these dates, divorce cases had to be

TABLE 1

Incidence of Divorce in Canada by Year:

Frequencies and Rates (per 100,000 population)

YEARS	FREQUENCIES	RATES
1921	558	6.4
1931	700	6.8
1941	2,462	21.4
1951	5,270	37.6
1961	6,563	36.0
1967	11,165	54.8
1968	11,343	54.8
1969	26,093	124.2
1970	29,775	139.8
1971	29,685	137.6
1972	32,389	148.4
1973	36,704	166.1
1974	45,019	200.6
1975	50,611	222.0
1976	54,207	235.8
1977	55,370	237.7
1978	57,155	243.4

Source: Statistics Canada, *Vital Statistics*, Vol. II, *Marriages and Divorces, 1975*, Ottawa, July 1977, Table 11, pp. 28-29. Statistics for 1976 and 1977 from an advance bulletin from Statistics Canada, December 4, 1978, p. 6; statistics for 1978 from another advance bulletin from Statistics Canada, September 4, 1979, p. 10.

2. D.M. Stetson and G.C. Wright, Jr., "The Effects of Laws on Divorce in American States," *Journal of Marriage and the Family*, 37, August 1975, pp. 537-547.

processed through the federal parliament and the only accept-able ground was adultery.[3]

By way of comparison with Table 1, the number of divorces in the U.S.A. reached one million for the first time in 1975. The rate per 100,000 population was 480; it had been 320 in 1969 and 220 in 1960. Two million and fifty thousand adults and well over a million children were involved in divorce in 1975. One marriage out of every three, on average, will end in divorce in the U.S.A.,[4] whereas the rate is closer to one in five in Canada, although there are wide fluctuations from province to province; some estimates have recently placed the attrition as one in two or three in Alberta. However, estimates vary depending on their basis: the total married population or the number of marriages each year. Americans had as high a divorce rate in 1960 as Canadians currently have and their rate is now well over twice that of ours, perhaps a presage of things to come in Canada. But Canadian rates may never go as high as the American rates because of differences in popula-tion composition and also because of the time element: Canada had a later start and the time differential may have allowed us to adapt to changing social situations in a less disruptive manner.

With regard to the frequency and number of divorces, the new 1976 census gives us a break-down of the national population according to their marital status, including the category of the separated. These figures are presented in Table 2. As we have already pointed out, divorced and separated people are not equally distributed among the provinces: they are over-represented in certain provinces which have had a higher divorce rate for quite a few years and under-repre-sented in others, such as in Quebec where "high" divorce rates are a relatively recent phenomenon.

3. R. Pike, "Legal Access and the Incidence of Divorce in Canada: A Sociohistorical Analysis," *Canadian Review of Sociology and Anthropology*, 12, 1975, p. 117.
4.   J.L. England and P.R. Kunz, "The Application of Age-Specific Rates to Divorce," *Journal of Marriage and the Family*, 37, February 1975, pp. 40-46. Moreover, it has also been estimated that over half of all *recent* marriages will end in divorce in the U.S.A.: S. Preston and J. McDonald, "The Incidence of Divorce Within Cohorts of American Marriages Contracted since the Civil War," *Demography*, 16, 1979, pp. 1-25.

TABLE 2
Canadian Population by Marital Status
1976

	NEVER MARRIED		MARRIED		SEPARATED		DIVORCED		WIDOWED		TOTALS
	F	%	F	%	F	%	F	%	F	%	
Males	5,666,590	49.49*	5,310,925	46.38	163,310	1.42	119,035	1.03	189,665	1.65	11,449,525
Females	5,006,005	43.36**	5,282,230	45.76	217,440	1.88	183,500	1.58	853,900	7.39	11,543,080
	10,672,595		10,593,155		380,750		302,535		1,043,565		22,992,605
	46.41%***		46.07%		1.65%		1.31%		4.53%		100.00%

*Percentages on the basis of total males in the population.
**Percentages on the basis of total females in the population.
***Percentages on the basis of the total population.
Source: 1976 Census of Canada, *Population, Demographic Characteristics, Marital Status,* Ottawa: Statistics Canada, Cat. 92-824, bulletin 2.5, Table 17. The percentages are provided by the author.

The percentages presented in Table 2 for separated and divorced persons may appear very small. However, it should be kept in mind that they were arrived at on the basis of the total male or female population of *all* ages, including babies. Had children been excluded, the percentages would have risen for all the categories except the never married. In 1976, nearly three out of every hundred persons were separated-divorced and 7.49% were formerly married (separated, divorced, widowed). In terms of sex, there were a greater number and proportion of separated and divorced women than men, in part because men remarry more and sooner, and in part because men have a higher mortality.

TABLE 3
Separated and Divorced Persons by Sex
in 1971 and 1976

| | SEPARATED | | | | DIVORCED | | | |
| | 1971 | | 1976 | | 1971 | | 1976 | |
	F	%	F	%	F	%	F	%
Males	162,060	1.50*	163,310	1.42	74,360	0.65	119,035	1.03
Females	209,305	1.94*	217,440	1.88	100,760	0.93	183,500	1.58
	371,365		380,750		175,115		302,535	
	1.72%**		1.65%		0.81%		1.31%	

*Percentages on the basis of total males and total females.
**Percentages on the basis of the total population for each year.
Source: 1976 Census of Canada, *Population, ibid.* The percentages are provided by the author.

It is even more instructive to compare the separated and divorced categories in 1971 to the same categories in 1976 and to relate them to increases in the overall population. In Table 3, when we look at the separated category, we observe a slight decline between 1971 and 1976: there were, in 1976, proportionately fewer separated men and women. It is possible that the comparatively higher separation percentages in 1971 are attributable to couples who had not yet entered the divorce stream, while in 1976 such couples enter divorce more rapidly and therefore do not remain for long in the category of the separated. It could also be that some people who were divorced in 1971 preferred to identify themselves as separated, since the latter has a less definite moral connotation, while, in 1976, with a greater public tolerance for divorce, such camouflage would not be judged necessary so often.

When we compare the sexes in the separated category in 1971 and 1976, we notice that, in both instances, there were more separated women than men; and that this difference is much the same in both these years. Actually, this statistic is somewhat strange, as, in theory, each separated woman should have a separated male counterpart in the population. In other words, each separated woman should have a separated ex-spouse somewhere so that the *numbers* should be equal for both sexes. If a separated woman divorces, she passes into the divorced category and so does her ex-spouse. And when the separated woman's husband dies, she becomes a widow—he is no longer a "live" statistic. What is the reason for the difference between the numbers of separated men and women? Is it because separated men more often live with another woman and pass themselves off as married? This is a plausible explanation, for if we return to Table 2, we see again that we have more married men than married women; and this without polygamy! Is this because separated women were easily located by the census, while a substantial number of separated men, being either too unstable or else transients, were not enumerated? Or is it because separated women admit to being separated more readily than men: the latter can pass themselves off as single or married. This is again possible because there were more single males than single females in Canada in 1976 (see Table 2).

When we turn to the category of the divorced in Table 3, we note that its numbers have increased substantially since 1971. This is due to the double fact that more people divorce each year, and that those who have divorced earlier but have not remarried remain in this category over the years. For these reasons, it is to be expected that the proportion of divorced people will increase for a few years to come, even if divorce rates stabilize.

The second striking fact in the divorced category is the

sexual difference. The proportion of divorced men has risen by
0.35, from 0.68 to 1.03, while that of women has increased by
0.65, from 0.93 to 1.58: nearly double the male increase. Again,
this statistic reflects the accumulation of women in the
divorced category because of a lower rate of remarriage than
that of men, a phenomenon to which we will often refer in this
text.

In order to obtain a complete picture of the *real* extent of
marital dissolution we also need to take desertion, whether
terminal or temporary, into account. Desertion has been
defined by the Canadian Welfare Council as "a separation of
the spouses which is against the will of one spouse ..."[5] In the
United States, Baber has estimated that there is one case of
desertion for every four divorces.[6] However, these figures may
well be conservative; Kephart, for one, estimates that there is
probably as much desertion as divorce.[7] Under Canadian law,
many desertion cases eventually end up as divorces after a
number of years. However, an examination of the legal
grounds used by petitioners leads me to the belief that perhaps
a sizeable percentage of desertions do not end up as divorces;
at least not for many years.

A final observation concerning overall divorce rates is that
second divorces have increased since the 1960's, but have
remained fairly stable since 1972. In 1975, 5.6% of all the
persons who were divorcing (5.3% of the divorcing men and
5.4% of the divorcing women) had already been divorced at
least once before.

PROVINCIAL DISTRIBUTION

Divorce rates vary enormously from province to province,
although geographic clusters appear. The lowest rates generally go to the Maritime provinces. Indeed, Newfoundland,
Prince Edward Island, and New Brunswick have rates that are
far below the national average, along with one Prairie prov-

5. Canadian Welfare Council, *A Study of Family Desertion in Canada,*
Ottawa, 1968.
6. R.E. Baber, *Marriage and the Family,* New York: McGraw-Hill, 1953, pp.
493-494.
7. W.M. Kephart, "Occupational Level and Marital Disruption," *American
Sociological Review,* 20, August 1955, p. 460.

TABLE 4
Incidence of Divorce by Province
for 1975, 1976, 1977, 1978:
Frequencies and Rates (per 100,000 population)

PROVINCES	FREQUENCIES				RATES			
	1975	1976	1977	1978	1975	1976	1977	1978
Newfoundland	380	424	456	427	69.2	76.0	81.1	75.0
Prince Edward Island	75	116	136	135	63.1	98.1	113.1	110.7
Nova Scotia	1,597	1,753	1,802	1,960	194.2	211.6	215.7	233.1
New Brunswick	758	938	961	1,153	112.3	138.5	140.0	165.9
Quebec	14,093	15,186	14,501	14,865	227.8	243.6	230.8	236.6
Ontario	17,485	18,589	19,735	20,534	212.6	224.9	235.7	243.1
Manitoba	1,984	1,941	2,085	2,189	194.8	190.0	202.2	211.8
Saskatchewan	1,131	1,207	1,474	1,428	123.2	131.0	157.4	150.7
Alberta	5,475	5,697	5,843	6,059	309.7	309.9	307.6	310.4
British Columbia	7,534	8,231	8,251	8,265	306.6	333.7	330.4	326.7
Yukon	43	67	59	65	206.1	306.8	274.4	299.5
Northwest Territories	56	58	67	77	148.1	136.1	154.7	176.6
CANADA	50,611	54,207	55,370	57,155	222.0	235.8	237.7	243.4

Sources: Statistics Canada, *Vital Statistics, op. cit.,* Table 11, pp. 28-29 for data for 1975; Advance Information Sheet, December 5, 1978, p. 6 for 1976 and 1977, and September 4, 1979, p. 10, for 1978.

ince, Saskatchewan, and the Northwest Territories. Nova Scotia's rates are higher than those of the other Maritime provinces.

By way of contrast, the highest rates go to provinces with higher per capita income, higher immigration rates, and a higher level of economic development and urbanization.[8] Indeed, if we compare rural and urban areas in 1976, we find that 1.53% of the urban population was divorced as compared to only 0.65% of the rural population. It is true that many rural dwellers migrate to cities in order to divorce or do so after divorce, either to escape stigma or to improve their economic condition and marital chances; these migrants contribute perhaps to the relationship between urbanization and divorce.

When we examine the distribution or prevalence of divorce across the provinces (rather than the incidence of persons who are divorcing within one year), we find that not all provinces are similar. British Columbia's population at one extreme is 2.13% divorced, with Ontario occupying a more intermediate position of 1.33% divorced, similar to the national average of 1.31%. Quebec, because it obtained a provincial court only

TABLE 5
Percentages of 1975 Divorces Which are Redivorces
by Sex and Province

PROVINCES	MEN	WOMEN
Newfoundland	1.8	1.1
Prince Edward Island	6.7	1.3
Nova Scotia	4.3	4.6
New Brunswick	3.4	3.3
Quebec	1.5	1.4
Ontario	5.2	5.5
Manitoba	5.5	6.0
Saskatchewan	3.5	5.0
Alberta	9.8	10.0
British Columbia	11.2	11.0
Yukon	7.0	9.3
Northwest Territories	3.6	3.6
CANADA	5.3	5.4

Source: Statistics Canada, *Vital Statistics, op. cit.*, Table 14, pp. 31-37.

8. See Pike, *op.cit.*, p. 130.

recently, showed a mere 1.05% of its population as divorced and New Brunswick, with low divorce rates, had only a 0.82% divorced population.

When we look at the distribution of recurrent divorce by province, we observe that the provinces with the highest rates of divorce also have the highest rates of second (or third) divorces, with the exception of Quebec which shows one of the lowest rates of recurrence. This may be related to the fact that it is only since 1974 that Quebec's divorce rate has caught up with the national average. Before that, Quebec's rates were already dramatically lower than those of Canada as a whole, for legal and religious reasons. Therefore Quebec has not yet had the time to show a high rate of subsequent divorces in its population.

AGE OF DIVORCED AND SEPARATED PERSONS

One important aspect of the profile of marital dissolution is the age groups in which divorced/separated people are distributed. We unfortunately do not have statistics on desertion but they are presumably subsumed under the separated category, although it is conceivable that many such persons identified themselves as married in the census. Because statistics on divorce and separation *by age* are found in two separate census publications, the age brackets are not uniform. Thus we have to present two tables, one for the divorced and one for the separated.

We looked at *overall* sex differences in Tables 2 and 3, and, in this respect, at trends in recent years. In this sub-section we look at sex differences by age groups. First, let us point out that the median age of divorced persons in Canada in 1976 was 42.7 years: 44.4 years for men and 41.5 years for women. (No median was provided for separation.) The figures in Table 6 represent all divorced persons in 1976 (prevalence), whether they had just divorced and were to remarry within the next three months, or had been divorced for many years, including those who will never remarry.

The number of divorced persons in the population diminishes drastically when people reach their mid fifties. This is

TABLE 6

Prevalence of Divorced Persons by Sex and Age Group, 1976: Frequencies and Percentages

AGE GROUPS	TOTAL		MALES		FEMALES	
	F	%	F	%	F	%
15-19 years	775	0.25	225	0.18	525	0.28
20-24	10,220	3.37	2,610	2.19	7,610	4.14
25-29	35,735	11.81	12,200	10.24	23,540	12.82
30-34	43,895	14.50	16,060	13.49	27,830	15.16
35-39	40,215	13.29	15,160	12.73	25,055	13.65
40-44	38,790	12.82	15,265	12.82	23,525	12.81
45-49	36,910	12.20	15,270	12.82	21,640	11.79
50-54	32,625	10.78	13,530	11.36	19,100	10.40
55-59	23,415	7.73	10,075	8.46	13,340	7.26
60-64	17,740	5.86	7,980	6.70	9,760	5.31
65-69	11,395	3.76	5,275	4.43	6,115	3.33
70-74	6,175	2.04	2,950	2.47	3,230	1.76
75 +	4,645	1.53	2,405	2.02	2,230	1.21
CANADA	302,535	100.00	119,035	100.00	183,505	100.00

Source: Statistics Canada, 1976 Census of Canada, Population: Demographic Characteristics. Marital Status by Age Groups, Ottawa, April 1978, Cat. 92-825, adaptation of Table 22. Percentages derived by author.

TABLE 7

Prevalence of Separated Persons by Sex and Age Group, 1976: Frequencies and Percentages*

AGE GROUPS	TOTAL		MALES		FEMALES	
	F	%	F	%	F	%
15-24 years	33,685	8.82	9,770	5.98	23,915	10.95
25-34	103,110	27.02	42,165	25.83	60,940	27.91
35-44	79,840	20.92	33,455	20.49	46,385	21.24
45-54	76,605	20.07	33,520	20.53	42,085	19.27
55-64	51,240	13.42	24,005	14.70	27,235	12.47
65+	38,070	9.97	20,320	12.44	17,750	8.13
CANADA	381,545	100.00	163,235	100.00	218,305	100.00

*The figures are slightly different from those of Tables 2 and 3 and may represent errors in Census computations; they are derived from different catalogues of the Census.
Source: Statistics Canada, 1976 Census of Canada, Labour Force Activity, Labour Force Activity by Marital Status, Age and Sex, Ottawa, September 1978, Cat. 94-805, Table 12. Percentages derived by author.

due to two main factors. First, people generally divorce when they are younger. In fact only approximately 12% of all divorces take place between spouses who are older than fifty. Second, since people divorce younger they also remarry younger, so that the majority of those persons who divorced several years ago are already remarried and are not included in this table.

Another observation is that the decline in divorced persons after the age of fifty is even more drastic among women than men, because women divorce earlier and remarry somewhat younger, and also because they become widows instead of divorcées: marriages which would otherwise have been dissolved by divorce are dissolved by death. Because of lower longevity among men, we see that the difference that we noted earlier in the numbers of divorced men and women diminishes drastically in the older age groups.

For both sexes, the age bracket that contains the highest proportion of divorced individuals is 30-34 years because this group encompasses the median age at divorce for women and follows the most common age at divorce for both men and women; that is, 25-29.

If we turn to Table 7 and examine the distribution of separated persons in 1976 by age groups and sex, we observe very similar trends. But it is somewhat surprising that the categories above fifty-five years of age still contain so many separated individuals. It would be interesting to know if these are preludes to forthcoming divorces. In this case, these figures would forecast somewhat higher divorce rates among older persons for the years 1977 and onward. Or do they represent many perpetual separations (including desertions) and temporary separations?

AGE AT DIVORCE, DURATION OF
MARRIAGE AND AGE AT MARRIAGE

Table 8 gives the ages of husbands and wives who were divorcing in 1975. Table 9 provides an overview of the trends in this area in terms of averages and medians. The average and median ages at divorce for both men and women have steadily decreased since 1969. They have decreased much more than the average age at marriage has: the latter has remained fairly

TABLE 8
1975 Divorces by Sex and Age Group:
Frequencies and Percentages

AGE GROUPS	HUSBANDS		WIVES	
	F	%	F	%
less than 20 years	44	0.1	294	0.6
20-24 years	2,685	5.3	6,301	12.4
25-29	10,442	20.6	12,352	24.4
30-34	9,980	19.7	9,293	18.4
35-39	7,470	14.8	6,434	12.7
40-44	6,083	12.0	5,102	10.1
45-49	4,884	9.7	4,037	8.0
50+	7,798	15.4	5,334	10.5
not stated	1,225	2.4	1,464	2.1
CANADA	50,611	100.0	50,611	100.00

Source: Statistics Canada, *Vital Statistics, op. cit.,* Table 16, p. 38.

stable in the past fifteen years. In 1975, women who married for the first time were on the average 22.5 years old (compared to 22.8 in 1950) and men were, on the average, 24.9 years old (compared to 26.7 in 1950).[9] By contrast, the average age at divorce has plummeted three years for women and four for men since 1969, and the change is even more striking if we look at the median age as indicated in Table 9. While the provinces hover around the national average and median age at divorce, Quebec has the oldest average age: 37.1 for women and 39.9 for men. This difference is not caused by a greater age at marriage in Quebec. It may be that divorce is a more difficult decision to reach in Quebec than in the rest of Canada because of Quebec's socio-ethical environment and this would mean that couples would remain married longer there before crossing the divorce threshold.

In 1975, 31% of divorces were taking place after ten to nineteen years of marriage, which helps to explain the difference between the average age at divorce and that at first marriage. The median duration of marriage before dissolution was 11.4 years in 1975, down from 12.1 years in 1972. Here too there are provincial variations, with Quebec marriages lasting

9. Statistics Canada, *Vital Statistics,* Vol. II, *Marriages and Divorces, 1975,* Ottawa, July 1977, Cat. 84-205, Table 3, p. 6.

TABLE 9
Average and Median Age of Divorcing Men and Women
1969-1975

| | WOMEN | | MEN | |
	AVERAGE	MEDIAN	AVERAGE	MEDIAN
1969	38.5	37.2	42.0	40.6
1970	36.9	35.0	40.2	38.5
1971	36.1	34.1	39.3	37.4
1972	35.6	33.4	38.8	36.7
1973	35.6	33.1	38.6	36.4
1974	35.5	33.0	38.4	36.1
1975	35.4	32.9	38.3	35.9

Source: Statistics Canada, *Vital Statistics, op. cit.*, adaptation of Table 18, p. 39.

an additional two years (median).[10] There seems to be a slight trend towards a shorter period of marriage before divorce. Twenty-two percent of all marriages are dissolved after five years of *legal* marriage.

Table 10 presents the details of the rate of dissolution by the number of years married. By way of contrast, in the United States the majority of divorces are granted within the first years of marriage.[11] For instance, in his study of divorce Kephart found that more than 40% of the couples in his 1,434 divorce sample had separated within the first three years of marriage and the peak of separations was in the first year of marriage.[12] However, there is a great variation from state to state[13] so that the distribution in certain states resembles that of the Canadian population.

10. L. Roy, *Le Divorce au Québec: Evolution Lente*, Gouvernement du Québec, Mars 1978, p. 15.
11. U.S. Bureau of the Census, *Current Population Reports*, Series P-20, No. 297, "Number, Timing and Duration of Marriages and Divorces in the United States: June 1975," U.S. Government Printing Office, Washington, D.C. 1976, p. 8.
12. W.M. Kephart, "The Duration of Marriage," *American Sociological Review*, 19, June 1954, p. 290.
13. See F.I. Nye and F.M. Berardo, *The Family, Its Structure and Interaction*, New York: Macmillan, 1973, p. 469.

TABLE 10
1975 Divorces by Duration of Marriage

DURATION	FREQUENCY	PERCENTAGE
less than 1 year	127	0.2
1 year	872	1.7
2 years	1,662	3.3
3 years	2,285	4.5
4 years	3,063	6.1
5 years	3,277	6.5
6 years	3,216	6,4
7 years	3,096	6.1
8 years	2,839	5.6
9 years	2,435	4.8
10-14 years	8,987	17.7
15-19 years	6,757	13.4
20-24 years	4,996	9.9
25-29 years	3,583	7.1
30+ years	3,356	6.6
not stated	60	0.1
	50,611	100.0

Source: Statistics Canada, *Vital Statistics, op. cit.,* adaptation of Table 19, p. 40.

In light of these statistics, Nye and Berardo concluded that "the first year or so of marriage is really the crucial period for establishing the basis"[14] of a stable relationship, although there are many circumstances which may arise later in a marriage, and which may even have been unpredictable at the inter-personal level, that can destroy a marital relationship, no matter how solid its initial basis was. For instance, in an Irish study of desertion 33% of the wives reported that the marriage had gone wrong from the very beginning.[15] Since many couples remain separated for several years before they divorce and since it tends to take upwards of twelve months on the average to obtain a decree after petition (the 1975 average was 13.5 months), the age at which the *real* divorce (that is, the emotional and physical divorce as opposed to the

14. *Ibid.,* p. 470.
15. K. O'Higgins, *Marital Desertion in Dublin.* Dublin: The Economic and Social Research Institute, 1974, p. 83.

legal one) occurs is probably on the average one to two years earlier. With this perspective the Nye and Berardo observation is pertinent.

Therefore, if we apply the American results and modify the Canadian statistics of Table 10 by using time of separation rather than time of divorce decree in order to calculate the real duration of these marriages as psychological rather than legal entities, the following emerges. As things stand, Table 10 shows a cumulative 22.2% of couples divorced within the first five years of marriage. But if we use a *moderate* estimation of the duration of separation prior to divorce (we have to use estimates as statistics do not provide us with a true separation period), we increase substantially the *de facto* proportion of marriages which were dissolved within five years. If a one-year pre-divorce separation is used, we have 28.6% of marriages which were dissolved within five years; with a two-year average separation, the proportion increases to 34.7% and with a three-year separation, it reaches 40.3%. The reality probably lies between the two extremes; that is, between 28.6% and 40.3%, since, as will be seen later in this chapter, 33% of the couples use the three-year separation period as their grounds for divorce. This means that at least 33% of the couples who divorce have been separated for a minimum of three years. However, we have no age distribution here, so that the overall meaning of this statistic is not complete, since it is possible that younger couples without children use grounds that differ from those of older couples with children. Therefore, younger *or* older couples could have a briefer separation period.

As we will see in Chapter 4, one of the important variables which is characteristically correlated with a high divorce rate is youthful marriage. As indicated by the percentages I have listed in Table 11, the same situation obtains in Canada. First let us consider the age at marriage of the wives: 43.15% of the 1975 divorces involved a woman who was younger than twenty when she married. By way of comparison, in 1975 only 28% of all new brides were under twenty at the time of marriage. Second, 13.35% of the divorces involved a man who was younger than twenty when he married, while nationally

TABLE 11
1975 Divorces by Age of Husband and Wife at Time of Marriage

AGE OF WIFE	TOTALS	AGE OF HUSBAND							
		UNDER 20	20-24	25-29	30-34	35-39	40-44	45-49	50+
Under 20	21,839	5,398	12,812	2,439	477	116	30	12	7
20-24	19,792	1,094	12,125	4,722	1,076	297	76	25	8
25-29	4,305	65	1,214	1,685	751	297	110	48	22
30-34	1,417	16	167	351	432	228	95	42	29
35-39	729	1	38	95	137	193	140	62	42
40-44	423	1	13	22	42	89	95	76	52
45-49	260	—	3	6	14	28	55	62	78
50+	341	8	2	1	5	10	18	33	226
Not stated	1,505	175	605	287	142	71	43	40	54
TOTALS	50,611	6,758	26,979	9,608	3,076	1,329	662	400	518

The "not stated" column for age of husband is excluded. Source: Statistics Canada, *Vital Statistics, op. cit.*, Table 17, p. 39.

only 8% of the new bridegrooms were under twenty at the time of marriage.[16] The comparison is not a perfect one since we do not have the age at marriage of all the couples who married the *same* year as the divorcing couples did. Nevertheless, the approximation is quite good.

The correlation between youthful marriage and divorce may have been stronger a few years ago or may be more evident in certain regions than in others; a study carried out in southwestern Ontario showed that 70% of divorcing wives had married when they were younger than twenty-one, while at that time the Canadian census showed that only 50% of brides had married at that age. The difference was even more striking among divorcing males as 75% had married below the age of twenty-five when only 50% of the males nationally had married that young.[17]

Another interesting relationship between age at marriage and divorce was established in the same study; it was found that couples who marry young divorce earlier than couples whose age at marriage is more advanced. Palmer writes: "Another characteristic of very young couples is their low tolerance of frustration—they are readier to give it up if the marriage does not give immediate satisfaction."[18] This reasoning seems to apply to the overall situation in Canada, for, as we will see in the chapter on remarriage, 60% of remarriages of divorcées take place before they reach the age of thirty, while the median age of all divorced women is 41.5 years. Therefore, those who marry young, divorce young and remarry young. Landis also found a similar trend in the U.S.A. People who had married very young tended to divorce, when the marriage was unhappy, more readily than those who had married above the age of thirty: the latter tended more often to stay in unhappy marriages.[19]

16. For similar results in 1973, see J.F. Peters, "Divorce in Canada: A Demographic Profile," *Journal of Comparative Family Studies*, 7, 1976, p. 337.
17. S.E. Palmer, "Reasons for Marriage Breakdown: A Case Study in Southwestern Ontario," *Journal of Comparative Family Studies*, 2, 1971, p. 252.
18. *Ibid.*, p. 253.
19. J.T. Landis, "Social Correlates of Divorce or Nondivorce Among the Unhappily Married," *Marriage and Family Living*, 25, May 1963, pp. 178-180.

If we look at the age at divorce and the duration of marriages in the United States, we see that teenage marriages are indeed a very important variable correlating with high divorce rates.[20] This is another point of similarity between the two countries.

PRESENCE OF CHILDREN

About 42% of divorcing couples have no children when they divorce, which means that close to 60% of divorcing couples do have children. Divorces involving children are therefore a more common occurrence in courts and make divorce more complicated, for the children themselves, the parents, the courts and welfare agencies. This also means that nearly 60% of divorcing people, but particularly women, become single parents, often for several years and sometimes even permanently. Table 12 presents a break-down of the number of children involved in divorce cases from 1972 to 1975. During those four years, the trend has been towards a smaller proportion of childless marriages ending in divorce, although that trend may be subject to fluctuations.

TABLE 12
Percentages of Divorce by Number of Dependent Children,
1972-1975

NUMBER OF CHILDREN	1972	1973	1974	1975
0	44.2%	43.4%	41.3%	42.4%
1	21.9	22.4	22.8	22.7
2	18.4	18.6	19.6	19.7
3	9.2	9.2	9.7	9.2
4	3.9	4.1	4.1	3.8
5	2.4	2.3	2.5	2.2

Source: Statistics Canada, *Vital Statistics, op. cit.,* adaptation of Table 20, p. 40.

20. See table reproduced in L. Scanzoni and J. Scanzoni, *Men, Women and Change,* New York: McGraw-Hill, 1976, p. 461.

One important question arising from Table 12 is whether people who divorce have a similar distribution of children to those who do not divorce. In other words, are divorcing people found disproportionately among childless couples compared to the rest of the population? And do couples with large families divorce less? The 1976 census shows that 30.1% of Canadian families do not have children under twenty-four years of age living at home.[21] By contrast, we see that in 1975 42.4% of the divorcing couples had no children at home. Divorcing couples are therefore considerably over-represented in the childless category. This stems from the fact that divorce or separation take place relatively early in marriage, before couples have children: 22% of the 1975 divorces had occurred within five years of marriage—see Table 10. However, this explanation has as its correlative the possibility that couples who do not have children are more vulnerable to divorce than others, and also the possibility that a number of couples delay having children because their relationship is not happy or secure.

Another method of studying the relationship between divorce and the presence of children is to look at averages. In 1975, divorcing couples had on the average 1.17 children while the average number of children in families in general was 1.8 in 1971 and 1.6 in 1976. Therefore divorcing couples have fewer children than the average.

An important question which has to remain unanswered for the time being is the age distribution of children involved in divorce, compared to the age distribution of all children in the population. In view of the great number of divorces occurring after only a few years of marriage, we can anticipate that a substantial number of divorces take place between couples who have very young children.

Another way of looking at the dramatic increase of divorce and at its after-effects is by examining the number of families which have two parents and those with only one parent, and by comparing their rate of change from 1971 to the 1976

21. Statistics Canada, Census of Canada, 1976, *Families. Families by Number of Children,* Cat. no. 93-823, Bulletin 4.4, Table 12.

TABLE 13

Family Types for 1971 and 1976 and Rate of Change since 1971

YEARS	TOTAL FAMILIES	HUSBAND/WIFE FAMILIES	MALE-PARENT FAMILIES	FEMALE-PARENT FAMILIES	TOTAL SINGLE-PARENT FAMILIES
1971	5,053,170	4,575,640	100,355	377,165	477,525
1976	5,727,895	5,168,560	94,990	464,345	559,330
Change Since					
1971	13.4%	13%	-5.4%	23.1%	17%

Source: 1976 Census of Canada, *Families. Families by Family Structure and Family Type*, Ottawa: Statistics Canada, Cat. 93-882, adaptation of Table 6.

census. Table 13 indicates that, while two-parent families increased by 13% in just five years, the number of male-headed families actually *decreased* by a full 5% while that of female-headed families increased by a staggering 23.1%. Unfortunately we do not have 1976 statistics for the number of such families resulting from divorces. In 1971, 112,665 of 477,525 households with one parent were a result of divorce: 22.5% of single-parent households were headed by a divorced parent; the rest were headed by widowed, separated, and never-married parents.[22] The female increase in Table 13 is directly related to higher divorce rates and, especially, to higher out-of-wedlock rates with mothers keeping their babies; the latter probably also contributes to the smaller percentage of male-headed families. In view of rising divorce rates and the increasing number of male parents who are granted custody, it is difficult to account for the decrease in the *number* of families headed by a man. However, the explanation may lie in the fact that men who become single parents remarry more rapidly than single-parent women or than divorced men in general; their families therefore return to the two-parent structure more rapidly than those of women.

It is also interesting to note that single-parent families increased most in Ontario, Alberta and British Columbia, the provinces with the highest divorce rates, and increased least in the Eastern provinces and Quebec, these provinces either having lower current divorce rates or, as in the case of Quebec, having only recently had a high divorce rate.

GROUNDS FOR DIVORCE AND PETITIONERS

The most common grounds for divorce in 1975 were:

        separation for not less than three years 33%
        adultery 30%
        mental cruelty 16.5%
        physical cruelty 13.9%

22. Statistics Canada, *Canada Year Book 1975*, Ottawa: December 1975, p. 171, Table 4.26.

These are the *legal* grounds for and not necessarily the real causes of divorce.[23] In fact, many people who use the first of these grounds separated because of adultery, while others who use the grounds of adultery never committed the act but pay a person to be their co-respondent, because they believe that a petition will be taken more seriously when adultery is involved. This belief is supported by facts; the average time for a case based on adultery is between three and twelve months, while it is in the vicinity of six to twelve months for a case based on noncohabitation. In 1969-72, 22% of adultery cases were processed in under six months, while only 13% of the cases based on grounds of noncohabitation were processed within this time-span.[24]

It is interesting to ponder on the question of who it is that initiates the divorce procedure—not the *legal* divorce, but the "real" one. That is, who decides to get out of the marriage? The man or the woman? An answer based on who *files* for divorce is inadequate. Which party is the petitioner is generally a mere legal formality and may present an unrealistic picture of the situation. No study has been made in Canada concerning the sex of the spouse who most commonly wants out. In the United States, it was found that about four of every ten couples who are divorced include one member who did not want the divorce.[25] Therefore, in 40% of cases, one spouse sets the procedure in motion. Since husbands have more money than wives, better jobs, more alternatives to meet persons of the other sex, and are less likely to bear total responsibility for the children if the marriage fails, we might expect that when a marriage is not satisfactory they will be more likely to be the first to suggest the possibility of divorce and then to seek it actively. However, Goode's study, published more than twenty-one years ago, found that 60% of the divorced women interviewed reported having been the ones who first sug-

23. Statistics Canada, *Marriages and Divorces*, op.cit., Table 21, p. 41.
24. Paul Reed, "A Preliminary Analysis of Divorce Actions in Canada, 1969-1972," Paper presented at the Annual Meeting of the Canadian Sociology and Anthropology Association, Edmonton, May 1975, p. 18.
25. L.A. Westoff quotes a National Council on Family Relations study but does not give the exact reference in her *The Second Time Around, Remarriage in America*, New York: The Viking Press, 1977, p. 21.

gested divorce.[26] Faced by this apparent paradox, Goode provides the following explanation:

> *We suggest, then, that in our society the husband more frequently than the wife will engage in behavior whose function, if not intent, whose result, if not aim, is to force the other spouse to ask for the divorce first.* Thereby the husband frees himself to some extent from the guilt burden, since he did not ask for the divorce. A by-product of this process frees him still more: the wife's repeated objections to this behavior will mean that there are family squabbles, and one almost constant result of repeated family squabbles is a lessened affection between husband and wife. In particular, of course, these squabbles mean that the husband can begin to think of himself as also aggrieved, as also sinned against.[27]

This explanation is quite consistent with current sex roles in our society which give men higher status, more alternatives, and a lower commitment to marriage. At first glance, social norms do indicate that men have a lesser stake in marriage than women. They may therefore take more chances on it. In fact, in a study, carried out in Toronto in 1972, of couples who engage in spouse swapping ("swinging"), I found that in seventeen out of twenty-five cases it had been the husband who had first suggested it, and that in sixteen cases out of twenty-five he had been the one who had reached the final decision.[28] It also became apparent that several husbands had used the pretext of improving their marriage as their reason for swinging. Under the threat of "We try it or we divorce," the wives went along.[29]

Goode also found that when the wife admits that the husband was the first one to suggest divorce, the median time

26. W.J. Goode, *Women in Divorce*, New York: Free Press, 1956, p. 135.

27. *Ibid.*, pp. 136-137. The first sentence is italicized in the original.

28. A.-M. Henshel (Ambert), "Swinging: A Study on Decision Making in Marriage," *American Journal of Sociology*, 78, February 1973, pp. 885-891.

29. A.-M. Henshel (Ambert), "Swinging: The Sociology of Decision Making," in *Marriage, Family and Society*, edited by S.P. Wakil, Toronto: Butterworth, 1975.

in terms of taking the first step to file suit was 5.4 months, while it was 12.9 months when the wife was the initiator.[30] This result is consistent with that of other studies which have established that the decision to divorce is less often reversed, and the divorce itself takes place sooner, when it is the man who decides upon it.

While Gunter does not offer explanations of the results of his study, he found that, with the passage of "no-fault" laws in Florida, the trend of which party petitioned for divorce changed. From 1962 to 1971, 62% of the petitioners were women. But after 1971, 64% of the petitioners were men.[31] Previously, with a question of fault inherent in divorce procedures, it looked less proper socially for a man to sue his wife for adultery, for example, since adultery is considered more reprehensible for women than for men. But with the passage of a no-fault law, men were freer to initiate divorce procedures legally. Moreover, Gunter found that when males initiated the divorce procedure after 1971, 85% of the cases were completed while only 50% of the procedures initiated by women were carried out.[32] Again, these data could be interpreted as an indication that when men want to divorce they are better able to go through with it than women; while women may recant because of conditions imposed by the man, because of financial difficulties, or because more women do not really want to divorce but resort to this action as a last step, hoping that perhaps their husbands' behaviour will improve.

We have no information with regard to Canadian divorce as to which partner first *wants* the divorce, but if we look at the sex of the petitioner, we see that wives are the petitioners in approximately 63% of cases. Even though Canadian laws have been reformed, we do not yet have a "no-fault" system and the sex of the petitioner in Canadian divorces is similar to that in Florida *before* it passed its "no-fault" decrees in 1971. However the duration of the *legal* process itself, once the suit is

30. Goode, *Women in Divorce, op.cit.*, p. 144.
31. B.G. Gunter, "Notes on Divorce Filing as Role Behavior," *Journal of Marriage and the Family*, 39, February 1977, p. 96.
32. *Ibid.*, p. 97.

filed, is not tied to the sex of the petitioners. Neither male nor female petitioners have an advantage in terms of the length of time it takes to obtain a final decree in Canada.[33] The legal process itself is neutral and non-discriminatory.

SOCIO-ECONOMIC STATUS, RELIGION, AND ETHNIC BACKGROUND

In terms of socio-economic status, Palmer's study showed that divorcing men had a lower level of education and income than males in general in their geographic area (London, Ontario). She also established that a major proportion of them were labourers and a lesser proportion worked in professional, managerial and skilled fields.[34] A similar inverse correlation between divorce and socio-economic status has also been established in the United States.[35] If we use any of the three main indicators of socio-economic status, education, income and type of occupation, American divorce rates are lower in higher education, income, and occupational brackets.[36] In terms of education, there may be a curvilinear relationship. "Men with very little education have a comparatively low likelihood of divorce; this likelihood grows with increasing education to a maximum in the groups that have attended or completed high school and declines for those who have (a) college (education) ..."[37] (This pattern did not apply to women, however.) The most striking differences occur within the varying income brackets. Those who are either unem-

---

33. Paul Reed, *op.cit.*
34. Palmer, "Reasons for Marriage Breakdown," *op.cit.*, pp. 255-256.
35. It should be noted that such data actually exist in the Canadian census but have not been published. I have requested the data but the relevant agency replied that "it is not possible to derive the cross-tabs of the kind you are interested in from the data we have." (Letter signed by a demographer in the Health Division of Statistics Canada.) Such cross-tabs may admittedly be costly to obtain; however, I have in the past obtained equally difficult and non-available cross-tabs from the same division (see Chapter 3).
36. W.J. Goode, "Family Disorganization," in *Contemporary Social Problems*, edited by R.K. Merton and R. Nisbet, New York: Harcourt, Brace, Jovanovich, third edition, 1971, pp. 492-493; L.C. Coombs and Z. Zumeta, "Correlates of Marital Dissolution in a Prospective Fertility Study: A Research Note," *Social Problems*, 18, Summer 1970, p. 95.
37. U.S. Department of Health, Education and Welfare, *Divorces: Analysis of Changes: United States, 1969*, Vital and Health Statistics, series 21, no. 22, April 1973, p.16.

ployed or with no income of their own have a rate of divorce seven times that of those whose income places them in the upper echelon. This finding seems to indicate that income, especially a low income, is the most salient aspect of SES in terms of divorce in the United States.

In our type of society, a low income is not only a source of relative disadvantage; it is also a source of raw deprivation and of tension. As we will see in the next chapter, economically disadvantaged persons are affected detrimentally by many situations which engender stress and strife. Marital and family life are directly affected when even the basics of life are not forthcoming. Each additional child becomes a burden emotionally and financially, and the traditional role of the man as the breadwinner is undermined.

Another social dimension on which we have no published data in Canada is religion. In the United States, Catholics have the lowest divorce rate, followed by those of the Jewish and Protestant faiths.[38] Lenski has hypothesized that homogamy, or similarity of background, may be greater among Jews, which would mean that Jews face fewer marital difficulties than Christians, who are culturally more heterogeneous.[39] Or, perhaps, it is possible that there is more cultural pressure placed on Jews to maintain their families intact. Landis, for one, found that Jews were most likely to remain in an unhappy marriage while people of no faith were least likely, and Catholics as well as Protestants fell between the two extremes.[40] While the divorce rate of Catholics is anywhere from one half to two-thirds that of Protestants, Catholics have the highest desertion rate.[41] This is directly related to Catholic doctrine concerning divorce. Thus, being of the Catholic faith does not prevent marital dissolution since Catholics resort instead to desertion, which means that their overall rates of marital dissolution are probably similar to those of Protest-

38. T.P. Monahan and W.M. Kephart, "Divorce and Desertion by Religious and Mixed-Religious Groups," *American Journal of Sociology*, 59, March 1954, pp. 462-465.
39. G. Lenski, *The Religious Factor*, Garden City, N.Y.: Doubleday, 1961.
40. Landis, "Social Correlates of Divorce and Nondivorce Among the Unhappily Married," *op.cit.*, p. 180.
41. Monahan and Kephart, *op.cit.*, p. 460.

ants and higher than those of Jews. These results may not apply to Canada since the province with the greatest proportion of Catholics is Quebec and its rate of divorce was somewhat higher than the national average in 1975 and 1976. Conversations with people in welfare work in Quebec also indicate a high incidence of co-habitation and desertion. However, what is applicable to French-speaking Catholics in Quebec may not apply to Catholics in other provinces.

We do not possess direct recent statistics on the relationship of ethnic background and language to divorce, but a study carried out in 1970 in Metropolitan Toronto provides some indirect evidence.[42] In that study, 103,815 pupils in elementary and secondary public schools returned a questionnaire. One of the results derived from their answers shows that 84.1% of children were living with both parents and 13.9% with only one parent (with another 2% living with neither parent). Therefore, 13.9% of children had only one parent at home, and it may be assumed, because of their age, that this meant separation and divorce rather than the death of a parent or out-of-wedlock pregnancies.

For those children born in Canada, 78.5% of those who spoke only English at home lived with both parents, compared to 91.2% of those who spoke English *and* another language. Nineteen percent of the children with an English-language background lived in single-parent families, while only 7.7% of those with another home language did so. A similar but less drastic difference was noted when children born outside Canada were considered. Of these, 15.6% lived only with one parent when English was their home language, while only 6.4% did so when English *and* another language were spoken at home. These results loosely indicate that in Ontario divorce (or separation and desertion) is more frequent among English-speaking persons, whether natives or immigrants, than among other ethnic groups who have maintained their language. Because at the time Toronto had a large Italian, French Canadian and West Indian population, it is possible that the

42. E.N. Wright, *Student's Background and Its Relationship to Class and Programme in School*, Toronto: The Board of Education, 1970.

correlation is also mediated by religious factors, or by ethnic/ racial factors in the group who speak only English.

CONCLUSIONS

The most salient point about divorce in Canada is that it has increased so markedly in the past decade and may not yet have reached a peak. Divorce is a new way of life for Canadians, children as well as adults. It is a social phenomenon that cannot be ignored even if it has not occurred in one's own family. And the same observation can be made about the increase in single-parent families in the aftermath of divorce. Such families are now found in all social classes, a fact that is evident in various types of residential units. For instance, if one lives in a large city, whether it be in a semi-detached house, a bungalow, a townhouse, or a high rise, one soon gets to know of the existence of several single-parent families in one's neighbourhood.

Other important features of the divorce situation in Canada are the varying divorce rates in the different provinces, the relationship between youthful marriage and divorce, the relatively brief duration of marriages before dissolution, and the high proportion of couples with children who divorce.

In the following chapters we will look at the sociological and psychological aspects of divorce. We will begin by inquiring into the causes of divorce.

3 The Causes of Divorce: Societal Causes

When we inquire into the causes of divorce, we operate on two levels. In the first instance we must deal with the visible causes of separation or marital dissolution; these are the apparent or immediate causes, the personal reasons. These are the rationales that the divorcing couples would give us were we to interview them and ask them what led to their divorce or to their marital discord. We might call these the individual causes of divorce. They include, among others, adultery, alcoholism, emotional problems, financial difficulties, over-involvement with one's work, drifting apart, and an increasing clash of values between the parties involved in a marriage. We seem to understand these reasons quite well; they deal with personal experiences and are thus recognizable to the lay-person. Some of these causes, such as homosexuality, adultery, and imprisonment, also serve as legal grounds for divorce.[1]

But beyond these immediate causes are more universal ones, stemming from the general conditions of a society: from ideological, cultural and economic conditions. It is these circumstances which, ultimately, create the atmosphere, the mood, or, if you wish, the environment that exert those various pressures on couples that make it easier or more difficult for them to lead a happy married life. It is these same

1. The legal grounds for divorce are those causes accepted by a legal system for a divorce decree. Many countries have no-fault divorce in which no reasons or legal grounds need be given: the marriage is legally terminated for reasons such as "irrevocable differences."

social variables that ultimately dictate which solutions couples opt for once their relationship becomes unsatisfactory: solutions such as trying to resolve the problem at all costs, remaining together unhappily, permanent adultery, mutual avoidance, desertion, separation, and divorce, to name only a few of the obvious ones. When we explore the reasons for higher divorce rates, it is to these societal variables that we first turn for an answer, for they have a bearing on the personal causes.

Whether we are studying the personal or the societal causes of divorce, we must deal with a set of interlocking variables: there is no *one* separate cause of divorce. Instead, there is a set of interdependent social and psychological circumstances that facilitate divorce; each circumstance "feeds" the others. There is no linear cause, especially at the societal level. Thus this chapter will be of small comfort to those who wish to pinpoint *one* "real" cause: not one but many threads make up the fabric of divorce.

This chapter will deal with the socio-cultural and social variables that are related to divorce. The following factors are generally fairly well agreed upon as constituents of the soil in which divorce will grow in this country: the individualistic and hedonistic mentality of the technological era; a general climate of liberalism; a reduction of religious influence and a greater acceptance of divorce in certain religions; a secularized view of marriage; the relaxation of divorce laws; the increased independence of individuals and a lessening of family pressures; more numerous alternatives for both sexes; social and geographic mobility; greater emancipation of women; a relative lack of psychological emancipation in men; increased longevity; the sub-cultural effect (pockets of high or low divorce rates); a surfeit of alternatives and choices that are offered to individuals; and poverty. We will review each of these variables always keeping in mind that the answer to the question concerning increasing divorce rates lies in a combination of these variables and not in any one alone. In the next chapter we will look into those immediate causes which specialists, social workers, and divorcing couples themselves find to be the most predominant *personal* reasons for a marital breakup.

INDIVIDUALISM AND HEDONISM

Several centuries of western civilization and philosophy have culminated in today's climate of individualism and hedonism. The philosophical emphasis in the West is on individual rights as opposed to the rights of the community that are stressed in Soviet societies, which also have high divorce rates but for reasons somewhat different from ours. In western societies, the emphasis is on self-fulfillment, on personal freedom and enjoyment. Other-orientation and couple-orientation are not stressed, even at the level of the family, as much as they were in the past.

In very recent years, individualism and hedonism have taken another form at the familial level: couples, especially women, are often encouraged and are deciding themselves not to have children. Children are seen as a burden rather than as offering a possibility for self-fulfillment. The slight but noticeable trend away from legal marriage into cohabitation is certainly also part of this tendency to seek the benefits of marriage while, in many cases, postponing its responsibilities. This mood entails living one's life *now*, often at the expense of the formation of durable human ties; at the slightest provocation these ties are assumed to be limitations on a supposedly unlimited potential for self-actualization; this concept of self-fulfillment is in turn fostered by the multiplicity of choices offered by technology and commercialism. Whereas in the past women were urged to find themselves through their husbands and their children, they are now urged to do so through their work. The pendulum has swung from one extreme to another.

Within such an atmosphere, amply fostered by the media in general, and especially by advertising, couples have less incentive to look together in the same direction and for each to seek fulfillment in the *other*. Couples tend to become two individuals; when the conjugal unit itself is forgotten, it becomes less important as a viable and durable entity. The "we-unit" gives way, the problems remain unsolved, and the couple, or one of the two spouses, wakes up to a new disenchanted reality. With the emphasis on individual fulfillment, the times are ripe for separation and divorce, rather than for the adoption of solutions that would strengthen the conjugal unit but might require accommodations on the part of one or both parties. As Epstein points out, there is nothing new about unhappy marriages: what is different is people's unwillingness to put up with them for very long.[2] And, we might add, people's unwillingness today to accommodate each other.

In a recent article, the Glassers emphasize that it is a lack of balance between the personal and the social which is the major problem, because in many segments of society the personal is taking precedence over responsibilities towards others. They give an example of the impact of this imbalance on the field of counselling by presenting the case of a woman, the wife of a forty-two year old professional man, who left both her husband and three minor children to return to university.

> Her professional counsellor was successful in making her feel very comfortable with her new-found freedom and independence. The very fact that the client sought help was an indication that she was not fully content with the decision she had made and that she still felt strong attachments for her family. But the possibility of her returning to them was never discussed. The comfort of the client's husband and children, who lived in a distant city, was of no concern to the therapist, and by the end of treatment, of no concern to the client either. Is this a successful outcome, and if so, for whom?[3]

GENERAL CLIMATE OF LIBERALISM

Added to this growing emphasis on individual gratification is a general climate of liberalism which has been unfolding for several centuries, first in Europe and then in North America. This climate of liberalism is reflected in areas other than the family as well. For instance, the penal system has passed from a mentality of retaliation for crimes committed to one of

2. J. Epstein, *Divorced in America*, New York: Dutton, 1974, p. 93.
3. L.N. Glasser and P.H. Glasser, "Hedonism and the Family: Conflict in Values?" *Journal of Marriage and Family Counselling*, October 1977, p.16.

rehabilitation; the educational system has gone from an emphasis on learning the basics to a pot-pourri of avant-garde concepts, and from discipline to individual "creativity"; western religions have evolved from structured bodies of beliefs to a more relaxed freedom of conscience. Similarly, in the area of marriage, we have passed into a time that allows for more accessible divorce and for a greater social acceptance of divorce.

We have entered a morally liberal era, a freer era, and within this context it is more acceptable not to have children, and to live together without marriage, alternatives that were condemned or frowned upon just a few years ago. It is also more acceptable to divorce, although divorce is still considered to be undesirable and carries a stigma in many groups. Liberalism has certainly not spread equally into all spheres of life, but it has definitely broadened our options, and this applies to the marital sphere as well.

REDUCED RELIGIOUS INFLUENCE

Following the advent of this climate of liberalism and individualism, the various churches and sects of the western world have seen their influence challenged and diminished in matters of family and personal life. A climate of lessened religious orthodoxy has swept through all the major religions of this civilization, and with it came, in many instances, a greater acceptance on the part of the clergy of divorce itself. Religious platforms were liberalized, although the Roman Catholic Church is still holding firmly to centuries-old beliefs, and religious prescriptions became more open-ended, leaving much to individual conscience or choice. Divorce was no longer subject to outright condemnation. Religions abandoned their moralizing stance in this respect, thus facilitating the faithful's freedom of choice;[4] divorce was relegated to the legal sphere.

At the same time, the faithful became less attached to their religion, and less ready to follow those prescriptions that

4. See V.J. Pospishill, *Divorce and Marriage: Towards a New Catholic Teaching.* New York: Herder and Herder, 1967.

would endanger their personal freedom and right to enjoyment of life, from nonconformist sex, to the contraceptive pill for Roman Catholics, to divorce. The judiciary and political systems have probably largely replaced religion in many people's minds as the arbiters of desirable behaviour. The sphere of the spiritual has receded in importance and with it the influence it once had on the everyday life of individuals and nations.

SECULARIZED VIEW OF MARRIAGE

Although most first marriages are still performed within a religious context, the reason is probably an attraction to a romantic notion of weddings rather than an attachment to marriage as a sacrament, as a religious institution, or a state blessed by God. At the same time, there has been an increase in marriages which are performed within a strictly secular context, either at City Hall, in court, or in a hotel. The important point is that marriage today is often regarded not as a sacred institution blessed by God and joining the partners irremediably in a covenant, but simply as a human relationship subject to the vacillations of human nature.

Many individuals no longer have or accept religious guidance in their marital lives. A secularized view of marriage has been adopted which makes the task of the individual conscience much easier when the question of choice arises. For instance, since marriage is no longer sacred, more couples now contract it knowing full well that it may not last: it may be fine for a few years but there will be something else after that if it does not work. Or some couples marry for the sake of convenience; either because of an out-of-wedlock pregnancy or for support, or to get out of their parents' home, or to be "like the others." A secularized view of marriage, synchronous with individualism, is bound to produce a greater proportion of marriages which are contracted on a very shaky basis in the first place and which are entered into haphazardly. And, in turn, this is likely to produce a lessened marital commitment. Moreover, a secularized view of marriage opens the door to divorce as an acceptable solution to an unhappy union.

RELAXATION OF DIVORCE LAWS

When a country through its laws makes divorce easier on a democratic basis, by placing divorce within the reach of the poor as well as of the rich, then that country will, for a decade or so, experience a radical upswing in divorce.[5] What follows is that many people who longed for divorce are finally getting the opportunity to do so and are taking it. This results in a backlog of cases to be processed and cleared. This is what happened in this country when, on July 11, 1968, the Divorce Act was reformed.[6] Divorce rates soared immediately and are still rising because it often takes quite a while for a new legal framework to filter down to the conscious reality of the everyday life of citizens. Moreover, when people no longer have to process so many papers and wait too long, and are no longer harassed by the court system when they petition, they will more readily than otherwise have recourse to divorce as a solution to an unhappy marriage. Stringent divorce laws can be seen as external barriers preventing divorce. Of course, this variable can have this effect only if the ideological barrier to divorce is lifted; if people come to believe that divorce is acceptable. This is precisely the attitude that the liberal and secular trends discussed earlier have fostered. In turn, the relaxation of divorce laws helps to enhance the social acceptability of divorce. Here again is an example of how these variables are inter-related and how we cannot use one of them in isolation to explain high divorce rates.

However, there are countries which relax their divorce laws in a token manner only; they make it *legal,* perhaps for the first time, as happened recently in Italy and in Colombia (South America), two Catholic bastions, but its accessibility is so costly and the process so cumbersome that only a few, usually the rich (who are not necessarily the ones who divorce the most) and the educated are able to avail themselves of this new right. In such countries, governments give lip-service

5. D.M. Stetson and G.C. Wright, Jr., "The Effects of Laws on Divorce in American States," *Journal of Marriage and the Family,* 37, August 1975, pp. 537-547.

6. T.J. Abernathy, Jr., and M.E. Arcus, "The Law and Divorce in Canada," *The Family Coordinator,* 26, October 1977, pp. 409-413.

acquiescence to public demand, while at the same time maintaining such restrictions on divorce as will ensure that the religious elements in the population will not be overly offended.

GREATER SOCIAL ACCEPTABILITY OF DIVORCE

Divorce certainly does not carry the stigma it used to. As divorce rates have risen, more divorced people are to be found in the population, and divorce has become more natural. Divorced people can no longer be stigmatized. Perhaps there is strength in numbers. Simultaneously, the greater social acceptability of divorce has led to fewer hardships for the divorced and divorcing individuals and has rendered the option of divorce more palatable; this, in turn, has probably contributed to increased divorce rates. And, as indicated in the previous section, a greater acceptability of divorce has led to a relaxation of the laws governing its accessibility, and this, in time, has led to further acceptability of the fact of divorce.

In Canada, there was, within a period of twenty years, quite a shift in favour of a relaxation of divorce laws. In 1943, a public opinion poll indicated that 24% of the respondents felt that divorce laws were too harsh; in 1966, 60% of respondents were in favour of relaxing the laws.[7]

We have become more permissive concerning divorce because its typical consequences are now less catastrophic.[8] There are not only more alternatives but fewer hardships. Moreover, the general social climate of acceptability or tolerance further reduces the number of problems involved in the divorce situation. The social costs of divorce have become fewer and less extreme. As Bernard puts it: "Social costs act selectively; when they are low, they release more people into the divorce population; when they are high, they release few."[9]

7. R. Pike, "Legal Access and the Incidence of Divorce in Canada: A Sociohistorical Analysis," *Canadian Review of Sociology and Anthropology*. 12, 1975, p. 120.
8. F.I. Nye and F.M. Berardo, *The Family, Its Structure and Interaction*. New York: Macmillan, 1973, p. 490.
9. J. Bernard, *Remarriage*. New York: Russell & Russell, 1971 re-issue, p. 97.

MORE NUMEROUS ALTERNATIVES

The current liberal and technological era has generated more alternative life styles for both men and women. The alternatives include the possibility of sex outside of marriage, within a loving and even acceptable context, by co-habitation or even by adultery. The personal ads of our dailies have recently accepted items such as:

> "*Married bisexual woman, 34, intelligent, educated, warm, is looking for same. Please write to Box ...*"
>
> "*Married man, successful businessman, 44, 6'1", 192 lbs., considered good looking, affectionate, is looking for a woman, marital status no problem, for discreet afternoon affairs. Box ...*"
>
> "*Professional, young man, 25, married but frustrated, is looking for older, mature female companion. Discretion assured. Write to Box ...*"[10]

Therefore, people no longer feel the need to confine their search for sexual gratification to a spouse.

In the past, a man needed a woman (a mother, sister, wife, or maid) to take care of his house, laundry, cooking and hostessing. Nowadays, the laundry is easily dealt with at the corner laundromat; catering services, fast food outlets and restaurants have alleviated his fears of an empty stomach. And, more positively, men are finally learning how to do housework and cook. In addition, in large cities, apartment living no longer demands sophisticated house cleaning: it can be done swiftly and even not done at all if the tenant is practically never there, as often happens with divorced men.

The other side of the coin is that it is now acceptable for a woman to earn a living; many women are trained to have at least one marketable skill before they enter marriage. This means that women have more alternatives than in the past as they are less dependent on their husbands for income. In addition, day care centres have helped many women find still another alternative to an unhappy marriage; they can go out,

10. These are composites of ads found in the *Toronto Star* and the *Globe and Mail* in 1979.

earn a living, and have their children cared for, sometimes extremely well, sometimes poorly, depending on the quality of the caretakers. Women can also go out by themselves, shop, even go to bars, especially singles' bars, without looking out of the ordinary and without violating any moral or even practical code of conduct.

More alternatives are also emerging in terms of alimony and child custody. The wife who has sacrificed her own ambitions, put her husband through professional school (often called obtaining one's P.H.T. for "putting husband through"), and then finds herself abandoned for a younger woman, is practically assured that the courts will, according to the new laws, compensate her, and perhaps even require that her ex-spouse put *her* through school and support their children during her schooling. Similarly, the impoverished husband of a successful career woman may be as likely today to get alimony from her if he is unemployed as vice versa. There are also more avenues opening up in terms of child custody. More children are granted to men than before, and joint custody is emerging as a strong force that allows *both* parents to share equally in the pleasures and the responsibilities of child rearing. Until now, all the responsibilities fell to women, since they generally got full custody, while the father inherited the "Sunday-daddy" role, a very enviable one for the harried woman left with two children, a small budget, and little time for herself, but a potentially unsatisfactory role for the Sunday-father himself.

Individuals, therefore, no longer need to remain in an unsatisfactory marriage to be sexually active, to be adequately fed, to go out, to have children. Technology and liberalism have presented us with a vast array of alternatives which make life, if not always pleasurable, at least bearable. Nye and Berardo explain this situation in terms of Thibault and Kelley's concepts of rewards, costs, and profits.[11] Alternatives allow for a comparison of what one has with what one could have.[12] As the alternatives proliferate, the costs of an

11. Nye and Berardo, 1973, *op.cit.*, pp. 500-503.
12. J.W. Thibaut and H.H. Kelley, *The Social Psychology of Groups*. New York: John Wiley, 1959.

unsatisfactory marriage appear greater and the rewards and profits lesser, while the alternatives themselves seem even more attractive in people's minds.

Certain authors also stress the suggestion that divorce is less costly today because *marriage* provides fewer outlets for sustenance and self fulfillment.[13] It has been said, in this connection, that the family is becoming more specialized in terms of the functions it fulfills: the family is focusing on personality needs and the early socialization of children, while leisure-needs, self-fulfillment through work, sustenance, and education, are provided for by other social agencies.[14] The family is becoming a more particularistic, psychological entity, whereas in the past it helped to structure society and its functions overlapped with those of society as a whole.

INCREASED INDEPENDENCE OF INDIVIDUALS FROM FAMILIES

Parents often feel embarrassed and betrayed when their children divorce. But offspring who have come of age are more independent from their families today, so that these parental pressures are not as powerful and, even when exerted, have little, if any, impact. Families are less able to dictate the behaviour of adults than in the past for several reasons; one of these is the individualism discussed earlier; another is that children are more economically independent than in the past and participate in fewer familial financial enterprises; also, families are smaller and therefore contain fewer members to exert pressure on a deviating couple; finally, social and geographic mobility make for a family fabric that is far more loosely interwoven than before.

By the same token, all of this is not an unmitigated blessing. It also means that individuals are less able to receive support from their families than in the past, although many ethnic groups or immigrant groups are an exception to this rule. It

13. K. Keniston, *All Our Children*, New York: Harcourt, Brace, Jovanovich, 1977, p. 21.
14. R.M. Williams, Jr., *American Society*, New York: Alfred A. Knopf, 1965, second edition, revised, p. 80.

means that persons cannot count as much as in the past on their parents for financial help: the latter have to take care of themselves, with a greater life-expectancy and, after a certain point, on shrinking financial reserves; this also means that families themselves are less willing to give moral advice and individuals are less trusting in turning to their families for advice and guidance. When children are a factor, it also means that people can expect less help in their care. Individuals are independent from precisely those family pressures that would contribute to the strengthening of marital bonds and would discourage open discord, especially as expressed through divorce.

All of this leaves a couple very vulnerable to external forces. Parental help can often go a long way to shore up the morale of a struggling couple, crippled with debts and battling child-hood diseases, and loving parental guidance can similarly offer the balm that would enable a couple in emotional distress to overcome a period of crisis. Because many people no longer have access to such a family structure, they have to turn to professionals for help. However, the professional approach, by contrast with the familial approach (when it is the right kind of family), is more detached. Professionals, while per-haps more qualified, do not tend to impart *values* to their clients nor to force them to *solve* problems in accordance with such values.

Therefore, increased independence from the family group may be related to higher divorce rates because one more barrier to divorce has been lifted with the loss of the family group as a powerful agent of social control. Moreover, couples often experience marital difficulties which, in a different situation, could have been remedied with the help of the family network.

GREATER SOCIAL AND GEOGRAPHIC MOBILITY

It has been posited, quite plausibly, that the increase in social and geographic mobility that we are experiencing in North America is conducive to marital disruption because of the strains imposed by these two kinds of social uprooting and the loss of support from one's former community that they entail. Relationships have been established between social mobility and the likelihood of divorce.[15]

First, let us define the terms and the dimensions of social and geographic mobility. Geographic mobility involves moving from one place to another. The further the place, the greater the dislocation, and the greater the necessity to readjust to a variety of new life circumstances. Social mobility, on the other hand, means the passage of an individual or of a family from one socio-economic level to another. It is "going up or down in the world." Upward social mobility is often synonymous with the accession to "a better social situation."

Both types of mobility are prevalent in North America and they often coincide, in that, in order to attain a higher social position (generally through an improvement in the *man's* position), a family or couple often has to relocate geographically. In such a double instance, although the rewards are great, the stress can be overwhelming; the individuals have to adjust to living in a new city and, moreover, they have to adopt a new life-style, one more suited to their recently achieved social position. They acquire a bigger house, live in a "better" neighbourhood, buy a new set of clothes, new cars, have to make new acquaintances and send their children to a more "suitable" school. Old friends are often discarded or lost, or are simply too far away, as is the extended family. The husband and/or the wife may have to work even harder at their new jobs so that they see little of each other; they may begin to develop two worlds in which they grow separately, eyeing each other from a distance.[16]

Moreover, when one moves away from one's community, one is no longer subject to its social pressures. Some couples take this opportunity, after a year or two, to initiate extra-marital relationships and to divorce. They might not have gone that far had they been back home, and perhaps neither of them would have been the less happy for it.

15. T.P. Monahan, "When Married Couples Part: Statistical Trends and Relationships in Divorce," *American Sociological Review*, 27, 1962, pp. 625-634.
16. I am presenting here the potentially negative aspects of social mobility, not the positive ones. It can also serve as a source of solidarity between a husband and wife.

EMANCIPATION OF WOMEN

This section requires more extensive treatment, for these days "women's liberation" is often *blamed* for soaring divorce rates. We have already seen that no single cause can explain divorce and this applies equally to the variable under consideration here. "Women's liberation" is a term and a reality that is charged with emotion and with prejudice, both favourable and unfavourable. First, let us point out that the emancipation of women from traditional roles is simply an aspect and a consequence of liberalism in general, of individualism, and of secular trends. If men were to benefit from these trends, so must women. Consequently, women slowly acquired the right to vote, to earn a decent salary, to be hired, as men were, strictly on the basis of their qualifications; they also acquired greater sexual freedom, still not comparable with that accorded to men, but great enough to shock many people who believe that a woman's place is near the cradle. Birth control and abortion have further enhanced female equality; the lowering of the birth rate is an additional contributing factor, for women with many children are more likely than others to be forced by circumstances to channel their energies solely into the mother-housekeeper role.[17]

More married women are committing adultery than in the past, although married men still significantly outnumber their female counterparts in this respect, if only because their work and their greater freedom give them more opportunities. The housewife at home at night does not have many opportunities to sleep with someone else, even if she wants to, while her husband out for a business drink has many such opportunities. (In a way, it is perhaps surprising that not more married men are adulterous, considering the opportunities.) In addition to the above development, more women than in the past simply walk out of their marriages or decide on divorce *themselves* because *they* are dissatisfied—again, such actions used to be male prerogatives. More strikingly, a greater, if still small, number of mothers in the past have left, abandoning

17. See my *Sex Structure*, Don Mills, Ont.: Longman of Canada, revised and expanded second edition, 1976, for a review of the situation, especially in Canada.

their children to the fathers. This development is shocking to people even though the number of deserting *fathers* is very high. There is obviously a double standard involved here: abandoning one's children *is* reprehensible, but it should not be regarded as more so for women than for men. In other words, along with the good in female emancipation comes the bad; women are acquiring rights that used to be male prerogatives, but some of these "rights" are not morally acceptable for either sex, not exclusively unacceptable for women.

The fact that women are now more equal under law, have access to birth control, have fewer children, are better educated, tend more often to be employed, are less dependent on men economically, and are freer sexually has made their reaction to marital life more similar to that of men. In fact, it has been found in the U.S.A. that there is a substantial increase in the incidence of separations as the wife's annual earnings increase.[18] Therefore, it is a valid observation that female emancipation facilitates divorce for women and consequently contributes somewhat to raising the overall divorce rate. However, this is not necessarily detrimental. In the past, more women than men remained in unhappy marriages (or were willing to do so) because they had no other choice. Now, the choices for both parties are closer to being equalized. And this is only "bad" if one operates on the assumption that women should suffer failed marriages more than men do.

Another interesting idea to consider is that it is divorce itself which leads to the emancipation of women who used to be more traditional in their way of life. Divorce is often the *cause* of women's liberation rather than the result. Let us examine the scenario. A woman finds herself on her own, perhaps with children. Perhaps she has never been employed before. She has to get a job, care for her children, pay the bills, have the car fixed, call the plumber when there is a leak, rearrange her social life, and start dating and entering into new sexual unions. She is a "new" woman. She discovers that she can get along very well, at times better than her ex-spouse can. And she often makes a healthier adjustment to divorce

18. H.L. Ross and I.V. Sawhill, *Time of Transition: The Growth of Families Headed by Women*, Washington, D.C.: The Urban Institute, 1975, p. 57.

than he does. She becomes interested in women's rights because she still has much to gain and she has so much to do. She may even join a women's group. Divorce caused the emancipation of such a woman. Not the reverse.

But there are sad cases where female emancipation is effectively the direct cause of certain divorces which would otherwise not take place. Although this should be discussed in our next chapter on the individual causes of divorce, we will mention it here. It often happens that a women becomes liberated too late in her life. Many women reach their thirties, get a job, meet new women, and for various reasons find themselves either involved in the women's movement or in great sympathy with it. With newly acquired expectations, they look at their own lives and are dissatisfied with what they see: a husband, a couple of children, a house. Misunderstanding the true nature of liberation, they feel that they are "just" housewives, and they want more. They ask for more and try to get it: more education, a job, more freedom from their children, a greater sharing of household responsibilities with a husband who may or may not be willing but is nevertheless bewildered by what is going on. The tension mounts, the frustrations pile up, the misunderstandings multiply and the explosion ensues: she or he wants out of the mess. This is why I said that such women, *in a way*, are emancipated too late: too late for their helpless children and often too late for their relationship with their husband; and, if not too late, too abruptly, too rapidly. Women and men should be emancipated earlier, so that innocent bystanders do not have to suffer. Unfortunately, the evidence coming from high schools indicates that teenage girls often view their future in a very unrealistic way: they think of getting married soon and having children; they do *not* think of becoming self sufficient or even of contributing to their future household income. Nor do they give any thought to their personal development and general education. In an age of individualism and of high divorce rates such attitudes are simply unrealistic.

LACK OF PSYCHOLOGICAL EMANCIPATION OF MEN

As the forces of liberalism, individualism, hedonism, and women's emancipation march on, all contributing to the undermining of the relationships of more and more couples, we must also deal here with the attitudes of men. We have talked of how the emancipation of women can relate to divorce. We must look at the equivalent issue with regard to men.

As things are, too many men have been brought up in a tradition of male privilege, of little boys who cannot cry, of teenagers who cannot show emotions and of grown men who cannot differentiate sex from love or tenderness. It used to be said that *women* mistook sex for love. Now it seems that while women are better able to differentiate between the two and want *both*, men know more about sex than about love and tenderness. Often they can expess affection only in bed or feel that, because there is a lot of sex in their lives, there is a lot of tenderness. Women have been trained to give tenderness and now want to receive it. More women are becoming dissatisfied at the terrible emotional deprivation they must endure married to husbands who can go to bed but cannot make *love*.

The inexpressive male has received some attention in research literature, mainly from a psychiatric point of view. Inexpressive men have been divided into two categories: the cowboy type and the playboy type.[19] The cowboy is the strong, silent, all-American he-man of the John Wayne type, as described by Manville, for instance.[20] His attitude toward women may be courteous but it is reserved.[21] The cowboy type cannot express the feelings which he does have and does not know *how* to relate to women as human beings. The playboy type, the Don Juan of the past, emphasizes enjoyment without responsibility or involvement. The playboy, however, does not seem to care for women.

19. J.O. Balswick and C.W. Peek, "The Inexpressive Male: A Tragedy of American Society," *The Family Coordinator*, 20, October 1971, pp. 363-368.
20. W.H. Manville, "The Locker Room Boys," *Cosmopolitan*, 166, 11, 1969, pp. 110-115.
21. Balswick and Peek, *op.cit.*, p. 364.

In conjunction with the above, it must be noted that, in increasing numbers, women are participating in the labour force on a par with men. Studies done in Canada, the U.S.A., France and even Soviet countries have all indicated that, when a wife becomes employed, her weekly workload increases by some eighteen hours while that of her husband increases on the average by only a few *minutes* per week, so minimal is his new contribution to the familial effort.[22] While women are working more, their husbands are, for the most part, not contributing substantially more to household duties and child-rearing; exceptions to this rule are, however, becoming more numerous. Such a situation is both unfair and bound to lead to a high level of frustration on the part of the woman . . . and to the possibility that she may look elsewhere for gratification or, at least, for a reduced burden.

Even in marriages where both parties are working, men tend to retain their old life-style while their wives are waiting for them at home with the children after finishing their own day's work. I find that working women in general, including career women, are much more willing than men are to arrange their schedules and even modify their career plans to make allowance for their marital and family life. Men stay at work later even when they could come home, almost by force of habit or as if they do not feel at ease in their own homes (perhaps because they are not there often enough and contribute so little to its daily functions). Men also participate in more business "evenings out" than women in comparable jobs. The latter are less willing to set their families aside. In many fields today, career pressures are as great for women as for men. In fact, they are higher for women because women generally have to really stand out to achieve recognition, while recognition at work comes more easily to men. On the whole, women tend to succumb less to the old stereotype of having to make it at all costs.

In other words, if men have the right to be dissatisfied with their wives and to look for greener pastures, women are

22. M. Meissner *et al.*, "No Exit for Wives: Sexual Division of Labour and the Cumulation of Household Demands," *Canadian Review of Sociology and Anthropology*, 12, November 1975, pp. 424-439.

quickly acquiring the same right. And many are already making known their dissatisfaction at the fact that their husbands fail to achieve their own full human potential, through a refusal to allow themselves to develop certain traits that, in the past, used to be considered feminine but are now widely accepted by psychologists as being simply *human* traits; traits which both sexes need in each other, and which both sexes should develop in themselves. Many marriages have already ended and many more will end as long as men fail to fulfill their full human potential and at the same time prove to be unsatisfactory marital partners for women. Also, many marriages will end with husbands threatened emotionally by and dissatisfied with their "liberated" wives, and seeking out women, or other wives, with more traditional outlooks on life.

INCREASED LONGEVITY

Since people live longer and in better health, each couple, if it does not divorce, will spend more years together. As Bell points out, a couple marrying today can, statistically, expect to live together for about thirty-five years on the average (statistics always speak in terms of averages), in spite of divorce and death.[23] For many, this may be too long, for, as most studies show, marital satisfaction tends to diminish in the middle years and to pick up again past the years of retirement. However, because of the prospect of a longer life span, couples who find themselves in the dip of marital dissatisfaction in their forties or even fifties may not wish to remain together, as they well might if they knew that they had only a few years left together.

The fact that people live longer means that they go through more stages in life than in the past. Life cycles used to consist of childhood and adulthood only; now they include young adulthood, middle age, the retirement years, and senior citizen status. Because of the diversity of personal and social situations inherent in these various stages, individuals' needs vary accordingly. Consequently, marital needs may also change so

23. R.R. Bell, *Marriage and Family Interaction*, Homewood, Ill.: Dorsey Press, 1971, third edition, p. 485.

that a partner who was just right for one stage may not be so for the next one. Moreover, an increased life-span means a different philosophy of life; one which must come to terms with the realization that one may have much time left to spend in retirement with a person one may no longer love or even like.

POVERTY AND LOW INCOME

We do not have Canadian studies in this area, but studies of other western societies indicate that divorce is most prevalent, and that desertion is perhaps even more common than divorce, in lower economic strata. A plenitude of studies have also found consistent correlations between low socio-economic status and emotional disorders, especially schizophrenia, general ill health, an inadequate utilization of medical resources, deliquency and criminality, and even reduced longevity. What the sum of these studies indicates is that life is more stressful and precarious when people have a low level of education and are economically underprivileged.[24] The combination of these two factors means that lower-status persons do not have the knowledge or the qualities required to cope with certain problems, or the necessary resources to turn to when needed.[25] Studies have also found a consistent correlation between low education (and income) on the one hand and marital dissatisfaction and divorce on the other.[26]

Poverty, either as a result of very low wages, or of relatively low wages coupled with a large family, or of unemployment, can be, for many people, tantamount to a crippling disease; a disease which leaves them empty and drained, and prevents

24. See R. Liem and J. Liem, "Social Class and Mental Illness Reconsidered: The Role of Economic Stress and Social Support," *Journal of Health and Social Behavior*, 19, June 1978, pp. 139-156.
25. L.I. Pearlin and C. Schooler, "The Structure of Coping," *Journal of Health and Social Behavior*, 19, March 1978, p. 17.
26. R.O. Blood, Jr. and D.M. Wolfe, *Husbands and Wives*, New York: Free Press, 1960, p. 229; L.M. Terman, *Psychological Factors in Marital Happiness*, New York: McGraw-Hill, 1938, p. 39; T.P. Monahan, "When Married Couples Part," *op.cit.*; R. Udry et al., "An Empirical Investigation of Some Widely Held Beliefs About Marital Interaction," *Marriage and Family Living*, 25, 1963, pp. 388-390.

them from effectively coping with their problems, either at an emotional or a practical level. Poverty can, directly or insiduously, attack family life and either destroy relationships or prevent them from ever taking a strong hold.

An impoverished couple has many more problems to cope with than a more privileged couple. The issue of money, or the lack of it, takes center stage. Tensions arise because of inadequate, overcrowded, noisy housing; because of lack of food; because of a lack of diversions; and because of a constant worry about the future. Tensions also arise because of unemployment or the fear of it, and sometimes from the necessity of being on welfare. A husband who loses the role of breadwinner often feels diminished, his self-esteem suffers; his wife may become intolerant of the situation; he may lose his authority over his children and their respect. Persons of lower social and economic status tend to sex-type the husband-wife roles to a greater extent than is done in other classes,[27] so that the male ego is even more bruised by his incapacity to hold the family together financially. It is indeed amazing that so many of these people pull through such crises still together and fairly satisfied with each other. However for a large number of them life is too difficult, the responsibilities too heavy, their emotional and physical resources too few, and the compensations non-existent. Separation and desertion follow. Divorce then takes place if and when money is available.

The women in such families are at even more of a disadvantage when they have children: they are uneducated, have few marketable skills, and whatever jobs they can find pay little. They cannot expect financial help from their former spouses and find themselves in housing projects that cater to people with similar problems and that are noisy and full of children. These women often watch helplessly as their children become difficult, diffident, and disappear, out of control, into the mass of children in the neighbourhood. Often these women have no

27. For instance, see L.B. Rubin, *Worlds of Pain: Life in the Working-Class Family*, New York: Basic Books, 1976, p. 125; M. Komarovsky, *Blue Collar Marriages*, New York: Random House, 1964; A.B. Motz, "Conceptions of Marital Roles by Status Groups," *Marriage and Family Living*, 20, 1950, pp. 136-162.

alternative but to remarry (if they can do so legally) as quickly as they can, or to live with a man, so that they are financially assisted. In the U.S.A., it has been found, in fact, that women who are less educated and have less money remarry more than other divorced women.[28]

SUB-CULTURAL EFFECT

This is a societal cause of divorce that is not generally mentioned by researchers. Certain cities (such as Los Angeles) and certain groups in the population (such as actors, some professionals, and artists) have extremely high divorce rates; 50% or more of their marriages end up in divorce. What actually takes place is that the factors that we have discussed in the preceding sections are concentrated in especially high doses in these areas and professions; factors such as individualism, hedonism, liberalism and mobility.

The inter-action of these variables exerts such pressure on the couples involved that a large proportion of them are always on the verge of divorcing, while others have just divorced, just remarried or redivorced. Much of the gossip which takes place in those groups focuses on marital situations, frailties, and failures. As one woman who once belonged to such a group commented to me, "You come to feel that you are the only ones who have never divorced and it really makes you feel odd. You practically feel a pressure to do it. In addition, you encounter so much hanky-panky that it is difficult to resist temptation no matter how good your marriage is." There is no stigma attached to divorce in such groups. On the contrary, there is almost an encouragement of it. Another woman, whose son attended a very liberal school in Canada, found that her child was the only one in his class whose parents were not divorced. Only six years old, he would often come home and say, "When are you going to divorce so that I can go and visit like the others?"

28. K.S. Renne, "Health and Marital Experience in an Urban Population," *Journal of Marriage and the Family*, 33, May 1971, p. 347.

SURFEIT OF CHOICES

Our society is consumer oriented. We buy and are urged to buy more and to go places; we are led to equate personal success with possessing things (big cars, big houses, pools, planes) and travelling to exotic places. We are confronted by a dizzying array of choices. We are offered so many products and so many opinions about so many products that we do not know which to choose, for each option appears more attractive than the next. We can move indefinitely from choice to choice and the potential seems limitless.

Moreover, this consumer-oriented society leads people to believe that a multiplicity of experiences is necessary in order to be "with it," happy, and self-fulfilled. North Americans are by far the biggest faddists in the world. No sooner has one fad taken hold (whether it be the hoola hoop, touch therapy, or vitamins) than another is introduced. People, especially those more affluent, feel compelled to try each because the promoters package their products in such a way that each product appears to be essential to one's self-fulfillment or personal growth. Many individuals hop from one product to the next as if on a constant merry-go-round, never knowing if they have achieved anything, and insecure about the fact that they have not already tried something else that is now en vogue. As Marianne Frankenhauser puts it, "Seizing as many choices as possible, utilizing every opportunity, is made to seem exemplary and desirable." This bombardment of alternatives leads to overstimulation or saturation. Our nervous systems may be offered more opportunities and may have to make more choices than they can cope with.

This unsettling situation is not only dangerous in itself in terms of inner peace and mental health but it also has its ramifications in the area of marriage. Many people in our population *cannot* resist alternatives. The next woman is always more beautiful. One type of woman has not yet been sampled. If a man remains with his spouse, he feels that he is out of touch with the times. Many men (women are as of yet less involved in this destructive game) judge their own merits by their "scores" and are constantly on the look-out for someone better, someone more beautiful, someone more "with it." The grass is always greener on the other side, but is also greener, as one book titles it, over the septic tank!

What we are pointing to is a form of neurosis, an individual problem to be sure, but the kind of problem that can only exist in the type of society we live in. As Janov has suggested, it is a neurosis based on pseudo-needs (material possessions as status symbols, for instance) to the detriment of more basic needs such as love and inner security.[29] This saturation, this over-stimulation of choices could not exist in a less mobile, less individualistic, hedonistic, and consumerist society, and in some cases it does contribute to marital failure and the recourse to divorce.

CONCLUSIONS

We have reviewed briefly the principal societal causes of divorce. Our major emphasis has been on the fact that these variables have to be studied in combination rather than singly to explain the current climate; a climate which has made for a soaring divorce rate. A review of these social factors provides us with a better understanding of the larger trends which foster, directly or indirectly, the more personal reasons for our high rate of marital unhappiness and, especially, which foster the adoption of divorce as a solution to this marital unhappiness.

In this chapter, we have linked high divorce rates and marital unhappiness to global social causes. This review also makes us realize that even if divorce were to be judged as a problem rather than as a solution to or result of a problem, societal remedies would be nearly impossible to apply because of the inherent complexity, comprehensiveness and interdependence, of the causal variables involved. High divorce rates may be one of the prices that a society subjected to the elements described in this chapter has to pay until such time as a balance is reached, if at all, between the various attractions and forces involved.

29. A. Janov, *The Primal Scream*, New York: Dell, 1970.

4 Personal Causes of Divorce

As pointed out in Chapter 3, the personal causes of divorce are those variables that the afflicted person will identify and that social workers and other professionals in the field of mental health will point to as having contributed to or precipitated the divorce. They are the tangible elements, objective or subjective, that led up to the divorce. Here too, we will see that these variables are rarely isolated. There is generally no single villain in a divorce case, but a whole series of them, and often divorce cases are a tragedy of errors and misunderstandings. Some causes, such as mental illness, alcoholism and adultery, are indeed so potent that they can practically act alone in destroying a marriage. But there are other marriages, afflicted with the same problems, that not only survive but recover and even thrive. Therefore the personalities and, especially, the ability to cope of the couples involved are an extremely important factor.[1]

Some of the variables discussed in this chapter might be described as "intervening" or intermediate as they are both social and psychological. They pertain to people's socio-demographic characteristics or background and affect accordingly the probability of divorce for those people. We will begin with these: very youthful marriage, brief acquaintance, unhappiness in parental marriages, dissimilarity of background, mixed-faith and non-religious marriages, and disapproval of the union by family and friends. We will then deal with the

1. These authors found coping mechanisms to be more important than personality traits: L.I. Pearlin and C. Schooler, "The Structure of Coping," *Journal of Health and Social Behavior*, 19, March 1978, p. 12.

personal variables: alcoholism, mental problems, total career immersion, failures in communication, sexual problems, adultery, children in first marriages, children in remarriages, emotional immaturity, mental and physical cruelty, and unrealistic expectations.

YOUTHFUL MARRIAGES AND PRE-MARITAL PREGNANCIES

Couples who marry in their teens run a greater risk of experiencing greater marital dissatisfaction[2] and of undergoing divorce.[3] There are several elements in this variable that account for this result. First, young people often marry as a consequence of pregnancy:[4] Christensen and Meissner have found that couples who marry following a pregnancy are twice as likely to divorce as others similar to them in terms of occupation, age at marriage, and type of wedding.[5] In many

2. G.R. Lee, "Age at Marriage and Marital Satisfaction: A Multivariate Analysis with Implications for Marital Stability," *Journal of Marriage and the Family*, 39, August 1977, pp. 493-504.
3. G.H. Elder and R.C. Rockwell, "Marital Timing in Women's Life Patterns," *Journal of Family History*, 1, 1976, pp. 34-55; R. Schoen, "California Divorce Rates by Age at First Marriage and Duration of First Marriage," *Journal of Marriage and the Family*, 37, August 1975, pp. 548-555; J.A. Weed, "Age at Marriage as a Factor in State Divorce Rate Differentials," *Demography*, 11, August 1974, pp. 361-375; L.K. Hong, "The Instability of Teenage Marriage in the United States; an Evaluation of the Socio-Economic Status Hypothesis," *International Journal of Sociology of the Family*, 4, Autumn 1974, pp. 201-212; L.C. Coombs and Z. Zumeta, "Correlates of Marital Dissolution in a Prospective Fertility Study: A Research Note," *Social Problems*, 18, Summer 1970, p. 94; K.E. Bauman, "The Relationship Between Age at First Marriage, School Dropout, and Marital Instability: An Analysis of the Glick Effect," *Journal of Marriage and the Family*, 29, November 1967, pp. 672-682; R. Parke, Jr. and P.C. Glick, "Prospective Changes in Marriage and the Family," *Journal of Marriage and the Family*, 29, May 1967, pp.249-256; G.R. Lee, "Age at Marriage and Marital Satisfaction," *op.cit.*; L.G. Burchinal, "Trends and Prospects for Young Marriage in the United States," *Journal of Marriage and the Family*, 27, May 1965, pp. 243-254; P.H. Jacobson, *American Marriage and Divorce*, New York: Rinehart, 1959; L.G. Burchinal and L.E. Chancellor, "Social Status, Religious Affiliation, and Ages at Marriage," *Marriage and Family Living*, 25, May 1963, pp. 219-221.
4. J.T. Landis, "Social Correlates of Divorce and Nondivorce Among the Unhappily Married," *Marriage and Family Living*, 5, 1963, p. 180.
5. H.T. Christensen and H.H. Meissner, "Studies in Child Spacing: Premarital Pregnancy as a Factor in Divorce," *American Sociological Review*, 18, 1953, pp. 641-644. In fact, they found that the longer after marriage the first child is born, the less the chance of divorce.

instances, these young couples would not have married had it not been for the pregnancy. They may not even love each other and may grow to resent their situation. The early arrival of the child only compounds their difficulties: they are young, inexperienced, uneducated and often unemployed. They are generally immature, mere children themselves. The child restricts their freedom, adds to their financial difficulties and forces them into an adulthood for which they are not ready and into roles which they did not have the time to learn, to internalize. Bacon has used the concept of accelerated role transition to explain the high rates of marital dissolution involving women who bear children very young. This concept is based on the "rapidity with which new and demanding social roles are activated, abandoned, and modified." Stress follows from any pattern of role transition which deviates from the socially prescribed norm.[6] Furstenberg has found that, in the case of pre-marital pregnancy, "marital histories ... show that disruption in the courtship process and limited economic resources are the most important factors contributing to marital dissolution."[7]

Second, even without such pregnancies, youthful marriage entails the union of two immature individuals who will soon grow up, and there are distinct possibilities that the directions each will take will differ as they mature. In addition, these individuals are too inexperienced to cope effectively with the challenges of life together, often in difficult socio-economic conditions. This leads to our third element:[8] people who marry during their teens often drop out of school, although not necessarily out of universities,[9] in order to earn a living, and are consequently faced with harsher financial conditions than people who marry later. Moreover, there is frequently another overlap between lower income and age at marriage: in many

6. L. Bacon, "Early Motherhood, Accelerated Role Transition, and Social Pathology," *Social Forces*, 52, March 1974, p. 334.

7. F.F. Furstenberg, Jr., "Premarital Pregnancy and Marital Instability," *Journal of Social Issues*, 32, 1976, p. 67.

8. R.M. Inselberg, "Marriage Problems and Satisfaction in High School Marriages," *Marriage and Family Living*, 24, February 1962, pp. 74-77.

9. A.C. Kerckhoff and A.A. Parrow, "The Effect of Early Marriage on the Educational Attainment of Young Men," *Journal of Marriage and the Family*, 41, February 1979, pp. 97-107.

countries, the age at marriage of brides is lower in less privileged classes,[10] thereby raising the divorce rates for these classes. It has been found that people who marry young, especially those who have children early, never make up for these early complexities: they remain poorer than other couples and do not tend to have the social mobility that their former schoolmates have. The fourth element in our discussion of youthful marriages is the educational factor from yet another viewpoint; studies have found that couples with higher education are happier.[11] Not only do many young couples never achieve a reasonable level of education, but their very lack of education at the outset of their life together is, as a rule, likely to thwart their chances of making it, although there are, of course, many exceptions to this rule.

There is also some evidence to suggest that people who marry in their teens are less well adjusted than those of their peers who marry at a socially more acceptable age;[12] that youngsters who marry have lower ego strength, and often come from an unhappier family background than similar people who marry later.[13]

The variables of education, employment, personality, age at marriage and pre-marital pregnancy are therefore intimately linked and reinforce one other. People who marry young will often have to discontinue their education to support their families or to take care of their children. For young people with a minimal education, employment is more difficult to secure

10. C. Gibson, "The Association Between Divorce and Social Class in England and Wales," *British Journal of Sociology*, 25, March 1974, p. 83.
11. R. Udry *et al.*, "An Empirical Investigation of Some Widely Held Beliefs About Marital Interaction," *Marriage and Family Living*, 25, 1963, pp. 388-390; T.P. Monahan, "When Married Couples Part: Statistical Trends and Relationships in Divorce," *American Sociological Review*, 27, 1962, pp. 625-634; R.O. Blood, Jr., *Husbands and Wives*, New York: Free Press, 1960, p. 229; L.M. Terman, *Psychological Factors in Marital Happiness*, New York: McGraw-Hill, 1938, p. 39.
12. F.M. Martinson, "Ego Deficiency as a Factor in Marriage," *American Sociological Review*, 20, 1955, pp. 161-164; J.J. Moss and R. Gingles, "The Relationship of Personality to the Incidence of Early Marriage," *Marriage and Family Living*, 21, 1959, pp. 373-377.
13. Martinson, *op.cit.*; J.J. Moss, "Teenage Marriage : Cross National Trends and Sociological Factors in the Decision of When to Marry," *Journal of Marriage and the Family*, 27, May 1965, pp. 230-242.

and financial difficulties are at a premium. All of these factors can only increase the potential for tension and dissatisfaction in the young couple. Moreover, these young couples often become dependent upon their parents and have to live with them, especially among certain groups in society. The cycle of poverty is perpetuated in their own children who also marry young and give them dependent grandchildren: "This 'telescoping' of generations precludes the economic recuperation of families in the middle years that later timing of marriage and parenthood makes possible."[14]

All in all, unless they receive the active support of a family group, the problems of very young couples, especially those with a child, are endless: how to find lodging, pay for it, cook, keep house, get a job, practice birth control, take care of a baby, find some leisure time, and still be able to communicate with each other. Their sex lives are often in a shambles as well because of ignorance, fear of pregnancy or venereal disease, and general immaturity. Therefore, youthful marriage and pre-marital pregnancies are highly complex issues involving many other variables and it is difficult to conclude which of these contributes the most to high divorce rates.

BRIEF ACQUAINTANCE

Statistics indicate that couples who marry shortly after having met each other, who do not get engaged, or have a very brief period of engagement, have greater chances of divorcing.[15] This situation is also a likely occurrence in the young marriages discussed above. There is a common-sense chain of causality involved. An acquaintance that is too brief simply means that the couple will marry without knowing each other. Unpleasant surprises may be in store for them, often soon after they have married, as one or the other partner stops the role-play of courtship and reverts to his or her natural personality. This change can be shocking for anyone unprepared for it. Disillusionment soon follows; arguments and

14. A. Fischer *et al.*, "The Occurrence of the Extended Family at the Origin of the Family of Procreation: A Developmental Approach to Negro Family Structure," *Journal of Marriage and the Family*, 30, 1968, p. 299.
15. H.J. Locke, *Predicting Adjustment in Marriage*, New York: Holt, 1951.

feelings of having been betrayed and lied to, set in very early in the relationship.

Even if this does not happen, couples with a brief acquaint-anceship have not had the time to explore each other's expectations of the relationship and they may soon find that their conception of their respective roles as husband and wife are drastically at odds and cannot be reconciled. They have not had sufficient time to experience each other in a wide range of situations, so that many aspects of their personalities have not had time to be expressed.

UNHAPPINESS IN PARENTAL MARRIAGES[16]

Parents who have an unhappy marriage may be passing on to their children maladaptive patterns of conjugal inter-action. By observing their parents' behaviour towards each other, children may learn mechanisms, and even attitudes, that are destructive in a relationship. Conversely, children who have had the example of two parents who tried to resolve their differences with love and trust, and who did their best to make each other happy, may be more competent later on in their own relationships because of the role modelling they received as children. In addition, because of a stable home environment, they may have more even personalities than some others. Consequently, it can happen that children who have perceived their parents to be unhappy have themselves personality traits that may be dysfunctional in a later conjugal relation-ship.

We do not know precisely how unhappy marriage and/or divorce in parents and divorce in children are connected. In order to provide a satisfactory explanation as to how this comes about, we would have to know how old the children were when their parents' marriage was unhappy; if girls are

16. I am here *at the outset* following some of the categories presented by Goode in his table entitled "Background characteristics associated with a greater or lesser proneness to divorce." The explanations, however, are mine. See W.J. Goode, "Family Disorganization," in *Contemporary Social Problems*, edited by R.K. Merton and R. Nisbet, New York: Harcourt Brace Jovanovich, 1971, third edition, pp. 500-501.

affected more than boys in this;[17] what type of marital "unhappiness" children have in mind when they report their parents to be unhappy, and what kinds of behaviour the parents exhibited in these instances; and whether, in the long run, divorce has fewer ill effects than an unhappy but stable parental marriage. It is also possible that if parents have divorced, children are more likely to accept this situation as normal, and will later have recourse to divorce themselves, more easily and more *rapidly* than in those cases where the parental marriage remained intact. We will look further at this variable in Chapter 7 where we will explore in great detail the effect that divorce has on children.

DISSIMILARITY OF BACKGROUND

It is easier to live with people who have similar values and habits to our own than with people who are very different. Although differences are exciting, when the gap between two people is too wide, misunderstandings, as well as irritation, puzzlement, annoyance and quarrels will easily arise. Such a situation can become very uncomfortable, especially when there is such a discrepancy of background that the spouses have little in common in terms of mutual interests, sexuality, and their conceptions of their respective roles as husbands, wives, and parents.

A certain commonality of values, interests, and habits is necessary in order to go through the daily routine relatively smoothly, and in order for people to relate to each other. Although there is still a great deal of controversy about this topic, a recent study of dating couples who break up found that, even at this level of interaction, those who terminated their relationships were from less homogeneous backgrounds.[18] The results of this study seem to support the

17. As indeed may be the case: Pope and Mueller reported higher divorce rates among females than males whose parents had been divorced. H. Pope and C.W. Mueller, "The Intergenerational Transmission of Marital Instability: Comparisons by Race and Sex," *Journal of Social Issues*, 32, 1976, p. 58.
18. C.T. Hill *et al.*, "Breakups Before Marriage: The End of 103 Affairs," *Journal of Social Issues*, 32, 1976, p.153. Extensive literature exists on what is called "mate selection" and on the basis for this selection, whether it is

argument that a certain similarity of background is necessary for couples.

Ackerman hypothesizes that marital stability is related to homogamy while instability is related to heterogamy or dissimilarity of background. He developed his theory to include the sharing of friends by both partners in a marriage as an element of marital stability, because shared friendships reinforce the similarity of values of the spouses.[19]

MIXED MARRIAGES AND NON-RELIGIOUS COUPLES

Theoretically, mixed marriages seem to be at a disadvantage because they generally do not benefit, at least at the outset, from the approval of the families involved. They also involve a dissimilarity of background and are likely to give rise to complicated decisions regarding the education of children, especially their religious education. If the spouses are religious but of different faiths, they will worship separately, thereby closing one avenue of shared interest.

However, mixed marriages do not seem to produce the same results for all religious groups. Studies such as those of Christensen and Barber in the United States indicate that Catholics and Jews who marry people of a different religion have slightly higher divorce rates than if they had married within their own religion; however for Protestants, mixed marriages do not seem to raise divorce rates.[20] Similarly, another study has found that Catholics who inter-marry have high rates of marital dissatisfaction while similar Protestants had the lowest degree of marital dissatisfaction; Jews are in between.[21] It has also been found that mixed marriages are more prevalent in remarriages than in the first marriages of

homogamy or similarity (and in what areas) or heterogamy or dissimilarity. A review of this literature is unnecessary for the purposes of this book.

19. C.Ackerman, "Affiliations: Structural Determinants of Differential Divorce Rates," *American Journal of Sociology*, 69, July 1963, pp. 13-20.
20. H.T. Christensen and K.E. Barber,"Interfaith Versus Intrafaith Marriages in Indiana," *Journal of Marriage and the Family*, 29, August 1967, pp. 461-469.
21. J.S. Heiss, "Interfaith Marriage and Marital Outcome," *Marriage and Family Living*, 23, August 1961, pp. 228-232.

divorced persons.²² It would be interesting to know if this greater religious disparity in remarriages plays any role in the success rate of such unions.

In the case of non-religious couples, what actually happens is that these couples are generally less conventional, more liberal, perhaps more individualistic, and certainly not bound by religious restrictions. These sociological forces combined in them mean that, if their marriage is not sufficiently satisfactory, they will be more likely than other couples to resort to divorce because they have fewer social and religiously inspired moral restrictions on them. Personal satisfaction will take precedence over other considerations that might deter religious couples from seeking divorce.

Let us look at religious couples and the possible reasons why they have a *low* divorce rate.²³ First, for them marriage is likely to be a religious matter, not a secular one; a covenant with God, and therefore, one not easily broken. Because of this they may work harder at making their marriages happy:

> *Persons to whom divorce and even separation are inconceivable, as in the case of members of certain religions, have a self-imposed limit beyond which conflict and tension cannot progress.*²⁴

They may be more willing to accept much unpleasantness in order to remain married.

Authors have speculated that the reason for the low divorce rates of religious couples is their valuation of the stability of marriage over personal happiness. In order to test this assumption, Kunz and Albrecht compared couples who were regular church-goers with couples who were lowest in all

22. E. Rosenthal,"Jewish Intermarriage in Indiana," *Eugenics Quarterly*, 5, December 1968, pp. 277-287; and "Divorce and Religious Intermarriage: The Effects of Previous Marital Status Upon Subsequent Marital Behavior," *Journal of Marriage and the Family*, 32, August 1970, pp. 435-440.

23. For data on Jewish groups, see C. Goldscheider and S. Goldstein,"Generational Changes in Jewish Family Structure," *Journal of Marriage and the Family*, 29, 1967, p. 269. Lee, *op. cit.*, also found a tendency for religious males (Catholic or Lutheran) to experience greater marital satisfaction: p. 501.

24. E.W. Burgess and H.J. Locke, *The Family*, New York: American Book Co., 1945, p. 580.

categories of church attendance.[25] They found that the former not only reported lower divorce rates, but expressed a higher degree of marital satisfaction and fewer role conflicts than the latter.[26] Such results may indicate that church-goers do indeed have happier marriages and remain together for reasons both of personal happiness and their belief in the permanency of marriage. A religious couple has one element in common that a non-religious couple does not have: they worship together and vividly share a common set of values which cement their relationship. The simple act of being married at a religious ceremony is inversely correlated with divorce.[27] Similarly, the education of children is easier for them because they have the certainty of religious beliefs to back them up.

DISAPPROVAL OF UNION BY FAMILY

A couple is not an isolated unit in society and they can benefit from the support of those dear to them as well as suffer from the withdrawal of this support. Couples who receive the approval of their families and of their friends are at a great advantage. They are part of a beneficent network and are in a position to receive help with child care along with moral comfort. Contrariwise, couples who do not have such support are not only deprived of something positive, but often family and friends may actively work at making their life together difficult and may even try to separate them by pulling in different directions. Such unions often occur among very young people and in cases of mixed marriage. Lowrie found that young brides who elope and marry out of their home state, usually without parental approval, have higher divorce rates than other young brides who have gone through an acceptable wedding routine.[28]

25. Religiosity is generally indicated by church attendance, an easier indicator than more subjective ones involving convictions and beliefs. Therefore, the variable of religiosity is ill defined and poorly operationalized. Nevertheless, the above results are of interest and relevance.
26. P.R. Kunz and S.L. Albrecht,"Religion, Marital Happiness,and Divorce," *International Journal of Sociology of the Family*, 7, July-December 1977, pp. 227-232.
27. Christensen and Meissner, *op. cit.*
28. S.H. Lowrie,"Early Marriage: Premarital Pregnancy and Associated Factors," *Journal of Marriage and the Family*, 27, February 1965, pp. 48-56.

Certain families can make it particularly difficult for their children to marry out of their faith and, when they do, the other spouse is often made to feel unwelcome and ill at ease, or is simply regarded as a stranger, at least until children are born—although for many couples the problems do not end even then. The following example could well apply to the previous section.

Daniel married a non-practising Catholic against his parents' wish. Although he was a lawyer and 26, they refused to attend the couple's non-denominational wedding. The couple was not invited to the next Bar Mitzvah in the family. His parents severed most of their ties with him and never saw his wife. Two children were born but the grandparents refused to acknowledge them, even though at that time the wife volunteered to have them raised in the Jewish faith so that the children would have a family. Five years later, Daniel ventured out of his law practice and invested heavily in an enterprise which failed. All the while he was keeping late hours and his wife was alone with the children most of the time. He started calling on his parents without his wife and when a financial crisis occurred, he accepted substantial sums of money from them. He became dependent upon them and, as a gesture of expiation or of acknowledgment, he reinstated himself within his family circle without his wife and children whom his parents still refused to see. The marriage deteriorated; the wife returned to school, completed her training, and requested a divorce.[29]

Familial disapproval of a union can also occur in cases of pre-marital pregnancy, social class disparity, age disparity, and racial difference, or when the spouse disapproved of has

29. Twenty interviews with divorced, separated and deserted persons were conducted in Toronto by the author in the fall of 1978 for the specific purpose of gathering case material for this book. The interviews focused on the causes of the marital breakdown, the respondent's reaction to it, adaptation processes and perception of his/her situation. In January and February of 1979, eight remarried couples were interviewed; all eight husbands had been previously divorced and five of the wives had. For the other three wives, this was their first marriage. Names have been changed to assure anonymity.

certain personality problems, is unemployed, or has fallen foul of social or legal authorities.

ALCOHOLISM

We are now entering the realm of those variables which people personally involved in divorce often cite as the major (if not necessarily the only) cause of the breakdown of their marriage. These variables are directly related to the personalities, the conduct, or the personal situation of the spouses.

Alcoholism, or addiction to alcohol, may in itself be the result of a poor and disruptive marital relationship; however, it may also contribute to the disintegration of a marriage. Alcoholism as a result of marital problems probably occurs among both men and women, while alcoholism as a direct cause of marital breakdown is generally, although by no means exclusively, a male problem. One out of every seven teenagers from divorced homes seen in Robson's study in Toronto had an alcoholic father.[30] Statistics indicate that hospitalized male alcoholics are more often separated and divorced than non-alcoholics.[31] For instance, in the population hospitalized for psychiatric problems in Canada in 1974, divorced men in the 20-39 age bracket had an alcoholism rate of 698 (per 100,000 population) compared to a rate of 93 for divorced women and a rate of 99 for married men.[32]

A conflict ridden marriage or, even one that is simply empty, devoid of feelings and of reciprocity, may cause such mental anguish to one or both partners that the more susceptible partner, either because of personal vulnerability or because of situational vulnerability (such as the lonely housewife syndrome), may resort to alcohol in order to lower anxiety, to make life more bearable, or as the only form of entertainment available. Both men and women can react to a bad marriage in this manner. In turn, alcoholism aggravates the situation by causing the spouses to drift further apart, by lowering their

30. B. Robson, *My Parents Are Divorced Too*, Toronto: Dorset, 1979.
31. R.A. Woodruff, "Divorce Among Psychiatric Outpatients," *British Journal of Psychiatry*, 121, 1972, pp. 289-292.
32. Unpublished figures on *first* hospitalizations obtained from the Health Division of Statistics Canada in 1976.

physical and psychological resistance to stress, by draining their financial resources, by placing a strain on their social life, and by endangering the well-being of the children. The burden placed on the family of the alcoholic is enormous.

In view of the fact that alcohol consumption in large quantities is, even now, more acceptable for men than for women, it is more often the man who will start drinking first, and then, because of this syndrome, burden and endanger the marital relationship. Men have more opportunities to go out, alone or "with the boys," and more opportunities to drink heavily than women do. It is more socially acceptable, for example, for them to sit at home and drink a lot of beer than it is for a woman, especially in front of the children. An alcoholic husband will drain the family budget, may endanger or lose his job, may often be absent from home, and is more likely to resort to violence and verbal abuse than is an alcoholic wife.

Similarly, the loneliness of a sour marriage and of divorce may lead people, especially men, to alcoholism, particularly if they were already fairly heavy drinkers. The family can be seen as a stabilizer which prevents deviations and, once people are deprived of this agency of control, they are more susceptible to such problems as alcoholism. Strauss has found that, while alcoholism itself certainly contributes to marital breakup, the stress and isolation that follow a breakup can either reinforce drinking behaviour or even instigate it.[33]

EMOTIONAL PROBLEMS

Emotional problems are both a cause of divorce and a consequence of (or reaction to) it. Lasting and deep-seated emotional problems are often the cause of divorce. Deep-seated emotional problems found in divorced persons were probably already present before the divorce (whether they caused it or not); for people who were healthy *before* the divorce, subsequent emotional problems are situational and will generally only be transitory. That is, post-divorce emo-

33. R. Strauss, "Alcohol and the Homeless Man," *Quarterly Journal of Studies on Alcohol*, 7, December 1946, pp. 360-404; R. Strauss and R.G. McCarthy, "Nonaddictive Pathological Drinking Patterns of Homeless Men," *Quarterly Journal of Studies on Alcohol*, 12, December 1951, pp. 601-611.

tional problems are reactive; a result of the stress engendered either by the marital breakup or by the problems of separation and of divorce. The longer emotional problems persist after divorce, the more likely it is that the individuals in question have deep-seated problems that were either active or latent before the divorce: in the latter case, the individuals were already predisposed to the problem and the divorce was only a precipitating factor, the "last straw."

Studies on mental health/illness have revealed that married men have the lowest rate of emotional problems, followed by married, widowed and never-married women, and widowed men. Divorced women have the next highest rate, followed by never-married men and, highest of all, divorced men. Gove surveyed the empirical literature on marital status/sex differences in mental illness and computed the following average ratios from the rates established for the studies included in his survey. The married category served as a basis of comparison for the other categories and represented a theoretical ratio of 1 so as to establish a ranking among all these gender/marital status categories.[34]

widowed women	: 1.43
never-married women	: 1.74
widowed men	: 2.53
divorced women	: 2.80
never-married men	: 3:13
divorced men	: 5:09

The most striking statistic is that of divorced men. It is five times that of married men (the latter having a ratio of 1). The rates for divorced women are also higher but the difference is less extreme. These results stem from studies using a wide range of indicators, including hospital statistics, community

34. W.R. Gove, "The Relationship Between Sex Roles, Marital Status, and Mental Illness," *Social Forces*, 51, September 1972, pp. 34-44. See, also, W.R. Gove and J.F. Tudor, "Adult Sex Roles and Mental Illness," in *Changing Women in Changing Society*, edited by J. Huber, Chicago: Chicago University Press, 1973. See, also, B.L. Bloom *et al.*, "Marital Disruption as a Stressful Life Event," in *Divorce and Separation*, edited by G. Levinger and O.C. Moles, New York: Basic Books, 1979, pp. 184-200.

surveys, psychiatric treatment in general, and visits to psychiatrists' offices. In Canada, studies by Gregory and Llewellyn Thomas have obtained similar results.[35]

TABLE 14

1974 First Hospitalizations for Psychiatric Disorders by Sex and Marital Status: Frequencies and Rates
(per 100,000 population)

SEX AND MARITAL STATUS	FREQUENCIES	RATES
married men	14,857	304
widowed women	2,419	321
married women	16,237	332
single women	7,402	387
single men	11,657	490
widowed men	938	491
divorced women	1,083	1,075
divorced men	1,020	1,372

Source: unpublished cross-tabulations supplied by Statistics Canada, Division of Mental Health, Anna Malhotra, analyst.

With the collaboration of the Health Division of Statistics Canada, unpublished material was used to compute rates of first hospitalizations for psychiatric disorders by sex and marital status for all persons above fifteen years of age. The rates were computed per 100,000 population on the basis of the 1971 Census while the numbers of individuals hospitalized are for the year 1974. Although divorced women and men are *numerically* the same in terms of first admissions, divorced women are more numerous in the population at large because they remarry less; hence their lower *rate* than men. When we examine the divorced category by age brackets (as predetermined by Statistics Canada), we see that for women and men

35. I. Gregory, "Factors Influencing First Admission Rates to Canadian Mental Hospitals III. An Analysis by Education, Marital Status, Country of Birth, Religion and Urban-rural Residence, 1950-52," *Canadian Psychiatric Association Journal*, 4, April, 1959, pp. 133-151; E. Llewellyn-Thomas, "The Prevalence of Psychiatric Symptoms Within an Island Fishing Village," *Canadian Medical Association Journal*, 83, 1960, pp. 197-204.

aged 20-39, the rates are 1,473 and 1,659 respectively, while for the age bracket 40-64, the rates show a sharp decline, especially for women: 824 to 1,365. It is possible that divorce is less stressful for a woman at middle age because her children are grown and she is thus faced with fewer role conflicts, demands on her time, and financial stresses. For men too, divorce seems to be related to higher rates of first hospitalization before middle age. Middle-aged men may be more secure in terms of their work and finances and this may lessen the impact of divorce on them. Or, perhaps, both sexes receive more support when they divorce later. However, these rates do not tell us anything about the *direction* of causality.

These are only rates for first hospitalizations for mental disorders. We have no comparable national statistics for visits to psychiatrists' offices, although we know that, each year, approximately 60% of office psychiatric consultations have a female as the patient in Ontario.[36] But we do not know the marital status of these women and men who seek psychiatric help outside the hospitals. Since married women have more money and more time than divorced women, we would expect that comparatively fewer divorced women would visit psychiatrists. But this is a hypothesis which has not yet been tested in Canada.

Researchers' overall conclusions are that divorce is related to higher rates of emotional problems. Along these lines, Renne found very high levels of psychological well-being among *happily* married people and lower levels among those who were unhappily married.[37] However, no one is certain which is cause and which, effect. To what extent do emotional problems cause marital unhappiness and divorce? And to what extent does marital unhappiness or divorce cause emotional problems? As we pointed out, divorced persons with lasting and severe emotional problems were probably also disturbed during their marriages, although in many cases

36. Information gathered from the Ontario Ministry of Health in 1977.
37. K.S. Renne, "Correlates of Dissatisfaction in Marriage," *Journal of Marriage and the Family*, 31, February 1970, pp. 54-67, and "Health and Marital Experience in an Urban Population," *Journal of Marriage and the Family*, 33, May 1971, pp. 338-350.

the relationship may have been so traumatic as to cripple a person emotionally. Some researchers believe that the high incidence of emotional problems among divorced people indicates a causal sequence from mental illness, to marital turmoil, to divorce.[38]

In this respect, it is interesting to note that all the studies on married people find married men healthier than married women. Yet, after divorce, the contrary happens and divorced men have higher rates of emotional problems than women. It could perhaps be that emotionally disturbed men contribute to the breakup of their marriages more than emotionally disturbed women do, and, once divorced find it more difficult to remarry, either because their problems are more severe or because they are not considered competent providers. A Vancouver study of multi-problem families found that a failure of family functioning had occurred in 63% of the families as a result of emotional problems in the husband; 37% of the wives had similar problems, although not necessarily in the same families.[39] Another possiblity is that women cope better after divorce than men. There are indications that they do in the long run, although immediately after separation or divorce women appear more traumatized. But, as the years go by the rates of emotional disorder in divorced men become progressively higher than those of divorced women, a fact that could support both the self-selection theory and the reaction theory, although after many years of adaptation to the divorce situation, the reactive theory seems much less applicable.

Pearlin and Johnson have also brought to light the interplay of economics and marital status; when they studied depression, they found that the difference between the married and the unmarried is greatest in conditions of economic hardship.[40] In other words, when people who are not married are economically deprived, they will be hit harder by emotional problems. Deprivation will make them more depressed, and

38. W. Briscoe, "Divorce and Psychiatric Disease," *Archives of General Psychiatry*, 29, July 1973, pp. 119-125.

39. United Community Services, Vancouver, *The Area Development Project*, n.d.

40. L.I. Pearlin and J.S. Johnson, "Marital Status, Life-Strains and Depression," *American Sociological Review*, 42, October 1977, pp. 704-715.

will also prevent them from coping adequately with depression caused by other factors.

In this context, it is interesting to look at the results of some British studies. To begin with, Hagnell and others found a certain psychological congruence in couples,[41] and this relative similarity was explained to be the result of interaction rather than of assortative mating,[42] although there is disagreement in this respect.[43] In other words, as spouses interact, their individual problems rub off on each other, so that they become more similar over the years in terms of mental health, rather than having chosen each other in the first place on the basis of the similarity of their problems. However, the acquisition of this congruence may be somewhat one-sided as it was found that wives with disturbed husbands develop emotional problems more readily than do husbands with disturbed wives:[44] because women are chiefly responsible for the care of families, when husbands are emotionally disturbed the strain is greater for women. On the other hand, when it is the wives who are emotionally disturbed, the husbands can escape much of the stress through their work. Moreover, a study by Briscoe and Smith found that fewer divorced women had had an emotionally disturbed spouse than divorced men.[45] One of the conclusions that can be drawn from this study is that the emotional problems of a wife are less well tolerated than those of a husband: a wife adapts more to the problems of her husband than vice versa,[46] and may be less willing to terminate a marriage because of the emotional dependency of her spouse.

41. O. Hagnell *et al.*, "Mental Illness in Married Pairs in a Total Population," *British Journal of Psychiatry*, 125, 1974, pp. 293-302.
42. N. Kreitman *et al.*, "Neurosis and Marital Interaction: I. Personality and Symptoms," *British Journal of Psychiatry*, 117, 1970, pp. 33-46.
43. E.S. Gershon *et al.*, "Assortative Mating in the Affective Disorders," *Biological Psychiatry*, 7, 1973, pp. 63-73.
44. Hagnell, *op.cit.*
45. W.C. Briscoe and J.C. Smith, "Psychiatric Illness, Marital Units and Divorce," *Journal of Nervous and Mental Disease*, 158, 1974, pp. 440-445.
46. Also relevant are the following: J. Collins *et al.*, "Neurosis and Marital Interaction: III. Family Roles and Functions," *British Journal of Psychiatry*, 119, 1971, pp. 232-242; B. Nelson *et al.*, "Neurosis and Marital Interaction: II. Time Sharing and Social Activity," *British Journal of Psychiatry*, 117, 1970, pp. 47-58; I.M. Ovenstone, "The Development of Neurosis in the Wives of Neurotic Men," *British Journal of Psychiatry*, 122, 1973, pp. 35-45.

TOTAL CAREER IMMERSION

By this is meant the condition of a person who is over-involved with his/her work, spends long hours away from home, arrives home late, may even have to spend some time at the office or on business during weekends and other holidays, may have to travel too extensively because of work, may not only come home late but, once home, simply immerse himself/herself in paper work and business phone calls. Generally, such persons are highly involved in or preoccupied with their jobs or careers, either for financial reasons, out of a love of their work, or because of a personality trait that makes them more at ease within the world of their employment than within the more intimate familial or conjugal world.

In the autobiographies that students in my classes have been writing for many years, many of them point out how little they saw of their fathers as they were growing up; the fathers were overly involved in their work or, if they were economically disadvantaged immigrants, the fathers had to labour long hours in order to make a living for the family, to raise its social status, to give their children a better life than their own, to pay the mortgages on successive houses of increasing size and "class." We postulate that if these students could remember having been deprived of a father as children, their mothers probably felt even more deprived of, in their case, a conjugal presence.

Until now, this has been an overwhelmingly masculine syndrome because men have always been encouraged to be good workers and have been the traditional breadwinners. By comparison, in the past fewer women were encouraged to aim high and, even now, few are so completely immersed as far as their employment is concerned. As pointed out earlier, professional women who have very demanding careers are much better able than men to make adjustments in these careers so that they have enough time to spend with their spouses and their children. Men seem to require their families to make adjustments for the sake of *their* careers more frequently than do women who have similar careers.

Whatever the sex of the "delinquent" spouse is, such a situation is increasingly being recognized by researchers as being detrimental to the well-being of the conjugal unit, because the spouse who is left out in the cold is quite likely to develop feelings of rejection, deprivation, loneliness, and of injustice. At the same time, the "work-aholic" spouse, if a man, is distancing himself from his wife through his over-involvement with his work and is diminishing his own ability to function affectively, thereby lowering also his effectiveness in the marital situation.

However, the impact of work involvement on a marriage differs according to several variables. For instance, Clark *et al.* found that, while a husband's number of working hours correlated with lower rates of sharing certain activities with the wife, this lowering did not exert any influence on the wife's perception of the husband as a good companion unless the wife had high expectations in this particular realm. They also found that when a husband has a high income, the wife is more satisfied with his role as a husband even if he does less housework. The authors speculate that "by earning more money, work-involved husbands gained resource power which allowed them to avoid housework."[47] In Great Britain, Pahl and Pahl as well as Young and Willmott found that wives of younger executives had higher expectations in terms of companionship and sharing than did older wives and that, consequently, these younger wives were more dissatisfied and felt neglected more readily.[48] Therefore, the degree to which work involvement on the part of a husband affects a marriage is related to the level of expectations of the wife.

It is also true that many men seek to escape a miserable marriage by immersing themselves in their work, but we are referring here to those cases where they have a decent relationship at the outset, and spoil it by being too distant from it. Work-aholism can be of same nature as alcoholism or drug addiction: it can be used as an escape mechanism; an escape from oneself and from the commitments of an ultimate relationship. The person whose mind is always preoccupied

47. R.A. Clark *et al.*, Husbands' Work Involvement and Marital Role Performance," *Journal of Marriage and the Family*, 40, February 1978, p. 18.
48. R. Pahl and J. Pahl, *Managers and their Wives*, Baltimore: Penguin Books, 1971; M. Young and P. Willmott, *The Symmetrical Family*, New York: Pantheon, 1973.

with his work has little time to think of others (except as co-workers) and little time for self-reflection. Such persons often lose touch with their own selves and, consequently, with others as well.

PROBLEMS OF COMMUNICATION

In our society, one of the facets of the marital relationship that is emphasized is companionship: husbands and wives are considered to be each other's best friends. The roles of husband and wife are, moreover, not as clearly or rigidly defined here as they are in some other societies where little need be clarified, because everyone knows his/her place. Consequently, in our society, spouses need to be able to communicate their own and understand each other's needs, desires and perceptions of mutual roles, otherwise misunderstandings, frustration, and tension will arise.

On the positive side, open channels of communication in a couple can only enhance their relationship as they will get to know each other very intimately, will share the joys and sorrows of everyday life, will discuss ideas, work, and children, and will plan the future together. As soon as problems arise between them, the couple is able to resort immediately to these channels of communication in order to resolve differences. By contrast, in a couple that is not used to ready communication, many problems will go unresolved or even undiscussed, and additional difficulties will arise from this situation.

The ability to communicate is also related to some of the variables that we discussed earlier, such as similarity or dissimilarity of background, alcoholism, and emotional problems. Such variables will themselves prevent open communication and a lack of communication may in turn, as in the case of alcoholism, precipitate the onset of these problems.

However, perhaps too great an emphasis has been placed by certain writers on total openness in marriage. As pointed out by Udry, the key to a successful marriage is *selective* communication rather than total openness. Studies have already shown that the venting of negative feelings has a disturbing effect in a marital relationship.[49] Spouses have to know each other well enough so that they know just how far they can go without hurting each other. There are things that are better untold. It is "the fruitful control and direction of the communication process which distinguishes satisfying marriages, not the volume of the material communicated or the amount of time spent communicating it."[50] Therefore, both lack of communication and inability to control the contents of communication lead to serious marital dissatisfaction. Many couples that I have interviewed mentioned this aspect of their relationship as a leading reason for their divorce.

SEXUAL PROBLEMS

The term "sexual problems" encompasses a wide variety of things in our society. In the old days, by contrast, fewer sexual problems were perceived. Homosexuality, bestiality, and total impotence or infertility were the only sexual problems that western societies accepted and labelled several decades ago. But with the advent of liberalism, individualism and, especially, hedonism, and with the rise of a more enlightened psychology, the field of sexual problems has widened considerably to include various sexual dysfunctions such as the inability to achieve or maintain an erection, premature ejaculation, difficulty in reaching orgasm, low sexual desires, passivity, frigidity in women, and even the inability of one partner to satisfy the other sexually.

In the past, more women than men were considered to have sexual problems, not only because much emphasis was placed on frigidity but also because the specialists in this area of health care were males who had been schooled within a very chauvinistic framework. Women were perceived as having been created for the pleasure of men and if they did not give that pleasure the failure was obviously theirs. In fact, in the past, men were only rarely perceived as having failed sexually

49. B.R. Cutler and W.G. Dyer, "Initial Adjustment Processes in Young Married Couples," *Social Forces*, 44, 1965, pp. 195-201.
50. J.R. Udry, *The Social Context of Marriage*, New York: Lippincott, second edition, 1971, p. 251.

as it was all too easy to find a scapegoat in the man's partner. Fortunately, new research has recently "discovered" that the number of genuinely frigid women is actually much lower than was assumed and that the problem, in many cases, resides with the male partner who is unable to arouse or satisfy the woman.

With the advent of the so-called sexual revolution and with the heightening of women's consciousness regarding their bodily functions and their general equality with men, psychiatrists report an increase in the number of men who go for consultation because they have difficulties in fulfilling their partner or in being satisfied themselves.[51] It is true that we are finding a few cases of women who have become too demanding sexually or who are derogatory about those men who are not accomplished "stallions." Objectively, these women are the counterpart of those overly demanding and accusatory males who were and are more at fault than the women they complain about. Unfortunately, the couples affected do not necessarily perceive the situation this way, and unnecessary feelings of inadequacy are created in the spouse who is most vulnerable in the relationship, generally the woman, and now, in educated circles, often the man.

One of the important functions of marital life in our society today is the mutual satisfaction of a couple's sexual needs. Sexual enjoyment is regarded as being of primary importance in contemporary society. This general attitude makes enormous demands of matrimony; many couples expect it to be an instant sexual nirvana. For some couples, instant sexual adjustment does indeed seem to take place because they have compatible bodies, rhythms, and predilections. However, for the majority of couples, at least a minimum of practice and of time is required to achieve a pleasurable balance, while other couples never seem to achieve it or else lose touch with it in the midst of other problems within the relationship. Couples are more impatient nowadays when confronted with dilemmas and are less willing, especially at and above the level of the middle class, to work through them or let them pass: they may

51. G.L. Ginsberg *et al.*, "The New Impotence," *Archives of General Psychiatry*, 26, 1972, pp. 218-220.

seek professional help, or just discuss the matter between themselves; they may read books, or they may decide to terminate the relationship, generally after all else seems to have failed.

However, it is unlikely that sexual difficulties by themselves are sufficient to cause a marital breakdown: if marital breakdown ensues, it is as the result of a multiplicity of problems, some perhaps neither overtly expressed nor even clearly perceived, and sexual problems are merely one part of a dysfunctional package. Similarly, sexual difficulties may be magnified by a couple and used as a cover-up for other more general problems of adjustment within the marriage. It is more acceptable in our society to blame "sex" than to blame ourselves and because sex can tend to become so specialized it appears to be more related to technique than to personality. In such instances, sexual problems may appear to be the major source of conflict in a couple,[52] but as Mowrer pointed out long ago, there is a tendency for marital conflict to be expressed in disguised form. Sex may be one of the forms conflict will take, but the conflict may involve all aspects of the marital relationship of which sexuality is only a part.[53]

ADULTERY

Sexual dissatisfaction and general unhappiness with a relationship often leads to adultery, especially among males who have more opportunities to meet suitable persons. At times, it is these opportunities which themselves lead to adultery. Extra-marital sex is generally related to lower marital satisfaction in the conjugal unit and to higher divorce rates.[54] In the United States, Gebhard estimated that in 1968 about 60% of all

52. S. Frank, *The Sexually Active Man Past Forty*, New York: Macmillan, 1968, p. 12.
53. H.R. Mowrer, *Personality Adjustment and Domestic Discord*, New York: American Book Co., 1935, p. 151.
54. S.P. Glass and T.L. Wright, "The Relationship of Extramarital Sex, Length of Marriage, and Sex Differences on Marital Satisfaction and Romanticism: Athanasiou's Data Reanalyzed," *Journal of Marriage and the Family*, 39, November 1977, pp. 691-703; R.R. Bell *et al.*, "A Multivariate Analysis of Female Extramarital Coitus," *Journal of Marriage and the Family*, 37, May 1975, pp. 375-384.

married men had, at some point in their conjugal lives, been unfaithful to their wives and that the equivalent figure for women was 35 to 40%.[55] These figures include marriages that will remain legally intact as well as couples who will eventually divorce, and, for both sexes, the overall adultery percentage is higher in the latter category, since adultery is more common among couples that will divorce than in marriages that will remain intact. For instance, in a more recent study, Hunt found that 52% of divorced women had had extra-marital sex compared to only 17% of women currently married.[56] And the trend is growing among women.

Depending on their tolerance levels and the dictates of their consciences, many individuals will, after months or years of sexual and marital dissatisfaction, resort to adultery. (Here, by adultery, we include homosexuality; it does not matter much the sex of the person: what is important is that a third sexual party or more is introduced into the union.) The presence of a third party generally tends to lower the degree of commitment that the unfaithful spouse has to the other. With an external outlet that may take up much time, the interest of the unfaithful spouse in his/her partner, and even in the entire relationship, diminishes. Extra-marital sex has become an alternative and divorce soon appears as another alternative. However, while this is perhaps a typical scenario, there are cases where extra-marital affairs lead to the strengthening of a marriage or to a greater tolerance of an otherwise unsatisfactory but unavoidable marriage.

Often, adultery leads to a long-term attachment, and the delinquent spouse may decide to leave his or her partner for the new person who is or seems more satisfactory. However, probably only a small percentage of adulterous relationships result in remarriages after a divorce has been granted: indeed, once the divorce is granted, the clandestine party's attraction often diminishes. In other situations, the offended party learns of the adultery, either by accident or because someone tells him/her, and may demand either a termination of the

55. As quoted in J. Epstein, *Divorced in America*, New York: Dutton, 1974.
56. M. Hunt, *Sexual Behavior in the 70's*, Chicago: Playboy Press, 1974.

clandestine relationship or a divorce. Often, the adulterous relationship only tips an already precarious balance and becomes the precipitating factor in divorce rather than the real cause of marital unhappiness.

Marital "indiscretions" as they used to be called for men years ago (for women, it was always called adultery), are viewed with varying levels of tolerance in different groups within our society. Certain immigrant groups, especially from the Mediterranean area, have a high tolerance for male indiscretions, especially with prostitutes, and their women have long learned to close their eyes to these whenever they become aware of them. Such marriages are generally characterized by a fairly rigid and clear division of roles, by a lack of companionship and shared activities (men tend to congregate among themselves or to go out together), and the woman's place is clearly within the home. In many instances, subordination to one's husband is an uncontested rule for women. In such a context, adultery has a very different impact and is unlikely to break up a marriage; nor are men likely to leave their legal wives for girl friends. In fact, girl friends do not have the status that the wife has, especially if the latter is the mother of a man's legitimate children.

However, as these immigrant families become assimilated in and assume the norms of our society, more women, and some men, and many of their children become less tolerant of this double standard, particularly when women are employed outside the home, a factor which increases their chances of becoming rapidly acculturated to the ideas of the receiving society. However, if these immigrant women remain at home, maintaining a language barrier (because of their sheltered lives many have lived in Canada for twenty years and still do not know either English or French) and a more general cultural barrier between themselves and the rest of society, we will have to look to their children and even their grandchildren to see a change in this respect and in the general attitudes to marriage of these sectors of our society.

CHILDREN IN FIRST MARRIAGES

The idea that the presence of children in a first marriage may, in certain instances, lead to divorce may seem almost sacrilegious because our society sets great store by the dictum that children are the cement of a marriage. Are they? Obviously not, since their presence does *not* prevent either marital disintegration or divorce. As we saw, nearly 60% of all divorcing couples have at least one child. A recent study has shown that there is a U-shaped relationship between marital stability and the number of children: women with large families and those without children are the most likely to experience marital instability while the lowest rates of divorce fall to women with a moderate number of children.[57] The relationship between divorce and large families may however be partly circumstantial: if other variables are controlled for, we may find that women with large families also married very young, have little education, and/or live in difficult socio-economic conditions.

Children are a very important element in the lives of most couples, and parents derive a great deal of satisfaction from their children, and from seeing them grow. Children can indeed bring a man and a woman closer to each other. The experience of *sharing* a child is very rewarding and contributes to personal growth as well as to the growth of a couple as a couple. However, there are also costs involved in having children and that these costs are escalating in this decade is obvious from the fact that family size is declining drastically in Canada. In 1976, there were, on average, 1.6 children in each family, as compared to 1.8 in 1971, the two lowest averages in the history of this country. Having children or not having children is, in this era, more of a conscious decision than in the past because of the advances in birth control methods and their general availability. Therefore, having fewer children is a choice which reflects couples' perceptions of the costs and rewards entailed.

What are the costs and rewards of having children? As

57. A. Thornton, "Children and Marital Stability," *Journal of Marriage and the Family*, 39, August 1977, pp. 531-540.

Hawke and Knox point out, trying to describe the rewards of parenthood is difficult. Indeed, parents often find it difficult to say exactly what it is they enjoy about having children, especially if they are somewhat ambivalent about the experience and if one or more of their children were unplanned. The rewards of parenting are "often intangible, very personal, and seemingly self-evident." By contrast, "the drawbacks of parenting are usually easy to define and discuss. Costs, hours of lost sleep, loads of laundry, missed social activities, and interruptions" of various activities,[58] including work and career among women and, in many instances, of the intimacy of the couple.

The overall well-being of poor families and families with relatively low incomes can be crucially affected by the number of children in them. Each additional child lowers the family's available resources of money, time, and attention. The same happens in more privileged families, but in these the financial costs are of a different nature. In such families, it is the luxuries of life, the frills, the leisures, which go out the window with each additional child. And today, fewer middle-class families are willing to do without the luxuries. They prefer to have fewer children and to give them more. In our society, children are, for many parents, the source of a vast array of difficulties, especially when finances, ill health, and behavioural problems are involved.

Many studies have been made on married couples in an attempt to determine the effect that children have on the marital relationship. For instance, Feldman found that a "dip" takes place in the marital satisfaction of couples with young children, while couples without any children showed greater marital satisfaction, at all levels, than couples with children.[59] Figley also found a low point in marital satisfaction in the

58. S. Hawke and D. Knox, *One Child by Choice*, Englewood Cliffs, N.J.: Prentice-Hall, 1977, p. 6.
59. H. Feldman, "The Effects of Children on the Family," in *Family Issues of Employed Women in Europe and America*, edited by A. Michel, Lieden: E.F. Brills, 1971, and "Marital Satisfaction over the Family Life Cycle," *Journal of Marriage and the Family*, 32, February 1970, pp. 20-28, by B.C. Rollins and H. Feldman. Also, W.R. Burr, "Satisfaction with Various Aspects of Marriage Over the Life Cycle: A Random Middle Class Sample," *Journal of Marriage*

years before children start leaving home.[60] However, when asked *directly* about the possible negative effects that children have on their marriages, couples are more circumspect. Only a few concede that children may have contributed to the deterioration of their marriage. Russell found that 6% and 8% respectively of husbands and wives felt so. Most studies agree that the arrival of a first child generally presents no severe crisis for a couple.[61]

Observational and correlational studies indicate that children do indeed have an effect on marital relationship and that this effect can be detrimental. For instance, Rollins and Feldman found that the presence of a baby reduces parents' communication by half,[62] while Miller found that companionship decreased with number of children.[63] There is less available time, the mother is more tired, and the care of the baby can be very demanding. Many husbands come to feel that their wives devote too much time to the baby and too little to them and many wives report a lessening of their husbands' attention to them.[64] The arrival of the first child is often what we might term the end of the honeymoon period and many couples find that they do not wish to settle for a more regulated and hum-drum marital life. Knox and Wilson found that wives reported fewer instances of marital improvement

and the Family, 32, February 1970, pp. 28-37; K.S. Renne, "Correlates of Dissatisfaction in Marriage," *op.cit.*; S.L. Nock, "The Family Life Cycle: Empirical or Conceptual Tool?" *Journal of Marriage and the Family*, 41, February 1979, p. 22.

60. C.R. Figley, "Child Density and the Marital Relationship," *Journal of Marriage and the Family*, 35, May 1973, pp. 272-282.

61. D.F. Hobbs, Jr., and S.P. Cole, "Transition to Parenthood: A Decade Replication," *Journal of Marriage and the Family*, 38, November 1976, pp. 723-731; J.H. Meyerowitz and H. Feldman, "Transition to Parenthood," *Psychiatric Research Report*, 20, 1966, pp. 78-84; D.F. Hobbs, Jr., "Parenthood as a Crisis: A Third Study," *Journal of Marriage and the Family*, 27, August 1965, pp. 367-372. However, other studies reported a period of felt severe crisis at that time: E.E. LeMasters, "Parenthood as a Crisis," *Marriage and Family Living*, 19, November 1957, pp. 352-355; E.D. Dyer, "Parenthood as a Crisis: A Re-Study," *Marriage and Family Living*, 25, May 1963, pp. 196-201.

62. Rollins and Feldman, *op.cit.*

63. B.C. Miller, "A Multivariate Developmental Model of Marital Satisfaction," *Journal of Marriage and the Family*, 38, November 1976, p. 655.

64. On the latter, see R.G. Ryder, "Longitudinal Data Relating Marriage Satisfaction to Having a Child," *Journal of Marriage and the Family*, 35, November 1973, pp. 604-606.

after the second than after the first child and more instances of marital dissatisfaction. The wives felt more tired, more drained, and had less time for their husbands.[65] Moreover, Rosenblatt observed couples in public places and found that those who were accompanied by children were less communicative with regard to each other: they touched, smiled and talked less with each other than couples without children.[66] Indeed, many couples point out that the presence of children has quite an impact on their sexual lives: they become constrained as to where and when. There is less spontaneity.

Studies by Russell and by Dyer pointed to interesting variable interactions. For instance, both Russell and Dyer found that there was a direct relationship between strength of the marital bond and higher parenthood morale.[67] Russell's results also indicate that when the father shows his concern for the mother's well-being by getting up at night to take care of the baby, parenthood presents very few problems. It seems that when couples have a good relationship they are better able to adjust to parenthood, and its stresses have fewer negative effects on their relationship. These results also seem to indicate that couples who are able to differentiate between their parental and their conjugal roles have a higher level of satisfaction. For instance, Russell found that those couples who are able to spend more time alone together in the evening are also those who negotiate parenthood more smoothly. She found that there is a two-way interaction among the variables, and that this suggests that the level of satisfaction in both parenthood and conjugal life is linked to the ability to have no more than the *desired* number of children, and to a couple's financial situation, including the quality of their housing. She also suggests that middle-class couples may experience less

65. D. Knox and K. Wilson, "The Differences Between Having One and Two Children," *Family Coordinator*, 27, January 1978, pp. 23-25.
66. P.C. Rosenblatt, "Behavior in Public Places: Comparison of Couples Accompanied and Unaccompanied by Children," *Journal of Marriage and the Family*, 36, November 1974, pp. 750-755.
67. E.D. Dyer, "Parenthood as a Crisis: A Re-Study," *Marriage and Family Living*, 25, 1963, pp. 196-201; C.S. Russell, "Transition to Parenthood: A Restudy," M.A. Thesis, University of Minnesota, 1972; C.S. Russell, "Transition to Parenthood: Problems and Gratifications," *Journal of Marriage and the Family* 36, May 1974, pp. 294-302.

gratification at the outset of parenthood than do lower-class couples. This may be because there is a more drastic change of life-style for the former than for the latter.

Having children is a mixed blessing, and for some couples, it is even a curse. Whether or not one likes the fact, having children changes a marriage, and, for many couples, the costs of the change may add up so drastically that they may not be able to bear the burden *together.* The only long-term solution for such couples is separation. However, even in these cases, it is reasonable to assume that child rearing is *only one* of the problems that these couples have.

CHILDREN IN REMARRIAGES

A greater proportion of second than first marriages end in divorce. Second marriages are more vulnerable. Is it because it is easier to have recourse to divorce when one has been through it once? Is it because, the second time around, one is less concerned about people's reaction? Is it because some couples remarry too rapidly after their first marriage and have not had time to put what has happened into perspective and to learn from the experience? Or is it that some people simply cannot handle an intimate relationship? Probably many of these reasons enter into play. However, there is an additional reason; one that was not discussed in the past but which is becoming increasingly recognized both by experts and by those individuals affected by it.

As the number of divorces increases, so too does the number of children involved in divorce and, consequently, in remarriage. While divorce and remarriage are difficult for children, these same situations are also complex for the adults involved. While we have to sympathize with the young ones trapped in these situations, we cannot leave unmentioned the fact that children exert a much greater influence on their parents' lives than was formerly believed. In the past, whenever children had problems, the finger was immediately pointed at parents, especially at mothers. But the emphasis has shifted and more and more studies are now recognizing that children can have a devastating effect on their parents' lives.

That the potential for conflict exists in the process of "familial reconstruction" can be seen in the many permutations that are possible when children are involved in remarriages. A reconstituted family can involve any one of the following combinations:

1. One spouse, generally the woman, has no children. The other new spouse, the husband, has children but they are in the custody of his ex-wife (this combination occurs frequently because men tend to remarry younger women, who are often childless).

2. One spouse, generally the wife, has the children of her previous marriage. Her husband has visiting rights, while her new husband does not have children.

3. One spouse, generally the wife, has the children. Her ex-husband has visiting rights, while her new husband also has children who are in the custody of his ex-wife.

4. Both spouses have custody of their children, with visiting rights for both ex-spouses.

5. Any of the above situations might exist, with the addition of a child born into the newly reconstituted family.

The potential for conflict is very great and will be discussed at greater length in the chapter on remarriage. However, let us just say here that it generally runs along the following lines: jealousy among the children of the two partners; dissimilarity of background among these children; dislike of the step-parent who is seen as usurping the place of the natural parent and who is often perceived by the child as competing for the affection of the child's natural parent; parents siding too obviously with their own natural children against their step-children and even against the new spouse who is the children's step-parent; step-parents disliking their step-children and resenting them as an imposition; natural parents (and even grandparents) using their children in an attempt to destroy the new relationship as a way of striking back at the ex-spouse. An example of this last case follows:

Andy is a bright, articulate, talkative ten year old. Perhaps because his father (Tom) has already been through two marriages and other relationships, or perhaps because he is indulged by his still un-remarried mother, his father (who sees the child during weekends), and his grandparents (he is the only grandchild), Andy has an overwhelming need for attention; he has grown into a manipulative little boy who participates readily in the schemings in which both parents engage against each other. He has been used and now he uses. His father remarried a woman with a four-year-old daughter. Andy did not get along well with the child, treated her rudely and unfairly. The new wife pointed the disruptive behaviour out to him. When the next visiting week-end approached, Andy and his mother decided that he was not going back to his father; they even got in touch with Tom's parents who did not approve of the remarriage on religious grounds. The child told his father that he could see him only at his mother's place or at his grandparents' place; the child's attitude was that if the worse came to the worst "I guess I won't see my father for a year; after that, he'll leave her and I'll be able to see him again." These words were prophetic. At first the father was justifiably angry at his ex-wife, his parents, and the child. But as the days passed, he became afraid of losing his son and, and by degrees, gave in to his requests. Tom's anxiety over his son did not diminish in the following weeks and he showered the child with attention while at the same time distancing himself emotionally from his new wife whom he came to perceive as the wedge between him and his son. The new wife felt hurt, abandoned, confused but nevertheless tried to work through the situation. The more she tried, the more Tom withdrew, becoming apathetic, cruel, insecure, involved with his son and his work to the exclusion of his new wife. After months of unbearable tension, the new marriage ended.

What we see above is a child being used by his mother and by disapproving grandparents against a weak father in an attempt to break up a relationship. Because the child had never been forced to adapt to new realities and had been subjected to too many disruptions, he could not tolerate another child and a woman who did not go along with all his whims. Andy, the child, became the willing transmitter and even the initiator of tension in the new relationship.

EMOTIONAL IMMATURITY

Some individuals have the emotional maturity of children; their development has been arrested. Others have limited emotions and emotional responses, either because they have lived in a very narrow socio-psychological environment or because of inherent emotional deficiencies. Immature people, by definition, tend to be unstable, unreliable, labile, unaware of their own needs, and particularly poor judges of others' needs; what characterizes them above all is their inability to fulfill the needs of others.

A marital relationship is a give-and-take situation and emotional immaturity precludes a satisfying interaction unless both individuals are equally immature and unaware of their own needs. In such a case, theirs will be a somewhat empty emotional life but they may have enough common interests to hold their relationship together. If nothing else, neither spouse will suffer from emotional deprivation at the hands of the other.

Emotional immaturity is probably most painful when one spouse is mature, sensitive and responsible, while the other is not. The former will be tremendously deprived, frustrated, and even abused. She or he will have to shoulder the burden of the relationship alone, and may have to take on additional responsibilities, such as financial management and the education of the children. There are, broadly speaking, two likely results to this situation. The mature spouse may suffer to the point where he/she can no longer endure the situation and separates. Or, the immature spouse may leave, desert, forgo all responsibility, or take up with another partner, thus in effect breaking up the relationship.

MENTAL AND PHYSICAL CRUELTY

Mental cruelty is an extension of the above but in a much stronger form. We have to distinguish between mental cruelty that actually took place in a marital situation and "mental cruelty" as legal grounds for divorce; up until a few years ago in the United States, in order to get a divorce, couples would file on the grounds of mental cruelty even if the real cause of the divorce was adultery—socially the former looked better than the latter. However, what we are concerned with in this section is real mental cruelty, whereby one spouse totally neglects the needs of the other in a punitive, maliciously hurtful, torturing or even sadistic manner. Mental cruelty may also involve the forcible instillation of unnecessary and overpowering guilt feelings in the other person; or a barrage of deprecation and put-downs so that the other party's sense of self is harmed and subsequently diminished.

Physical cruelty, singly or in combination with mental cruelty, is easier to define. It entails such actions as punching, battering, twisting of limbs, refusal to help or feed a desperately ill or crippled spouse, throwing the person about, burns (such as with cigarette butts), and the use of pain in sex when the other person does not enjoy it. Physical cruelty in marriage is usually inflicted by the male because men tend to be more aggressive than women, by social sanction and example, and in addition, are generally bigger and stronger than their spouses. In Toronto, it is estimated that 25,000 wives will be assaulted by their husbands in 1979 and that 2,500 husbands will be attacked by their wives.[68]

In the past, very few wives complained of such treatment because it was considered highly embarrassing socially. Moreover, even if they complained, they received very little support from anyone and their husbands were likely to retaliate with increased violence if the complaints of their spouses came to their attention. Since then, various agencies have launched an educational campaign aimed at these women in an attempt to make them understand that their predicament is not a shameful one, that it is to be found in all strata of

68. S. Katz, *Toronto Star*, March 10, 1979, p. C5.

society, and that they should seek help. The police have, in certain cities, become more sympathetic to the plight of these women, and many half-way houses or hostels have been set up for them and their children, to help them while they receive counselling and stabilize their lives.

Mental and/or physical cruelty can lead to divorce depending on a number of additional variables such as the level of tolerance for these acts in the cultural groups the spouses belong to, the alternatives available to the physically and/or emotionally battered spouse (for instance, wives who are employed outside the home will leave more readily than non-employed wives), the presence of children and whether or not they are also battered and/or affected by the marital strife, and by the external support available to and received by the assaulted spouse.

UNREALISTIC EXPECTATIONS

As we have mentioned several times already, with the exception of mothering and employment, our society does not define the role of husbands and wives in a very rigid manner. There is so much room for both individualism and fantasy that many persons have unrealistic expectations of marriage, one way or another. Some see marriage as a constant, Hollywood-type honeymoon, a rose garden without thorns. Such persons are either unprepared for the problems which arise naturally in a relationship, or are unable or unwilling to solve these problems when they do arise. And at the other extreme are those individuals who expect marriage to be rather like a business proposition; a formality, a contract, which in no wise diminishes their freedom and in no manner increases their obligations.

Unrealistic expectations are often tied to the upbringing of individuals. For instance, it is likely that adults coming from families that were torn by strife will not have learned what normal family life is, unless they have been exposed to other models on a regular basis. In this regard, it would be interesting to study the marital expectations of the children of divorce and to compare them with those of children of happy unions.

In similar vein, it frequently happens that highly intelligent people or, at the other extreme, people of lower intelligence, suffer from a lack of realism, especially when it comes to the affective or emotional realm. Often, highly intelligent people become very intellectual, take pleasure in learning, in highly abstract concepts, theories, and ideas, but remain distant from, or are unable to come to terms with, emotional and affective realities. This situation is aggravated in their adult life as they engage in and immerse themselves into their intellectual and professional pursuits to the detriment of their intimate relationships. Such persons often have the tendency to offer or take refuge in intellectual clichés in place of necessary genuine emotions. And at the other extreme are those who do not have the intellectual equipment necessary for an understanding of the roles of their society, including conjugal roles. They may enter marriage totally ignorant of even the most fundamental realities of life, expecting that all will be well. Either of these extremes exacerbates the situation when spouses hold conflicting attitudes about their roles as husbands and wives.[69]

CONCLUSIONS

As this chapter has stressed, it is impossible to isolate any single social or personal factor as the "cause" of divorce. At the base of the pyramid is a foundation of inter-related socio-economic and cultural variables which have shaped people's attitudes to, expectations of, and responses to marital life, dissolution and divorce. At the top of the pyramid are those psychological or personal variables, which, in a series of interactions, are usually seen as the immediate causes of divorce by the parties concerned as well as by the various specialists whose work it is to help and treat these families.

The effect of many of the individual causes of divorce could be substantially diminished if couples took a longer time between original acquaintance and marriage, married at a later age, were more educated, and lived in more satisfactory

69. A. Jacobson, "Conflict of Attitudes Toward the Roles of the Husband and Wife in Marriage," *American Sociological Review*, 17, 1952, pp. 146-150.

economic circumstances. Similarly, if marital education was more widespread, it could perhaps alleviate or anticipate problems of communication, sexual adjustment, and dissimilarity of background.[70] Parental education could also serve as "preventive medicine" for those problems created by the presence of children, whether in first marriage or in remarriage.

Such measures would, however, neither abolish unhappy marriages nor eradicate divorce; the roots of both are ultimately to be found in the societal causes discussed in the previous chapter, and in the vagaries inherent in the frailties of human nature. High divorce rates and the frequent termination of informal conjugal arrangements are perhaps the unavoidable cost that a society with the values described in the previous chapter has to pay if and when marital discord arises.

70. For a discussion of pre-marital as well as divorce counselling, see G. Shipman, "In My Opinion: The Role of Counseling in the Reform of Marriage and Divorce Procedures," *Family Coordinator*, 26, October 1977, pp. 395-407.

5   The Process of Divorce

It is not only necessary to understand the sociological background to and personal causes of divorce, but it is also
important to inquire into the processes. How do people get
there? How do they pass from early marital bliss, to unhappy
marriage and divorce? Actually, it is probably easier to have
an unhappy marriage than to have a good one. In our society, a
good marriage requires love, understanding, concern, adaptation. A bad marriage carries no such requisites. Tongue in
cheek, I tell my students that I believe the difference between a
Ph.D. and a Mrs. lies in the fact that the Ph.D. is harder to get
and the Mrs. is harder to keep. (Unfortunately, there is no
comparable punch line for men since men do not change title
when they marry: they remain Mr.). In fact, were it not that the
focus of this book requires us to look closely at *unhappy*
marriages, it would be more important to look at good
marriages, both because they are less common and because,
although they are certainly more rewarding, they are a more
difficult accomplishment. Marriage *per se* is not a state to
envy: only happy marriages are enviable.

   Many bad marriages endure for life while many middle-of-
the-road marriages, tolerable but uninspiring, end in divorce.
Some people, for reasons of religion, ideology, culture,
children, lack of money, or fear of social disapproval remain
together no matter what, while others, either less constrained
by these variables or less tolerant of mediocrity and personal
unhappiness, are less inclined to stay in a situation that does
not bring them what they are seeking and divorce. Tolerance
levels differ and so do opportunities: not everyone who wants

a divorce obtains one; similarly, many persons who divorce want to remain married while their partners do not.

We will start by examining some of the factors that contribute to unhappy and empty marriages; then, we will look into separation and desertion, and will conclude with an examination of divorce itself.

THE UNHAPPY MARRIAGE

It is no simple task to define a bad marriage: people's feelings about their marriages are very subjective and individual. In fact, there is evidence that in many cases husbands and wives disagree about the quality of their own marriage.[1] Women generally report their marriages to be unhappy more often than men and wives more frequently express dissatisfaction with their relationships than do their husbands.[2] The same result was obtained in studies involving dating and engaged couples who were in the process of breaking up: not only were women more likely to perceive problems in the relationship but they were also more likely to be the ones who precipitated the break-up.[3] This dichotomy probably results from the fact that women are more dependent upon marriage as a source of gratification in general and of emotional gratification in particular. Studies have indeed established that marriage is more important for women's happiness than for men's,[4] so much so that, in many instances, women equate overall happiness with marital happiness.[5]

Women are therefore more likely to pay greater attention to their marriages and to be more easily hurt or disappointed by

1. C. Safilios-Rothschild, "Family Sociology or Wives' Sociology? A Cross-Cultural Examination of Decision-Making," *Journal of Marriage and the Family*, 31, 1969, pp. 290-301.
2. K.S. Renne, "Correlates of Dissatisfaction in Marriage," *Journal of Marriage and the Family*, 32, February 1970, p. 56.
3. C.T. Hill *et al.*, "Breakups Before Marriage: The End of 103 Affairs," *Journal of Social Issues*, 32, 1976, p. 147.
4. J. Bernard, "The Paradox of the Happy Marriage," in *Women in Sexist Society*, edited by V. Gornick and B.K. Moran, New York: Basic Books, 1971, p. 87.
5. N.M. Bradburn, *The Structure of Psychological Well-Being*. Chicago: Aldine, 1969, pp. 150, 159.

marital inadequacy. Indeed, fewer married women than men hold jobs, and when they do, most tend to see this role as being only tangential to their overall sense of personality. In other words, women more than men subsume themselves in marriage only. Moreover, women are socialized, from a very early age, to be affectionate and sociable: what is generally called expressive. Because of this, they have a greater ability to notice potentially troublesome aspects of their marriages, while their husbands, being both less sensitive to emotional factors and less dependent on the relationship, will not have the same responsiveness.[6]

Many studies have also reported that women make more concessions in marriage and adapt to it more than men do.[7] In fact, both husbands and wives report that is the wife who makes the greater adjustment in marriage.[8] The principle of lesser commitment[9] or of lower interest[10] on the part of men is applicable here. At least one study has found that *both* husbands and wives regarded husbands rather than wives as the source of marital problems.[11] However, women believe that their own inability to adjust to these problems is a shortcoming on *their* part.

Because boys are brought up to become breadwinners and women to become wives and/or mothers, because boys are brought up to be "strong" and "masculine" and women to be expressive and emotional, the two sexes often have very different expectations when it comes to the selection of a spouse. For instance, men place greater emphasis on sexuality

6. Of course, there are many exceptions to these generalizations, but these do not negate the validity of these observations for the population in general.
7. R.O. Blood, Jr. and D.M. Wolfe, *Husbands and Wives, The Dynamics of Marital Living*, New York: Free Press, 1960, p. 23; L. Rainwater and K.K. Weinstein, *And the Poor Get Children*, Chicago: Quadrangle, 1960, pp. 68-69; E.W. Burgess and P. Wallin, *Engagement and Marriage*, Philadelphia: Lippincott, 1953, p. 618; A.-M. Henshel (Ambert), "Swinging: A Study of Decision Making in Marriage," *American Journal of Sociology*, 78, January 1973, pp. 123-129.
8. Burgess and Wallin, *op.cit.*, p. 618.
9. P.M. Blau, *Exchange and Power in Social Life*, New York: Wiley, 1964.
10. W.W. Waller and R. Hill, *The Family*, New York: Holt, Rinehart & Winston, revised edition, 1951, p. 191.
11. R. Lee and M. Casebier, *The Spouse Gap*, New York: Abingdon Press, 1971, p. 31.

while women stress emotional elements such as affection and love. Consequently, in marriage men expect of their wives far more interest in sex while women expect their husbands to be more emotional.[12] This difference of orientation leads to frustration, disagreements, a resort to other means of obtaining fulfillment, and often to divorce. Similarly, because of the divergent roles that men and women fulfill in society, and because of the different advantages and restrictions that these roles convey and impose, men and women tend to develop dissimilar and even incompatible personalities.[13] Men generally nurture their working and worldly qualities to a greater extent than women do, while women stress their familial identity, often to the detriment of other aspects of selfhood. This situation, again, leads to a gulf between spouses.

Therefore, within one marriage, one spouse may be fairly satisfied with the relationship while the other feels restricted or deprived. What is good for one partner is not necessarily so for the other. And what is good or tolerable for one couple may not be so for another couple. We will dispense with the extensive literature which attempts to define and reconcile terms such as marital satisfaction, marital stability, marital happiness, marital success, and, even marital adjustment, and will simply describe the bad marriage as *one in which either one or both spouses are unhappy or dissatisfied and would, if given complete freedom of choice, choose to be single or to be married to someone else.* We will focus here on those factors that make for an unhappy marriage and on some of the common causes of unhappiness within relationships.

The factors that make for a bad marriage again differ from couple to couple: much depends on what is important for each couple and for each partner within a relationship. But there are, nonetheless, some generalizations which we can make. We can, to begin with, enumerate those variables which are often found in relationships that are not happy: lack of communication, disagreement concerning mutual roles, lack

12. N. Foote, "Matching of Husband and Wife in Phases of Development," *Transactions of the Third World Congress of Sociology.* 4, 1956, pp. 24-34.
13. G. Gurin *et al., Americans View Their Mental Health.* New York: Basic Books, 1960, p. 110.

of attention and inadequate time devoted to the other partner and to the relationship, self-centeredness, personality problems, affective and/or sexual coldness or incompatibility, differences in habits, goals, and values, sexual segregation, and interference by a third party, either as the result of extramarital affairs or the intrusion of intolerant in-laws. These are some of the things characteristically encountered in unhappy relationships. But what we need to explore at greater length in this chapter is the *processes* involved. In other words: *how* do people reach this point in their married lives?

Two persons usually decide to marry because they know or think they know that they are right for each other, and they will together fulfill their mutual hopes about marriage. So, they get married. What happens between time A (marriage) and time Z (the separation or decision to divorce)? Within the analytical framework of exchange theory, Levinger points out that an imbalance between costs and rewards sets in:

> *The dissolution of intimate relationships is often marked by a drastic shift in perceived rewards or costs. When relationships are on the upswing, mutual rewards are believed to be highly probable and thoughts of costs are suppressed; later, during disenchantment, one or both partners find the old rewards less probable, and unanticipated costs are now discovered.*[14]

Except in those instances of sudden and dramatic changes or occurrences, the process of marital disintegration is so gradual that the spouses recognize it only when it is very advanced. As Fullerton points out, there is no single specific point at which a marriage turns sour: "There may be a sudden *recognition* that something is terribly wrong, but it is usually an awareness that has been repressed for a long time."[15]

14. G. Levinger, "A Social Psychological Perspective on Marital Dissolution," *Journal of Social Issues*, 32, 1976, p. 25; G. Levinger, "Marital Cohesiveness and Dissolution: An Integrative Review," *Journal of Marriage and the Family*, 27, February 1965, pp. 19-28. See also, F.I. Nye *et al.*, "A Preliminary Theory of Marital Stability: Two Models," *International Journal of Sociology of the Family*, 3, March 1973, pp. 102-122.
15. G.P. Fullerton, *Survival in Marriage*, New York: Holt, Rinehart and Winston, 1972, p. 411.

Often, traits that were found interesting, intriguing, unusual in a partner become irritants as the initial phase of excitement wears off. Qualities that were appreciated because they complemented the partner's own personality become threatening when the couple is faced by the normal problems of marital life. Accusations may be made gently, or harshly, and the other partner suddenly learns that precisely those traits he or she had been cherished for are a thorn in the side of the other partner. While most couples adapt to the situation and a new equilibrium is reached, many couples do not and this is the beginning of the long downhill run.

In some instances, the couple did not know each other very well, either because of too brief a premarital acquaintance and/or a youthful marriage, or because they had expectations that were unrealistic. Marriage is a shock, and it can also be the more or less rapid discovery that one is married to a stranger, that the person one loved was quite different from the person one is married to, or that marriage is simply not what one expected. It may also be the self-realization that one is not what one was trying to pass for. Such marriages can remain calm or become tumultuous. What they share, in either case, is disillusionment and even bitterness. One or both spouses feel cheated. Many of these couples separate rapidly while others remain together for longer periods, either because the discovery process takes more time for them, or because they may take longer to accept a reality which is initially too painful to even acknowledge. Others never separate: some adapt, while others merely tolerate, sometimes with the aid of other gratifications, such as their children, alcohol, extra-marital affairs, and over-involvement in various activities, especially work. Children can serve as very important sources of delay in the total disintegration of a marriage. In at least one study, they were found to be the only satisfaction that unhappy couples shared.[16] When children leave and parents are left alone, they may realize that they have very little in common. Theirs is an empty nest in the true sense: not only empty of children, but of love. There is a gulf

16. E.B. Luckey and J.K. Bain, "Children: A Factor in Marital Satisfaction," *Journal of Marriage and the Family*, 32, February 1970, pp. 43-44.

between the spouses and they do not know each other well
enough to bridge it.

> *This may happen especially in a marriage where the couple
> have used the children as their primary way of relating to
> each other or as a buffer between them on points of conflict.
> When the children leave home the spouses, in their psych-
> ological nakedness, confront each other across the gap
> which has always been between them and which was
> temporarily filled by their children.*[17]

A similar disillusionment and even bitterness can set in in
couples who, while they once knew each other well, changed
as the years went by, each in his or her direction. In Lillian
Hellman's *Toys in the Attic*, we hear: "Well, people change and
forget to tell each other. Too bad—causes so many mistakes."
Needs become different, and so do aspirations. This may give
rise to conflicts, overt or latent, and, after a while, communication channels slowly break down. Lack of interest and even
resentment set in and the gulf between the two partners
becomes irreparable. Such was the case of Bob and Alice who
divorced when they were thirty-three and thirty respectively.

Bob and Alice had a typical dating and engagement period.
She went to nursing school while he trained to be an
electrician. They married at twenty-three and twenty after
having known each other for nearly six years. Alice remained at her work in a hospital until their son was born
four years later. She then became a housewife and at first
found the change as well as the presence of the baby
immensely enjoyable. During those years, Bob decided to go
into business with a partner and they rapidly prospered. In
fact, their success was too rapid and the couple moved into a
larger home three times in five years. Bob and his partner
expanded their firm and longer hours of work followed. The
business became Bob's chief concern. At first Alice did not
have the time to feel left out as she busied herself with the
baby and the decorating of their successive homes. She took

17. Lee and Casebier, *op.cit.*, p. 138.

a course in home decoration at a nearby community college and decided to go on to do a B.A. at the University, taking evening courses. She actually did not notice Bob's absence very much but became ill at ease in his presence as she felt that they had so little in common. She was not, after all, interested in money, big houses, and the fast life that Bob was now dreaming of. She wanted what was meaningful work for her and did not even dare talk to him about it until financial matters dictated that she broach the subject: she needed money to pursue her studies and had to talk to him about her work plans. He was shocked, and adamantly opposed to "any wife of mine ever taking a job." Quarrels followed for a few weeks, both people resenting each other deeply; he, because he felt he had given her more than they had ever dreamt of, she, because she felt trapped and limited by him. One night he walked out, slept at a hotel, and returned home the next evening to find the house deserted and a note requesting a divorce taped to the television set.

There are other instances in which couples, as most do, start with the best of intentions, but one or both of the partners have emotional problems or conflicts that either surface repeatedly, or else flare up abruptly at a phase of their life together, requiring a sudden and, in some cases, intolerable change from one or both parties. One example encountered by this author is the case of a couple in which the woman had been in and out of a mental institution since the beginning of their marriage. After years of financial difficulties, household and child care responsibilities, work changes, and lack of emotional support, the husband decided to leave the relationship and seek another one elsewhere. Other examples are those of couples in which both members function very well and are happy, until one day, after two or three years of marriage (more in some cases), monotony sets in, a few routine problems arise, and one of the two cannot cope with the situation.

Debby and Irving had been married for two years when she became pregnant accidentally. Irving was not yet ready to support a child financially as he had two others from a previous marriage. He did not force her to get an abortion but, after many discussions during which he firmly held his ground, she decided to obtain one. She always regretted it, and from time to time referred back to the matter, while he, on the other hand, felt no sympathy for her feelings and had no regrets. Nevertheless, the first glow of their relationship had been tarnished and Irving was finding it difficult to live without that initial excitement. At the same time, he was doing nothing to repair the rift with his companion and was becoming noticeably cool to her. Debby one day told him that, although she did not want him to cheat on her, she would not be hurt if he had casual affairs while away at conventions. Actually, she did not even want that but she was afraid that he was already cheating, as he had done in his previous marriage. He joked to reassure her, but at the next convention he did have a brief affair. Bolstered by his initial success, he sought others once he returned to town and started seeing women quite often. Debby sensed that something was going on but he always denied everything even after she once saw him coming out of a house with a woman and challenged him about it. Their communication problems mounted and they sought, at her request, marital counselling. But Irving was no longer happy about their relationship and felt burdened by her regrets and her (justified) suspicions about his affairs. He did not really want to change. Although he liked his second wife, they eventually separated, but continued dating and sleeping together occasionally. He had no intention of going back to her, while she lived under the illusion that he would. Finally he decided to marry someone else, thereby ending their separation with divorce, rather than the reconciliation she had hoped for.

As mentioned at the outset of this chapter, many problems surface at the empty-nest stage of a marriage, and at the time in the life of a man where a career is at a standstill. Deutscher believes that those couples who were able to provide support for and to relate well to each other early in their life together will continue to do so at this very crucial period in their lives.[18]

18. I. Deutscher, "The Quality of Post-parental Life: Definitions of the Situation," *Journal of Marriage and the Family*, 26, 1964, pp. 52-59.

Accordingly, one might generalize that there is continuity in couples' lives; difficult early years of marriage may often forecast subsequent marital disintegration. However, the reverse occurs so often that such generalizations are not particularly helpful, in that they make no allowance for the many extraneous factors, unpredictable when a couple first marries, that may enter into play.

The above examples and illustrations should serve as adequate demonstration of the fact that what begins as a loving marriage can easily deteriorate to the point where separation follows. And though the path of marriage may be downhill, there are almost invariably uphill trends, as couples try to patch things up, that mask the progression. There are many roads from a good marriage to separation and divorce, a combination of highways and sidestreets, main and secondary factors linking bliss and disillusionment. This period of painful transition is what Paul Bohannan has called the first station of divorce, the emotional divorce or the deteriorating marriage. The emotional divorce "occurs when the spouses withhold emotion from their relationship because they dislike the intensity of ambivalence of their feelings." These two people "grate on each other because each is disappointed." It seems that women suffer more than men from the trauma of this period, while men are more severely strained once the process of divorce begins.[19]

SEPARATION

Separation takes place when the two spouses begin living apart, generally in separate residences. Many couples choose to draw up a legal separation agreement, spelling out each other's rights to separate personal life and, where money is a factor or children are involved, specifying both parties' rights and obligations. Some couples file for divorce immediately upon separation or very shortly thereafter while others wait until they wish to remarry or until their three-year separation period is nearing an end. In many instances, one of the two

19. D.A. Chiriboga and L. Cutler, "Stress Responses among Divorcing Men and Women," *Journal of Divorce*, 1, Winter 1977, p. 98.

spouses, usually the husband, already has another partner, and for that spouse the separation means the beginning of a new relationship. Thus, for one spouse, separation is predominantly positive, and it is the other spouse who has to cope with the emotional realities of separation—and, often, with new and difficult financial responsibilities as well.

Separation is a period of upheaval, of unsolved problems, of uncertainties, and often of attempts to re-establish the relationship. Many couples go through several separations before either definite reconciliation or divorce. Other couples separate at some stage in a genuine attempt to solve their problems: a 1969 study of 150,000 people in a New Jersey city revealed that 13% of the married couples there had at some time separated.[20] However, once a couple separates the likelihood of divorce, soon or later, is very great: close to 90% of separations are the prelude to an eventual divorce.[21] Notwithstanding this fact, separation often occurs while one or the other partner hopes that a reconciliation will follow, as can be seen indirectly from data found in the U.S.A. Two National Fertility Studies, one in 1965 and the other in 1970, established that about a quarter of twice-married women had given birth between separation and divorce;[22] the births tended to cluster closely after the marital disruption period, suggesting both the possibility that these were "last chance" pregnancies and the possibility that some resulted from extra-marital affairs that had led to the separation.[23]

Separation is the discovery of one's solitude (if one is alone or alone with children), of financial restrictions and even of poverty; it is a period of tremendous difficulty where children are concerned; it is a constant flow of demands, of new situations and attempts, successful and unsuccessful, at

20. L. Pratt, *Family Structure and Effective Health Behavior, The Energized Family*, Boston: Houghton Mifflin, 1976, p. 154.
21. B.L. Bloom *et al.*, "Marital Separation: A Community Survey," *Journal of Divorce*, 1, Fall 1977, pp. 7-19.
22. N.B. Ryder and C.F. Westoff, *The Contraceptive Revolution*, Princeton, N.J.: Princeton University Press, 1977, and *Reproduction in the United States, 1965*, Princeton, N.J.: Princeton University Press, 1971.
23. B.R. Rindfuss and L.L. Bumpass, "Fertility During Marital Disruption," *Journal of Marriage and the Family*, 39, August 1977, pp. 518-519.

adaptation. It is the time when one is both closest to one's marriage and yet so very distant from it. It is the time when all the frustrations and injustices of the previous relationship are vivid, omnipresent, and often exacerbated by visits, phone calls, and letters, especially when children and financial matters are involved. Separated persons, in spite of all the problems they have had in their marriages, are often still attached to their spouses and may wish either to be reunited with them or to express their anger at them.[24] Studies find that it is during the period of separation that adults have the greatest health problems.[25] Some studies have also found that separation is often hardest on women and that their levels of anxiety and their rates of emotional problems rise sharply in this period, while it takes longer for men to be hit by this new reality.[26] However, not all studies are in agreement. Chiriboga and Cutler state that

> ... the whole process of separation is highly traumatic, generally more so than is the stress associated with the marriage ... the troubles associated with the marriage represented old, familiar problems that had been faced for a considerable period of time. Shifting gears from the state of couplehood ... created a demand for much new learning.[27]

And in terms of sexual differences, they add:

> Men, however, appeared to be more vulnerable than women to the stresses of separation, particularly in dealing with the emotional issues at stake ... Their emotional vulnerability may stem from the tendency for men in American society to deny or suppress the existence within themselves of emo-

24. R.S. Weiss, "The Emotional Impact of Marital Separation," *Journal of Social Issues*, 32, 1976, p. 135.
25. For instance, W.J. Goode, *Women in Divorce*, New York: Free Press, 1956, p. 187; B.L. Bloom *et al.*, "Marital Disruption as a Stressful Life Event," in *Divorce and Separation*, edited by G. Levinger and O.C. Moles, New York: Basic Books, 1979, p. 187.
26. For instance, K.S. Renne, "Health and Marital Experience in an Urban Population," *Journal of Marriage and the Family*, 33, May 1971, p. 340; Chiriboga and Cutler, *op.cit.*
27. Chiriboga and Cutler, *op.cit.*, p. 104.

> tional problems. *They use such buffers as work or excessive*
> *social activity as a means of avoiding the problem en-*
> *gendered by the divorce. Women, more in touch with their*
> *emotional life ... may hit an emotional low more quickly,*
> *but may also be faster in resolution.*[28]

In fact, psychiatrists, family counsellors, and other observers of the situation have found that many men had actually been looking forward to separation and throw themselves into it with zest, only to be hit later by loneliness, dissatisfaction, and frustration, in many instances because the bachelor scene does not meet with their expectations or becomes a meaningless routine. It is especially difficult for men who had been dependent on their wives for their daily material well-being, for they are not used to taking care of themselves. However, those men who used to share in household activities with their wives have an easier time of it as they are less helpless.[29]

During separation, the individual has to learn all over again to live alone. Some even have to learn how to survive in terms of eating, cleaning, laundry. Many have to go to work, or look for work, or go on welfare, all the while having full responsibility for children for the first time. Many women have never been employed prior to separation, have either inappropriate skills or none at all, and do not even know how to go about looking for employment. Some become immediately impoverished, a feature that is most common with desertion. For many, separation is the single most difficult time in terms of missing the other partner while at the same time being so angered by him or her. It also involves the potentially traumatic task of announcing the news to relatives and friends and having to readjust many relationships. It may entail getting used to new neighbours, new schools, day care, and so on. It may mean taking the streetcar rather than driving. And aggravating all these problems is the fact that, often, the marriage is still uncertain: many still harbour hopes, sometimes justified, usually in vain. It is a time of daydreaming

28. *Ibid.*, p. 104.
29. E.M. Hetherington *et al.*, "Divorced Fathers," *Family Coordinator*, 25 1976, pp. 417-428.

about what might be, what might have been, and what could still be if only he or she . . .

When Jennifer's husband left her, she told him that, apart from the few encounters necessary to sort out some fiscal loose ends, she would have no more to do with him. She had been so unhappy with him, so repressed, so deprived of love that she felt it would be useless and destructive to think of him and even more so to talk to him over the phone and see him. Yet, she says, there are those evenings when "I lie down wondering what he is doing. Wondering if he might not want to try again, idealizing the few beautiful moments we had together." At times, she fantasizes that he is attempting to get her back—all the while being able to tell her interviewer that such daydreams are hurting her and have no grounds in reality whatsoever: *he* would not try to get her back but he would love it if *she* asked him to take her back. "Would he take you back?"—"No, of course not! But he would relish that victory."

Separation is also an extremely confusing period for children; not only are they affected by the problems that beset their parents at this time but they have just suffered the total or partial loss of one parent, and generally feel insecure about the future and their parents' feelings towards them. They also often have to adapt to a new and perhaps less adequate house, new schools and playmates. If not, they have to explain their altered situation to old acquaintances, or lie their way through the situation. If the mother has to go out and work, children may find themselves with little supervision and with little support if they get into trouble or feel lonely.

Finally, separation is also a difficult period for many of the *new* partners or dates of the former spouses. A newly separated person who starts dating is often so wrapped up in the problems of the past marriage that he or she does not do justice to the new partner(s), may be suspicious of them, may judge them according to the ex-spouse's deeds and personality, or may be afraid to get involved again, at the expense of the emotional investment that the new person makes. These

problems often set in motion self-fulfilling prophecies, as the
brief case below illustrates.

Harold fell in love, at least superficially so, with a woman
who was all that he had always desired. Once he had
married her, he became less affectionate and giving, as he
was afraid of becoming too involved with her and of being
hurt by her as he had been by first wife. He withdrew from
her, more and more, and kept his distance emotionally. She
tried to make him understand the source of his problems—
and he *did* understand it intellectually. But he was unwilling to give another marriage a real try and unwilling or
unable to "let himself go." Separation followed very rapidly.

DESERTION

Desertion is much like separation, except that it is more acute:
all the problems are magnified because of the suddenness and
unexpectedness of the situation, and because of the lack of
legal recourse in many such cases. No one who is deserted can
be ready. It is always a surprise, often an unpleasant surprise,
sometimes a devastating shock. In some instances it is a relief,
especially when the deserted party has been beset by financial
problems caused by the presence of the other spouse, such as
in chronic unemployment, alcoholism, gambling, or spending
money on other women or men.

A person who deserts probably has a different personality
configuration and/or socio-economic situation to that of the
person who seeks divorce. Benson states:

*It would certainly be misleading to suggest that deserters
are sensitive men who flee their families to find tranquility.
In most cases they have never known much personal
organization, and desertion is just one more step in the same
troubled direction that their lives have already taken.*[30]

Skarsten points out that "many deserting husbands are
inadequate and depressed males who characteristically han-

30. L. Benson, *The Family Bond*, New York: Random House, 1971, p. 274.

dle problems by withdrawal." They often come from a background of desertion themselves and such husbands frequently are rather isolated and not integrated into the appropriate social networks.[31]

Desertion, it has been said, is the divorce of the poor: unable to pay for separation and divorce fees and unable to support an ex-wife and children, impoverished men desert. However, in his study of Philadelphia, Kephart found that desertion patterns were on the whole very similar to divorce patterns in terms of social class. For instance, he found that 43.6% of the white desertions took place in couples from the upper vocational half of society.[32] It is quite possible, however, that reasons for desertion among relatively affluent men are different from those of lower-class men. For instance, the former may wish to force their spouses into more rapid divorce by impressing upon them the irremediability of their own decisions, while the latter may desert more for financial reasons. Indeed, a study done in Toronto in the early 1960's found that financial difficulties, including a husband's failure to support the family, were a highly significant contributing factor.[33] Also it is easier for a working-class man to desert without a trace than for an established businessman or professional to do so. Nevertheless, even the latter can establish themselves in another province where they will be difficult to trace, and, especially, will be induced to support their families only with difficulty.

I would suggest the following double hypothesis for Ontario and perhaps even for Canada in general: among men, desertion tends to be more frequent among lower-status persons. Deserting wives, however, come predominantly from the middle and upper strata. Men desert in great part because of economic conditions while women desert to start a new life, "find themselves," and for other reasons related to the concept of self-fulfillment. Desertion among wives, as we will see

31. S. Skarsten, "Family Desertion in Canada," *Family Coordinator*. 23, January 1974, p. 23.
32. W.M. Kephart, "Occupational Level and Marital Disruption," *American Sociological Review*. 20, August 1955, p. 461.
33. J.L. Topp, *Parents Without Partners*. Master's Thesis, School of Social Work, University of Toronto, 1963.

below, is on the increase: it is a new phenomenon and probably has, at its basis, somewhat different contributing factors. It is also assumed that deserting wives either have the ability to support themselves or the legal know-how to compel their husbands to contribute to their support. Indeed, in a *Psychology Today* article, the runaway wife was described as being in her mid thirties and of good economic means.[34]

Some men do desert with their wives' prior knowledge and may even tell their children beforehand. But most simply never return one night. Some leave, return with a bit of money, and then leave again when the supply is exhausted. This makes for a highly insecure situation for all the parties concerned, but particularly for women, since men have, traditionally, been the ones who have deserted. Lerner has suggested four reasons for this phenomenon: the greater responsibility that women have for the care of children, women's economic dependency on their husbands, the fact that women are less aggressive than men, and the fact that women accept fewer roles that are non-familial in nature.[35] However, agencies which specialize in the location of missing persons in the U.S.A. report that the number of runaway wives they are seeking is actually greater than that of husbands.[36] This is certainly an indication that more wives desert now than in the past, but it may also indicate that more leave children behind than in the past and that the newly burdened husbands are more willing to report and seek their missing wives than used to be the case. Women, however, more often give a warning sign, or tell husbands and children beforehand.[37]

Children generally do better in those instances where the deserting parent has been able to assure them of his or her love before leaving; something that deserting mothers may do more often than deserting fathers, since the former would have had

34. M. Cassady, "Runaway Wives," *Psychology Today*, 42, 1975.
35. S.H. Lerner, "Effects of Desertion on Family Life," *Social Casework*, 35, January 1954, pp. 3-8.
36. *The New York Times*, February 23, 1975; M. Bralowe, "Runaway Wives," *Wall Street Journal*, October 1, 1975, p. 5.
37. R. Todres, "Runaway Wives: An Increasing North American Phenomenon," *Family Coordinator*, 27, January 1978, p. 19.

a greater responsibility for the children. Such a gesture may alleviate the deserting party's feelings of guilt and also make it less difficult for the remaining one to cope with the situation.

Desertion is a very broad term, encompassing several different situations. At one extreme are those persons who leave home, never to be seen or heard of again. The remaining spouse is not only beset by financial difficulties, but may be completely bewildered by the situation. She may even believe that some misfortune has befallen her husband and may live for months and even years praying for the miracle that will bring him back. The deserted individual may be in a legal limbo and may remarry only after years have elapsed or on proven desertion. Many persons of the opposite sex may refrain from forming a lasting relationship with the deserted spouse, in the fear that the other spouse might return, with ensuing legal complications.

Then there are those who leave just as abruptly, but, sooner or later, give sign of life: a letter, a phone call, a small cheque, a card on a birthday, and there are those who follow the same pattern at departure but return occasionally for a brief visit. There are those who return for a while and then desert again and those who explain to their families what is happening and never return permanently. The latter, however, are the most likely to remain in contact with their families and even to visit them. If there is any overall pattern it is that of occasional absences which become longer and more frequent until, one day, the man never returns.[38]

Deserted mothers often concentrate in public housing projects, along with separated or divorced mothers whose ex-spouses do not contribute to the household income. It is estimated that only 20% of the parties who are supposed to contribute to the family they left do so on a regular basis, and that 30% do not contribute a cent. Between these extremes are those who either contribute erratically or else very small sums. Therefore, the notion of the exploited man who has to support two households is grossly exaggerated. There are, indeed, a few instances of rich husbands who are exploited by

38. R.E. Baber, *Marriage and the Family,* New York: McGraw-Hill, 1953.

greedy wives but these cases are actually rare. What leads us to believe that they are so frequent is the fact that the media inform us whenever such a case occurs on a grand scale, but do not do so for the thousands of cases where the family is left penniless.

The deserted family must deal with some very specific problems over and above coming to terms with the suddenness of the situation. First, the family seldom has the legal support that is so important, especially when financial difficulties are involved. Unless the missing spouse is found, the deserted party may be left without direct financial assistance and with welfare as their only recourse. The family must also face difficult problems of self-definition and identity, especially when the whereabouts of the deserter are not known. It is also more complicated for such families to plan for the future than for those involved in separation cases. Should the spouse return, as often happens, even more insecurity lies ahead, given the high rate of recidivism.[39] And to this situational uncertainty must be added the feelings of worthlessness that the deserted spouse will experience if he or she interprets the desertion as a sign that he or she has failed the missing spouse[40]

THE DIVORCE ITSELF

When legal divorce occurs in Canada, the former spouses have generally been living apart for a minimum of three months and more often for from six months to three years. While the divorce is a rite of passage, it does not require the traumatic adjustments that the separation itself did. However, the finality of the decree can be a terrible blow for the partner who did not want the divorce and even for the one who sought it Some people remarry within a year, and for them the psychological problems of the separation and of the divorce are minimized as they concentrate on the development of the new relationship. However, the rapid remarriage of one spouse i yet another adjustment that the other spouse has to make, an

39. J.E. Steigman, "The Deserted Family," *Social Casework*, 38, 1957, p. 168.
40. Lerner, *op.cit.*, p. 6.

the un-remarried spouse may have a difficult time coping with all the problems involved, especially when there are children and visiting rights have to be acceded to or invoked while no one is yet used to the idea of the new relationship.

The divorce procedure, the legal phase of divorce, can also be quite painful, especially when spouses are at each other's throats to obtain as much as possible on one side and give as little as possible on the other.

> *Why people behave so badly is tied up with what they expect when they marry, what they eventually get, and the expensive and unpleasant legal process of divorce, which, when prolonged and dramatized by lawyers who enjoy a spirited battle and want the most for their clients, makes everything worse and encourages hostility. Also, once one or both members of the couple decide they no longer want to be married, it seems to signal the unleashing of all the frustrations each carried silently through the marriage. There is no longer any reason not to be as drastically unreasonable as one feels like being.*[41]

When custody of children or visiting rights are contested, the situation becomes very emotional and manifestations of hatred often follow. It is, at such times, almost inevitable that parents will, to some extent, use their children as pawns out of the fear of losing them or losing their love, and in order to get back at the other spouse through them.

Bohannan distinguishes, in addition to the emotional divorce which begins during marriage and continues during separation and even for many years after divorce, five other "divorces:" the legal divorce, the economic divorce, the co-parental divorce with the attendant problems of custody and of access to the children, the community divorce, and, finally, the psychic divorce which he defines as follows:

> *Psychic divorce means the separation of self from the*

---

41. Westoff, *op.cit.*, p. 44. As one illustration of the role played by lawyers, see E. Baguedor, *Separation. Journal of a Marriage*, New York: Simon and Schuster, 1972, chapters 4, 10, and 11.

personality and the influence of the ex-spouse—to wash the man right out of your hair ... While it is the most difficult it is also the ... most constructive. ... Each must regain—if he ever had it—the dependence on self and faith in one's own capacity to cope with the environment, with people, with thoughts and emotions.[42]

How people feel after divorce depends on a multitude of circumstances. Foremost are the feelings one has towards the ex-spouse and how one is treated by and treats him or her. The spouse who remains attached to the ex-partner has the more difficult time. However, when both can sit down and iron out the problems of children and money, the burden is lessened. Much also depends on who remarries first, and when, on the children and the custody arrangements, the new spouse, financial matters, living arrangements (such as the house and the neighbourhood), one's relationship with relatives and friends, one's work (or lack of), one's personality, and the new sexual relationships that one forms. It has been found, for instance, that separation and divorce are made much easier by increased levels of social participation. In fact, stress is inversely related to participation, and the critical period seems to be some six months after separation. It has also been established that men become socially active more readily than women do because of "greater opportunity for making social contacts on the part of the males, and perhaps greater loneliness."[43] Women participate even less when they have childen, probably because they are too busy and have no money for sitters, and also because their children prevent them from sinking into complete loneliness. The following table indicates, on one side, the variables that increase the likelihood of a smooth adjustment to divorced life and, on the other, those that are likely to create difficulties. Most of these points will be discussed in the next chapter.

42. P. Bohannan, "The Six Stations of Divorce," in *Divorce and After*, edited by P. Bohannan, New York: Doubleday, 1970, p. 53.
43. H.J. Raschke, "The Role of Social Participation in Post Separation and Post Divorce Adjustment," *Journal of Divorce*, 1, Winter 1977, p. 135.

Factors facilitating emotional adjustment in and after divorce.	Factors creating emotional difficulties in and after divorce.
No strong attachment to former spouse	Attachment to former spouse which is not reciprocated
Reasonable time lapse for remarriage	One spouse remarries immediately after, or had already been living with someone prior to, the divorce
No children	Children
If children, cooperation between parents	If children, difficulties between parents over custody, visits, support, child rearing
No financial ties, independence	One spouse contributes to the support of the other and resents it
No financial problems	Financial problems: difficult for both spouses
	One spouse left without support
	Mother has to go to work for the first time
	Children left largely unsupervised
Children maintain good ties with non-custody parent	Children have doubts about feelings of non-custody parent
Children see non-custody parent regularly	Children do not see non-custody parent regularly
Kin and friends are supportive	Kin and friends are not supportive
No legal difficulties	Legal problems, at times exacerbated by lawyers
Good living conditions	Moving into poorer living conditions
Satisfaction with work	Unemployment or problems at work
	Alcoholism
	Drug addiction
	Emotional disorders
	Physical illness
Involved in various activities	Inactive, secluded, and lonely
Good new sexual relationships	Difficulty in forming new sexual relationships
Satisfactory sexual life	Getting into bad sexual relationships
For women: nontraditional sex roles	For women: traditional sex role attitudes[44]

44. P. Brown and R. Manela, "Changing Family Roles: Women and Divorce,"

CONCLUSIONS

In this chapter, we have concentrated on the processes that first lead people into bad marriages, and then to termination of them. The focus has been on the mechanisms involved. While we saw that it is no hard thing to end up in a bad marriage, it is more difficult to be party to a good divorce. Few people are ecstatic about divorce, although they are often happier about it than they were with the ailing marriage that led up to it. Most people pass through a mourning period, either at separation or at divorce. In this respect divorce does cause some problems, especially under the circumstances enumerated above. But, for most people, an unhappy marriage gives rise to even worse problems; at least in a divorce the problems vanish after a while, except when children are involved and visiting rights are complicated or there are nagging doubts about the well-being of the children in question.

Divorce is always a phase, a rite of passage away from an unhappy marriage. But a bad marriage is a *condition* for many couples. It is a phase only if it improves (rarely enough) or if divorce follows. And thus we return to the theme of our introductory chapter: unhappy marriages, whether intact or breaking up, *are* a social problem. Divorce is one solution, albeit not a solution of unmitigated joy, to this problem.

Journal of Divorce, 1, Summer 1978, p. 315; also, P. Brown *et al.*, "Sex Role Attitudes and Psychological Outcomes for Black and White Women Experiencing Marital Dissolution," *Journal of Marriage and the Family*, 39, August 1977, pp. 549-561.

6 The Life of the Divorced

Life after divorce or, for that matter, during separation, is always drastically different, at least in the short term, especially for the partner who moves out, or for both if they both relocate upon separation or divorce. However, the extent of this difference is very much dependent on whether there are children present, on financial matters, on the durability of relationship with one's family and friends, on the individual's ability to cope with change, and on what kind of life-style the person adopts at the time. As individuals reintegrate themselves within their old networks or within new ones, as they stabilize their lives, form new meaningful relationships with the other sex, improve their financial situations, and as old wounds slowly heal, the lives of divorced persons normalize and they become able to integrate into their lives those aspects of their old and new life-styles that will allow them to cope with their current needs and situations.

The life of the divorced can be divided into the following categories: emotional or inner life (tied to relationships with children, former spouses, relatives, friends, work associates and new or current neighbours), leisure activities, and relationships with the other sex, or with the same sex if the divorced person is homosexual. In other words, the categories are almost the same as those we would enumerate for married persons, with a few differences. In fact, for the spouse who keeps the children *and* is also fortunate enough to retain the original dwelling, outward life is not substantially different—and can in fact improve considerably, once all the tensions and frictions leading up to and contingent upon the divorce passed.

At another level, the life of the divorced can be discussed in terms of three dimensions; these are the three dimensions of "singlehood:" temporary or transitory singlehood through which nearly all divorced persons pass; permanent or long-term singlehood as a conscious choice on the part of the individual; and what we will call unwilling singlehood. A fourth dimension is remarriage which will be discussed separately because the persons involved are, by definition, no longer divorced.

More books and journal articles than in the past are being written about single life.[1] At the meetings of various learned societies, there are special sessions and workshops on the subject. While more people today remarry, the high divorce rate nevertheless means that many people are single for at least a few years of their adult lives. Many divorced persons choose to remain *de facto* single or legally single (even though living with someone) for quite a while after divorce while some choose to do so permanently, and others find themselves in a situation of unwilling permanent singlehood. We will examine each of these three situations in turn. We will concern ourselves here only with people who are single because of divorce, separation and desertion, and not with the entire single population.

TEMPORARY OR TRANSITORY SINGLEHOOD

Nearly all divorced persons go through a period, however brief, during which they live as single persons, even though they may have children and a lover who lives elsewhere. Individuals in this category are between marriages, and gear their lives towards remarriage. Most of them are aware of the fact that eventually they will want to settle down with

1. For books, see M.A. Singleton, *Life After Marriage: Divorce as a New Beginning*, New York: Stein and Day, 1974 (a "guide book"); M. Adams, *Single Blessedness*, New York: Basic Books, 1976; P.J. Stein, *Single*, Englewood Cliffs, N.J.: Prentice-Hall, 1976; J.L. Block, *Back in Circulation*, New York: Macmillan, 1969; C. Napolitane and V. Pellegrino, *Living and Loving After Divorce*, New York: Lawson Associates, 1977.

another person. They do not see themselves as "single" people as they have only just been divorced and, moreover, think of remarrying later. In fact, some remarry so rapidly after a divorce that they never even have the opportunity of seeing themselves as divorced. Temporary or transitory singlehood may last from a few months to a decade or so, and some people in this category may sooner or later decide that they actually prefer a single life-style after all, and may cease to seek marriage. In such cases their "in-between-marriages" attitude will change to a mental set of permanent bachelorhood, and they will move into our second category.

In terms of life-style, there is probably little difference at the outset between the three categories of singlehood. Differences appear with time as some people come closer to forming permanent relationships while others make the choice to remain single. But transitory singlehood differs most strongly from permanent singlehood in that persons in the former category soon begin to look actively for a partner, and at some point this search becomes serious and focused.

PERMANENT SINGLEHOOD

Although many individuals in this category will eventually remarry, what is important here and distinguishes them from people in our other categories is the fact that they do not *intend* to remarry (and, often, do not even intend to form very lasting relationships) and actively *plan* on remaining single. Some become activists for the single cause and join various groups such as Single Society International or Parents Without Partners. If they are educated, they may write about single-hood, do research on the subject, and participate in conferences about it.[2] Their point of view is that the status of the single person has to be elevated and recognized in a society in which the preferred state is that of matrimony. It has even been argued that what defines the status of the divorcee is that he or she is still marriageable: "Its boundary is not given merely by termination of a marriage but by the presumption of

2. Peter Moore, "Enjoying the Eccentric Family," *The Single Parent*, 15, July-August, 1972, pp. 5-7.

marriageability."[3] This approach is heavily influenced by the norms of a society which views marriage as more desirable than singlehood. The life-style of the permanently single will generally, in this framework, be indistinguishable from that of singles who have never married and do not intend to. Only the presence of ex-spouses and of children render divorcees different. In this respect, it would be interesing to know whether the presence of children tends to motivate people to remarry or to remain single and whether there is any difference between men and women in this respect.

As illustrations of permanent singlehood, we will examine three very different cases.

Margaret divorced at thirty-two. She has one child, aged seven at the time of the divorce, and her former husband has always contributed his share of child support. Margaret had a B.A. in Business Administration before she married and, dissatisfied with her marriage when her child was four, she returned to school and completed a M.B.A., got an excellent job and was soon promoted. She now earns, at thirty-eight, over $40,000 a year, has a very well appointed townhouse, good circle of female friends, and is never short of male company. She is very attractive and young looking. She travels extensively, often taking her daughter with her. She has been proposed to several times and has already refused to remarry. She is very satisfied with her life and sees no reason to change it. From her point of view, why should she? She feels she lives in the best of all worlds: she has a well adjusted child, is extremely happy in her work, is secure with the thought that she can easily obtain male company, and her sex life is satisfactory, although at times sporadic. Above all, she enjoys her freedom and feels that remarriage would only take time away from all those things she enjoys, in that she would have to take care of a husband's domestic and social needs. She especially appreciates the fact that she feels so much in control of her own life and she fears that marriage would only diminish her sense of self.

3. W. Weissleder, "No-Illusion Marriage and No-Fault Divorce," *Canadian Review of Sociology and Anthropology*, 11, 1974, p. 218.

Margaret is very representative of a new type of woman: those who are educated, have high or satisfactory vocational status, a good income, frequent male company, and who do not *wish* to remarry. It has been found that women in this category are less likely to remarry than less educated women with a lower income.[4] It used to be believed that no single woman *chose* to remain single. As Havens, however, puts it:

> If one rejects the common notion that females with high incomes are simply the "marital rejects" or "pathetic misfits" of society, then a possible interpretation is that those females are less willing to enter into and/or maintain marital commitments. In other words, many of these females choose not to be married.[5]

Other authors (e.g. Srole *et al.*) have even posited that the type of woman who is selected for marriage and for remarriage may not be the strongest one, but the traditionally most "feminine" one; that is to say, the more dependent and childlike one.[6] In the past, it had been assumed that educated and well established women could not find men to match them. This does happen, but these days such women often *voluntarily* choose to remain single after divorce. A male researcher, while pondering how healthy marriage is for women, suggested that many women remarry simply because they have no other options when they are unskilled and uneducated.[7] To complement the perspective, Adams has hypothesized that if a woman is to lead a happy and successful single life she must be economically independent as well as socially and psychologically autonomous, without dependent children.[8]

4. K.S. Renne, "Health and Marital Experience in an Urban Population," *Journal of Marriage and the Family*, 33, May 1971, pp. 338-350.
5. E.M. Havens, "Women, Work and Wedlock: A Note on Female Marital Patterns in the United States," *American Journal of Sociology*, 78, January 1973, p. 218.
6. L. Srole *et al.*, *Mental Health in the Metropolis*, New York: McGraw-Hill, 1962, p. 180.
7. Srole *et al.*, *ibid.*
8. M. Adams, "The Single Woman in Today's Society: A Reappraisal," in *The Women's Movement*, edited by H. Wortis and C. Rabinovitz, New York: John Wiley, 1972, pp. 89-101.

The next two case studies are of men.

Paul divorced at twenty-nine after a five-year marriage. They had no children and his ex-wife could support herself. He decided that it was time for a general change in his life and, in spite of his age, was accepted in medical school. He was too busy to even think of remarrying and it was only slowly, as the years went by, that he realized that he did not want to remarry and thoroughly enjoyed the single scene. He cannot exactly be considered a swinger because his profession does not allow him sufficient time for that. However, he pays far more attention to his physical appearance and sexuality than men generally do, and he is always willing to plunge into a new relationship. His relationships are always brief and broken by his pursuit of a more exciting woman. He is now forty-five and a well established medical specialist.

The last case is that of Mark, age forty-two at the time of this interview.

Mark divorced three years ago. His ex-wife had custody of their two children, aged twenty and eighteen, who are now both employed. His ex-wife is remarried and Mark is therefore entirely free of financial responsibility. He is a skilled worker and is currently employed by Bell Canada. He is a sports addict and spends almost all of his free time watching horse- and auto-racing. In the little spare time he has, mainly in the winter season, he reconditions cars, at times races them, or sells them. He has had a couple of steady girl friends but he is not very interested in dating: "I like girls but I just don't have the time for them."—"No, I don't believe I will remarry, I've got too much to do."

Robert Bell defines five categories of divorced persons who do not get remarried. However, his typology does not separate those who *choose* singlehood from those who are "chosen" by it. He differentiates between what he calls the bitter, the frightened, the overdemanding, the rejected, and the adjusted (the latter being close to what has been discussed in this section).[9]

There are several variables that will determine an individual's choice of remarriage or singlehood. These "pushes" and "pulls" toward singlehood, as Stein describes them, actually consist of the weighing of the relative advantages of being married or single.[10] They may also involve a negative perception of what marriage is (a trap, sexual limitation) as well as a sometimes erroneous positive perception of the excitement and variety of singlehood. Remarriage rates will nonetheless remain high as long as there are important functions that can only be fulfilled acceptably within marriage and voluntary singlehood will increase when acceptable alternatives exist.[11]

UNWILLING SINGLEHOOD

At the outset the attitudes of unwilling singles may in no way differ from those of transitory singles, although their lifestyles may differ, and it may be that it is this difference in lifestyle which prevents them from meeting eligible persons. It may also be that certain personality configurations (including emotional disorders) or attributes (unattractive physical appearance) prevent them from finding a mate. However, the latter is probably a more common occurrence among singles who have never married than among divorced singles— because the latter have already "made it" once. Some people who were very unstable during their marriages may continue to be so after them, and, consequently, may be considered poor risks by persons of the opposite sex; alcoholism would certainly fall into this category. Advanced age is also a detrimental factor, especially for women who divorce late. This is because men tend to remarry younger women and the pool of available males is greatly reduced for older divorcées (earlier death among men also contributes to this situation). Many divorcées are housekeepers, with children, no market-

9. R.R. Bell, *Marriage and Family Interaction*, Homewood, Ill.: Dorsey, 1971, third edition, pp. 527-529.
10. P.J. Stein, "Singlehood: An Alternative to Marriage," *Family Coordinator*, 24, October 1975, p. 500.
11. For a similar formulation, see Weissleder, *op.cit.*, p. 226.

able skills, and little money, and this militates against remarriage by limiting their opportunities to meet men.

We will present four case studies of persons who did not choose to remain single after a divorce but were chosen by singlehood because of a variety of circumstances.

Rosemary is such an example. Married at eighteen, divorced at thirty-eight, with five children ranging from seventeen to seven, she is a high-school drop-out who was never employed. Rosemary spends all her time at home, except when she visits her mother, goes to the grocery store, or to the welfare department. Her former husband contributes practically nothing to his ex-family's livelihood and she lives in a public housing project, surrounded by women like her, with too little money, too many children, and no opportunities. After five years of desertion and divorce, she would very much like to remarry: "Perhaps I could get out of here and live a little better. I am so tired of raising kids by myself. But who wants a welfare woman with five kids?"

Very different is Sharon's case:

She had completed one year of University before marrying, at the age of nineteen, a newly-graduated lawyer. They had three children and at thirty she found herself abandoned for another woman. Her husband was remarried, a year later, to yet another woman and had a child with her. However, he is both wealthy and extremely attached to his children, and has therefore always supported his ex-wife and three children in fine style. Sharon has been unable to find another man of her faith who could support her in this manner. She has a housekeeper, a very large home, a car, is well dressed and her children attend a private, religious school. She has much leisure time, swims, and plays tennis regularly. She occasionally dates but is never satisfied with the social status of her partners. At any rate, she herself admits that no one has proposed to her in all these years. She is now forty.

Neil would also very much like to remarry.

> Divorced eight years ago at thirty-three, he drifted into alcoholism. His health has deteriorated and he has aged prematurely. He is generally depressed and pays very little attention to his physical appearance. He does date from time to time, but from *his* description of these encounters, it is quite obvious that he always manages to offend the women by his boorishness and tactlessness. Moreover, his income is unsteady and he does not have enough to go out a great deal. He would like to marry "to have a woman take care of me. I need a good cook."

Finally, Mary is another fairly common case: the older divorcée.

> At sixty, Mary is a secretary for a legal firm; she divorced four years ago. Her children were married and she moved into an apartment. Her former husband died of a heart attack soon thereafter. Mary has never had a real date in all these years. At first she did not care, then she really got involved in the older single scene through various clubs, but to no avail. Now she is resigned to her situation and foresees that she will never remarry, although she would like to: "Men my age are either married or they are going out with younger women or they are dying out. Older men are in senior citizens' homes."

It is this group of singles who are the most lonely. They are also probably the ones, especially among men, who suffer most from emotional problems, either as a consequence or as a cause or both of their unwilling singlehood. At bottom, they also often harbour an unconscious ambivalence towards marriage and may be too "choosy" for their own good in the long run and for the wrong reasons (at least from the bystander's point of view). They also suffer more from relative deprivation because they wish to have what the others have, namely a partner to whom they are married.

INNER LIFE

In this section, we present an overview of the main threads which run through the inner life of divorced persons. These threads are interwoven with the rest of the life of the individuals as is discussed in the subsequent sections of this chapter, and as was presented in a schematic manner at the end of Chapter 5. One of the first tasks that confronts separated/divorced persons is to detach themselves from their former spouse, if this is not already done. The process can be extremely painful, for both the person who decided to leave and for the person who stayed behind unwillingly. The person who is abandoned, who may not have wanted the separation, and who may not be ready for it, feels betrayed and confused, is afraid of the future, lonely, and often experiences a plummeting of his/her sense of self-esteem.[12] That person may have to resort to drugs (tranquilizers or stimulants) or alcohol to cope with the resulting anxiety, may get overinvolved in work and in social activities, or immerse her entire life into that of her children; she or he may lean heavily on parental support and on old friendships, although many of the latter tend to crumble away when a couple separates.

Often a spouse will leave for another partner. There may be guilt feelings involved, but that spouse is generally at a tremendous advantage emotionally as he (it is, so far, more often the man than the woman) has a new home, with a loved person in it, a foundation for self-esteem, emotional and sexual outlets, and emotional support.

The spouse who remains in her married neighbourhood, especially with children, has to cope with neighbours' enquiries or inquisitive looks, with neighbourhood children's reaction to the plight of her own children, while at the same time taking care of all the details of the house by herself. In large cities, these problems are of short duration and the

12. A group of single parents studied by Hansen and Grills showed a variety of these feelings; Grills also found that employment helped relieve some of these. F.C. Hansen, *Parents Without Partners,* Master's Thesis, School of Social Work, University of Toronto, 1963; C.C. Grills, *Parents Without Partners,* Master's Thesis, School of Social Work, University of Toronto, 1963.

situation of the partner who moves out is probably difficult for a longer period of time because more adjustments have to be made. However, as we will see in the next section, more often than not even the spouse who has custody of the children has to move and the move generally involves downward socio-economic mobility.

Often, one of the two partners' self-esteem has been badly battered both by the other partner and by the relationship or its failure. The fact of finding oneself alone and divorced in a society which values marriage as much as ours does may compound that lowering of self-esteem. In addition, many people do not know what to say to divorced persons or how to react to them. There is no institutionalized way of reacting to divorced persons in the way there is for married persons. This may further depress these individuals and contribute to their loss of self-respect. However, as their situations stabilize, as they adapt to their new lives, and, especially, as they form new and meaningful relationships, self-esteem may return to its original level and may even top that level if the person is much happier now than he/she has been in many years.

Divorced persons may be in an emotional limbo for a long time following the separation because of what they had to suffer in the married relationship. Some may react by withdrawing from the opposite sex emotionally or maintain relationships purely for sexual reasons; others may become exploitative, as a defense mechanism, so that they will not be hurt again; others may decide never to have a long-term and deep relationship again, while others literally jump into a new relationship, blindly, as an escape from the past: the latter is often referred to as being "on the rebound."

When financial conditions are difficult, children's demands time-consuming; lodging substandard, and when there is little support from family or friends, the emotional life of the divorced person can be extremely difficult: there are too many burdens to bear, too few joys, too much work; the person becomes tired, depressed or agitated, restless or apathetic, has an acute sense of betrayal, unfairness, and loneliness. However, many of the emotional sufferings that divorced individuals undergo could be avoided were society and people in general more prepared to accept the situation, to see it as normal, and to be willing not to regard the divorced as a separate species with esoteric social needs.

RELATIONSHIP WITH CHILDREN

There are several patterns of relationship with regard to children. In cases of outright desertion, and in a few particularly difficult, contested, and bitter cases of divorce, a parent may sever all relationship with child or children. The abandoning parent may or may not feel guilty, depending on his personality. One such man recalled that his divorce had been so bitter that he had not seen his child in sixteen years. The boy had been abandoned with the mother when he was only a few months old (after the mother had refused to take her unfaithful husband back). The man added, "I always expect that, one day, someone will ring at my door, I will open it, and this big boy will punch me in the nose." He professed never having regretted his separation from the child.

At the other extreme is the parent who receives sole custody of the child, while the other parent is either entirely absent or has visiting rights or sees the child only during weekends. The parent with custody generally has the opportunity to maintain a closer relationship with the children and has by far the greater control over their education. But when poverty is involved (and we should remember that over 33% of female headed families live below the poverty line), that parent usually the mother, is often overwhelmed by the odds against her, and her life with her children can be very difficult. She may need to take employment and, on her return home, cook and prepare the house for the next day; the children are not supervised to the extent that they should be, and in the teenage years, frequently give considerable difficulty to their mothers. When the neighbourhood is rough, they run a higher risk than other children of becoming delinquents and of dropping out of school. Such a mother's relationship with her children may be one of bickering, anger, harsh words, tears, or withdrawal. However, when economic conditions are more favourable and the woman is less overworked and receiving a reasonable degree of support from her environment, her relationship with her children is likely to be close and rewarding. Such a parent has an advantage over the parent without custody, as the children prevent her from becoming too lonely and give her an entrance into a better regulated emotional reality than that of the foot-loose bachelor.

Another problem faced by the parent with custody arises when the time comes for her to form relationships that are sexual in nature, especially when children are in their teens. Certain adults find it inhibiting to have children around while others prefer children to remain unaware of their activities. Many parents are concerned about the potential effect that their sexual and dating life can have on their children: "I wonder what my daughter will think about all my male friends, especially what she will do in two or three years when *she* starts dating." In fact, a study has found that children of sexually active women are themselves sexually active at a younger age. Several complications can arise in this respect. The first one is the danger of teen pregnancies and premature marriage for the daughters of divorcées. The simple fact is that, while a forty-year-old woman or man should be mature and experienced enough to cope with an active and varied sexual life, the same cannot be said of a fourteen-year old. There *is* an age for everything and this may perhaps be the best tactic to use: to explain honestly to the teenager that everything has a time and that, for now, he or she is not yet ready to imitate the parent. At times like these parents need strong values, open channels of communication with their children, and should have been able to impart their values to their children in the past, otherwise it may be a little too late to start at this point.

There are also a few parents who share custody. The children may live with one for a week or for part of a week; or they may live with one parent for part of the year. Generally, such ex-spouses do not live far from each other so that the children's lives at school and with friends can have continuity and can run smoothly. Such arrangements, when well organized, may be the best ones as the children benefit from the attention of both parents, and each parent receives the support of the other and also has a considerable amount of free time which allows each to develop other relationships, pursue work interests, rest, and have some leisure time. However, shared custody also has the potential for a great many disruptions in the children's lives, especially in terms of schooling, friends, and discipline.

Then, there are various other arrangements, such as those parents who have free access to their children and generally see them a few times each week, including at least one full day during the weekend. Again, such situations can be very beneficial to the child and to both parents. The visiting parent maintains a close relationship with his children while the custody parent gets some free time; a very important factor, especially for women who are encumbered with home and child care responsibility. Other non-custody parents get their children only once a week, or on alternate weekends, or even only once a month. The less the parents see children, the more likely they are to feel insecure in their relationship with their children, to fear losing their love, to feel helpless as far as their upbringing is concerned.

The role of the non-custody single parent is also very problematic. The best description of the shape that the role often takes can be found in a chatty but excellent book by Epstein from which I quote at length:

> One of the consequences of visitation is to compartment-alize the role of fatherhood, to make it an all-absorbing task, in a way that it almost never is under normal conditions. A married father might spend an hour or so playing with his young son or daughter, or even on a weekend or holiday an entire afternoon, but then again weeks might go by when he does nothing of the kind, and no one would judge him a poor father. The irony is, a full time father is under no pressure to work at fatherhood full time, while a divorced father, when he has his children visiting him, is under an inner pressure to work at fatherhood double time. . . .But being a father, being a son, being a daughter, these are not weekend or summer or Christmas things ... (Fathers are found) at amusement parks, at fastfood franchise joints, at the toy

departments of discount stores, at the beach, at all the places where for children pleasure is promised and where for adults time spent with their children may be killed quickly if not necessarily efficiently . . .[13]

Single parenting after divorce will vary immensely depending on a series of variables. Most important are economics, the availability of human resources such as helpful relatives and friends, and the sex of the single parent. In an article on single fathers, Mendes also found that an important determinant was the issue of choice. She finally divided her sample into those fathers she called "seekers," those who had actively sought the custody of their children, and the "assenters," those who did not initiate the process of becoming single parents.[14] Number of children, age of children, their health, and the age and health of parents are also salient factors in the single parent's experience.

As in the above case study of Margaret, in our age of sexual inequality, women who have children and are very involved in their work may find, after divorce, that they have more time to devote to both as well as to themselves. They may enjoy the freedom of living alone, of finding out how well they cope, of not having to constantly seek someone's approval, of neither having their lives revolve around the schedule of a man, nor of having to cater to his domestic needs. They may also enjoy bringing up children by themselves as they may feel that they can be more consistent in their practices without having to listen to someone disparage their methods, as so often occurs with couples. Such women may settle for lifelong singlehood or for singlehood that will last until their children are gone. They will be happy mothers, productive in their careers, with time for themselves, and they may also have various relationships of a sexual nature, some of which may be deep and lasting but allow them to live independently.

13. J. Epstein, *Divorced in America,* New York: Dutton, 1974, pp. 292, 293, 288.
14. H.A. Mendes, "Single Fatherhood," *Social Work,* 21, July 1976, pp. 308-312.

RELATIONSHIP WITH FORMER SPOUSE

This is a very complex issue because it is often overlaid with emotion and because it encompasses a vast range of alternatives. At the separation stage, many couples still date each other and even sleep with each other, especially when one or the other expects a reconciliation. This is often called a trial separation, just as there are now trial marriages. But, after divorce, such arrangements are less frequent, because at least one of the two spouses is oriented toward the future, which generally means finding *another* partner.

During the separation, before the divorce, and particularly for those spouses with children and/or with complicated separation agreements concerning money or other material possessions, the relationship is often bitter, quarrelsome and full of recriminations, and each spouse may try to use the children to get back at the other, may have excessive recourse to lawyers (who often add fuel to an already heated situation in order to benefit from it), and may attempt to make parents and friends take sides. Generally, once issues are legally or personally settled, things cool down. But there are many couples who maintain grudges after years of divorce, even after one or both have remarried, especially where maintenance and children are concerned. The children are often the vehicles of this tension, either willingly or unwillingly. Atkin and Rubin have called divorce "the tie that binds."

> Cutting the bonds of matrimony in no way means cutting the emotional bonds that weld together a man and a woman . . . mixed-up feelings of love, hate, guilt, anger, resentment, spite and jealousy can hold a divorced couple in bondage to each other for years. . . . Ironically, for some ex-partners those very hang-ups that made it impossible for them to live together amicably may be the forces that keep them tied to each other. . . . The emotional shackles of divorce are generally so well disguised that both parties may be quite unaware of them.[15]

15. E. Atkin and E. Rubin, *Part-Time Father*. New York: The Vanguard Press 1976, p. 21.

As they point out, achieving complete divorce is a difficult process, especially when children or money are involved and, in many cases, the two become interchangeable objects of barter in what has been called "the alimony game."

The remarriage of one spouse before the other is often the source of a recurrence of conflicts. When there are children, the ex-spouse may be afraid of the effect that the new mate will have on them or even may be afraid that the children will become attached to the new partner. There is more to it though. As Epstein aptly puts it: "It is not that most divorced people wish their ex-spouses ill; it is that they detest the idea of their finding greater happiness than they themselves do."[16]

Many couples remain good friends after the relationship has been severed, phone each other from time to time, or write, or talk about business, or inquire after each other, even when children are not involved. When this is the case, such friendliness generally tends to wane as one or both ex-spouses remarry, often because the new spouses find the former relationship a threat to their current marriage. Remaining "good friends" is both an asset and a liability. It is a liability when one of the ex-spouses is still attached to the other and even secretly hopes for a reconciliation. The friendship prevents that ex-spouse from becoming sufficiently psychologically free from her/his past to build toward the future. And it comes as a shock to him or her when the other one remarries.

At the other end of the spectrum are those ex-spouses who cut their ties with each other completely. It is as if the marriage had never existed and their focus is on the present and the future. Generally, such couples have no children, no alimony or maintenance is involved, and they often live in different cities. Some are remarried while others are not.

In other words, there is a range of possible relationships between former spouses. What is important to stress here is that while some types are neutral or constructive, others are destructive and can do a great deal of harm where children are involved.

16. Epstein, *op.cit.*, p. 224.

RELATIVES

Parents and other kin are often dismayed when they learn that a couple has separated or divorced. Some parents may see it as a blot on the family's escutcheon and may even threaten to disinherit a son or daughter if reconciliation does not ensue. In fact, in a few families with wealth, a couple may wait ten years before divorcing in order to preserve their inheritance. Generally, parents and kin rally around their own child in the event of marital dissolution and it is rare for them to maintain any kind of regular relationship with the other spouse.[17] When there are children in a marriage, the situation is different, a cold politeness or even warmth to the other spouse is the order of the day as the grandparents have a vested interest in maintaining a relationship with their grandchildren. Also, the parent with custody may choose to stay on good terms with the other spouse's parents in order to ensure help, gifts and inheritance.

After the initial shock has worn off, parents and relatives can be a great asset for the divorced person if he or she lives in the same city as they do; they can provide the divorcee with a place to go, with someone to confide in, with help in the care of the children, and so on. Relatives in the same city are especially helpful for the parent who has custody of children: in them, the children will find additional sources of love and parents will have a source of help and of emotional support, someone to talk to about the children. However, it may also happen that the divorced person returns to the fold of his/her family in a kind of regression; as if out of a need to go back to childhood and avoid responsibilities. The family can then become a protective cocoon that will prevent the individual from building an independent life, especially with a person of the other sex.

17. J.W. Spicer and G.D. Hampe, "Kinship Interaction After Divorce," *Journal of Marriage and the Family*, 37, February 1975, pp. 113-119.

FRIENDS

The divorced couple's relationship with friends is subject to greater variability than that with relatives. They are likely to lose friends. At first the reaction may be sympathetic, if a little awkward and puzzled. A number of irrational responses take place in friends' minds when they learn of a divorce, since this divorce stirs in them quite a range of feelings regarding their *own* marriages.[18] Men often report receiving more help from their friends, especially when they have custody of their children, than women do. Men at first may be invited to dinner because it is assumed, often rightly, that they cannot cook, while divorced women do not generally benefit from such assistance because it is assumed that they can take care of themselves. In addition, it is generally the wives (who are the ones who cook) who suggest that the friend be invited. But these same wives may prefer not to invite a *female* friend who is divorced as they may see her as a competitor for their husband's attention. Many divorced women report that, suddenly, married female friends invite them less and keep them away from their husbands. As time goes by, divorced persons are either increasingly excluded by their old circle of married friends or else slowly exclude themselves as they come to feel more and more out of place.

Single life can therefore bring a certain degree of social isolation, especially if the adult in question is unemployed. Making new friends is more difficult in middle ages than it was during the prime of youth because, after a certain age, we have built our lives, have already established a network of friends, and we find that other eligible or potential friends have done the same and are already busy with their long-time friends, with their relatives, and with their children. Therefore, the divorced person who chooses a long period of bachelorhood is well advised to seek people in a similar condition. This, in itself, can be awkward and unpleasant for there are few places where one can meet such persons, except in singles' bars and clubs; places which repulse many people

18. A.A. Miller, "Reactions of Friends to Divorce," in *Divorce and After*, edited by P. Bohannan, New York: Doubleday, 1970, pp. 57-59.

because of their superficial and plastic atmosphere. Parents Without Partners and One-Parent Families Associations of Canada are other outlets, but their activities and structure do not suit everyone.

Nevertheless, after a while, divorced persons tend to find others who are in their situation and form a new network of friendships, albeit a transitory one, until they remarry. Often, one former spouse has relied heavily on the friendships already established by the other spouse: these friends will tend to remain loyal to the spouse they knew first and the other spouse may find himself or herself quite isolated. Relationships with one's friends depend in great part on the social milieu one grows up or lives in. In certain milieux, where divorce often occurs, or where people are more liberal and themselves of varied marital status, friendships need not be altered. This type of environment can make room for both divorced persons as autonomous, separate individuals without imposing on either the awkwardness, the out-of-place feeling, that many others report experiencing.

WORK AND FINANCES

It is a great asset for divorced persons if, first of all, they have steady employment and, second, if they like their work. Divorce involves the division of a household; many economic difficulties follow, especially where child support is concerned. In many cases of desertion, difficult economic conditions already existed. Many men desert because supporting a family is too much of a burden for them, especially when they have a girl friend elsewhere. But even in relatively well-to-do middle-class homes, divorce is costly.

Divorced persons who have work they really like will have something to fall back on, at least temporarily. They may take advantage of the gap in their personal lives to work harder at their careers for a while and to advance rapidly, a factor that can enhance their self-esteem. However, there is a potential danger here, especially for those persons, as we indicated in Chapter 4, who were already too involved in their work. The danger lies in the fact that they may never find the time to rebuild their emotional and personal lives: their work may become all they have and all that matters.

There are individuals whose psychological configuration is such that they are too independent to live with another adult all the time. For them, marriage is constraining and confining. They need freedom to structure their own time, to make their own living arrangements, and even to bring children up by themselves. They like to "do their own thing," and divorce is beneficial to them. This personality profile is commonly that of artists and career people, especially those who need to travel a great deal, maintain odd hours or who are extremely committed to their work.

Being single, especially a single parent, as a result of desertion, separation, divorce and out-of-wedlock pregnancy, and, even more, being a *female* single parent, too often means one problem: poverty or relative economic disadvantage. For instance, over half the families with two children headed by a single mother are in a low-income category, and the percentage rises with each additional child. In 1967, while 17% of families headed by a man (generally with both spouses present) were poor, 36.3% of families headed by a woman were poor. While only 7.5% of all families were headed by a woman, 14.8% of low-income families had a female head.[19] In 1973, the average income of female heads of households was only slightly more than half that of males, $7,413 versus $13,204.[20] In Quebec in 1976, 20% of all divorced women were on welfare.[21] There are also indications, supported by American evidence, that deserted and separated women are poorer and more often dependent on welfare than married and divorced women.[22] Moreover, separated and divorced women are not poor necessarily because they have emerged from a marriage with a low-income man: indeed, a study of welfare recipients for dependent children in the United States discovered that

19. Report of the Royal Commission on *The Status of Women in Canada.* Ottawa, 1970, pp. 319-320. For similar conclusions for the year 1961, see J.R. Podoluck, *Incomes of Canadians,* Ottawa: Dominion Bureau of Statistics, 1968.
20. Statistics Canada, *Canada Year Book 1975.* Table 6.6, pp. 255-256.
21. L. Roy, *Le Divorce au Québec: Evolution Lente.* Gouvernement du Québec, Mars 1978, p. 36.
22. K.S. Renne, *op.cit.,* p. 347.

the fathers were not concentrated in the low-income categories but paralleled the occupational distribution of men in the general population.[23] Female-headed families are poor, not only because of the lower education of women, fewer marketable skills and lower income, but because the fathers do not support their children. Many of these women therefore experience a steep drop in socio-economic status because of the failure of their marriages.

LIVING ENVIRONMENT

We are dealing here with two situations: those divorced persons who move out and have to readjust to a new environment and those who remain within a neighbourhood and have to adjust their new marital status to the old environment. After a divorce, it often happens that both spouses move to a new location to make a fresh start. However, when the house does not have to be sold and when there are children, it is often judged preferable to remain in place so as to disturb the children as little as possible.

The spouse who moves out is generally the man, and he usually leaves with little furniture, at least by comparison with what the couple had in common. In addition, the male has usually received little training in housekeeping so that it is often difficult and even irritating for him to set up his new apartment in such a way that he will feel at home in it. He will consider it to be a temporary situation, not a home and will therefore go there just to sleep and watch television.

The most important element to point out is that single-parent families resulting from divorce or separation are found disproportionately in public housing, indicating the state of their finances as well as the difficulties inherent in their new life-style. In 1970, 35.1% of tenant families in Ontario Housing in Toronto had only one parent and over one-third of those on the waiting list were in the same category.[24] While government

23. Reported on p. 500 of R.A. Brandwein *et al.*, "Women and Children Last: The Social Situation of Divorced Mothers and Their Families," *Journal of Marriage and the Family*, 36, August 1974, pp. 498-514.
24. Figures provided to D.E. Guyatt, *One-Parent Family in Canada*, Ottawa: The Vanier Institute of the Family, 1971, p. 43.

housing is a great help to these impoverished families, generally headed by a woman, it also carries a stigma: these projects are "housing for the poor." The density of children in these projects is high, supervision difficult or impossible, and delinquency rates often high. Moreover, high-rise living has been correlated with psychological strain in women.[25] All these factors are very demoralizing for the divorced parents involved. The wish of most is to get out of their surroundings.

LEISURE ACTIVITIES

There are certain problems related to singleness past a certain age in our society. The preferred social status here is that of marriage, especially for women. The entire social fabric revolves around couples: parties, dating, dinner with married friends, children's plays at school or recitals at dance schools, and travelling (the "single supplement" in the latter case is a perfect example), to mention only a few. This becomes especially obvious for women in terms of social outings; a woman alone in these conditions is often either eyed suspiciously or is considered fair game. The "husband snatcher" epithet applied to the single woman does not seem to have a counterpart among single males, who are less often seen as threats to intact marriages.[26] Often, even among friends, a single person is made to feel out of place. An interviewee narrated an amusing but enlightening anecdote which illustrates so well a certain prevailing mentality. The well-meaning hostess of a party was introducing the guests to one another. She would introduce a woman, then locate her husband, and say, "This is the man she belongs to." When the interviewee's turn came, the hostess said, "And Cathy does not belong to anyone."

Single life also implies inferior status in many people's minds. There is still in Canada today the antiquated prejudice that the single person has *failed* to find someone or has been rejected. The person who has never married is an even more

25. A.R. Gillis, "High-Rise Housing and Psychological Strain," *Journal of Health and Social Behavior*, 18, December 1977, pp. 418-431.
26. D.K. Orthner *et al.*, "Single-parent Fatherhood: An Emerging Family Life Style," *Family Coordinator*, 25, October 1976, p. 432.

conspicuous target here, especially in the case of women. In the results of a small survey I carried out in 1972 on students' sex role attitudes, 30% of the 113 who responded to the question said that they tended to take unmarried women of thirty-five years and above less seriously than unmarried men of the same age. Unmarried women were depicted in pitying terms ("they *lack* something" or "I feel sorry for her") while nothing even remotely comparable was expressed with regard to bachelors.[27]

The divorced person has at least "made it" once and his or her single status is taken to be temporary. However, if divorced singleness lasts beyond a certain number of years, the unavoidable comment, especially to a woman, is again: "What I don't understand is why such an attractive woman as you never remarried." The secret assumption is that there is something abnormal in the person who does not remarry. After a number of years of divorce, people will again wonder what is wrong with the divorcee. Few people, especially the married or the recently separated/divorced/widowed, seem to understand that anyone could *choose* to remain single. Men seem to have even more difficulty accepting this of women, perhaps because they are suspicious of women who can make it alone, even with children. For a man, a woman who chooses to live without a man is somehow dubious. "Is she a lesbian?"—the question crops up with predictable regularity.

Often, the male who moves into an apartment and does not feel at home there, will spend most of his time away from it, something which is easier for men to do than for women since women do not have quite as much freedom as men and since there are many places where they cannot go unescorted without being annoyed or even endangered. The typical life of many such men is to stay at work as late as possible, go for drinks, and then eat out or skip eating, a factor which contributes to a disbalanced diet and makes them more vulnerable to various ailments, including a general depression of the nervous system. Others may go from bar to bar, looking

27. A.-M. Ambert, *Sex Structure*, Don Mills, Ont.: Longman of Canada, second edition revised and enlarged, 1976, p. 158.

for girls, at times only looking, too afraid to pick one up, even afraid of catching V.D. They return home late unless they want to watch television. They often sleep little, adding to their general fatigue. Many dread the weekends because, without work, these are the loneliest times of all.

Many women also lead a life-style similar to that described above, although it should also be said that this pattern of activity does not apply to all men. Those women who lead this kind of life are usually those without children and with perhaps enough money to allow them to nightclub. They range from secretaries to career women. But most women either tire of that scene sooner than men (it carries more dangers for them) and rebuild their lives in a new apartment, or else spend a considerable amount of time at home with their children and with other women. In fact, perhaps one of the major problems of the divorced woman with children is that she does not have the time for leisure activities if she is employed, or else does not have enough money to go out, buy nice clothes, and pay a sitter. In addition, the woman with children at home may feel guilty about leaving them in order to go out and have a good time.

Leisure activities are especially problematic when the divorced person is an alcoholic or becomes one. Without the shelter of a real home, of a wife or husband, and of the direct responsibility for children, such a person will sink deeper into that dark world, thus endangering his/her health, financial situation, and even job. Moreover, alcoholics have a more difficult time forming new, meaningful relationships both because of their problem and also because they are less reliable and attractive partners.

RELATIONSHIP WITH OTHER SEX

This area will eventually determine which path the divorced person will take: cohabitation, remarriage, or bachelorhood. That divorced people usually resume some form of relationship with the other sex can be seen in a study by Gebhard who found that 82% of divorced women in his sample had had sexual intercourse since divorce and that only 12% of these had confined their activities to just one man.[28] These statistics would indicate that divorced women have a higher frequency of sexual interaction with men than never-married women and even than younger women (18-21) who are not yet married. However, despite the statistics, the situation is not the same for both sexes. Not only is it more difficult for women to commence new relationships with the other sex because of reduced opportunities, but there is also a double standard which cheers the divorced man on and suppresses the divorced woman.

> *A newly divorced man vigorously on the make is a phenomenon everyone agrees to understand; there is a tradition of sorts for it, the binge allowed the emotionally wounded man. The newly divorced man is even permitted a period of misogyny, of cynical and destructive feelings toward women. Yet even in the most liberated circles, similar behavior on the part of a newly divorced woman is not tolerated. Should a newly divorced woman indulge herself in a binge of emotional dishevelment similar to that allowed the newly divorced man, including a period of cynical and destructive feeling toward men, she, too, would be in a tradition of sorts, though one for which no sympathy exists—the tradition, that is, of the manhater, the bitch, the ball-buster.*[29]

Many people have already established relationships, sometimes sexual, before they divorce. The relationship at times endures and remarriage follows rapidly. This would seem to be reflected in American statistics which show that approximately 25% of the divorced remarry within one year of the decree.[30] More often, the relationship breaks up rapidly but the ex-spouse is now used to being back and functioning in the dating market. In fact, a problem that is quite frequent

28. P.H. Gebhard, "Post Marital Coitus Among Widows and Divorcees," in *Divorce and After*, edited by P. Bohannan, New York: Doubleday, 1970, pp. 89-106.
29. Epstein, *op.cit.*, p. 236.
30. P.C. Glick and A.J. Norton, "Perspectives on the Recent Upturn in Divorce and Remarriage," *Demography*, 10, August 1973, pp. 301-314.

among newly separated and divorced people, especially if they have had little warning and if their milieu has not provided them with anyone who is also divorced as a role model, is that they do not know where to find partners or how to behave in "single" circumstances. These difficulties are illustrated in the following case:

> Linda is now living alone for the first time since her twenty-five years of marriage. She is forty-two and her two children are both married. Her husband left her rather abruptly, without much psychological preparation but, fortunately, with a decent income and the house. Although Linda resumed work five years ago, she had always defined herself as a housewife. Still youthful looking and attractive, she would like to have male company, but "I've never been out alone in my entire adult life. I am completely out of it." Also, she had always been faithful to her husband "and it is difficult to visualize myself with another man." She would feel ill at ease, awkward with another man. "I feel old fashioned in the area of sex. I wouldn't know how to behave, how far to go on the first date or the second, or when to do it all and what to do. It was easier when I was younger: there were more rules and less freedom. Now anything goes and it is as if I was out of it." Obviously, adapting to the dating game will be the most difficult part of her new existence. Her own daughters would cope with the situation better because they were brought up in a different world.

There are many persons who become "swingers" for a while, often for a very long time. In fact, many married men contemplating divorce envy this life-style and try to emulate it after their separation, often much to their disappointment. Many divorced people go through a stage of playboy and playgirl, latching onto one person after another, bed-hopping. For some, this is cathartic: they may have been very sexually deprived in their marriages and the fact that they *can* attract many partners boosts their self-esteem which may have been battered in their married relationships. This phase can also be educational, in terms of learning about one's own sexuality and that of the opposite sex. However, most people soon tire of this life-style and yearn to form one deep relationship. The problem is that if they have played the swinger for too long, they may have acquired habits which may not serve them well in a meaningful friendship. And, finally, there are those who opt for perpetual swinging and are still hard at it at sixty, trying to pass for forty-five, bolstered by Grecian Formula and face lifts. These individuals generally tend to be insecure: with advancing age, their desirability and consequent status in the swinging scene is in doubt. They become afraid of age, because they have little of substance to look back on and advancing age seems to promise only emotional sterility.

Most individuals who divorce, however, are more interested in forming one relationship that will give them love, security, and a home base. They may play the singles' scene (bars, clubs) for a while but generally feel uncomfortable within it and see it as a very artificial situation. They become progressively more intent on finding one particular person rather than on having many dates. Often, the onset of a lasting love relationship also signals the onset of renewed mental and physical well-being in the divorced person. But there are individuals who like variety more than others do and such a trait is best accommodated within the single life-style. The single person can form more relationships that are sexual in nature than can the married person. It is possible that *one* deep and exclusive relationship gives more personal security than several for the majority of people. However, there are people who feel insecure and trapped as soon as they enter into such a relationship. Their normalcy is not the question. The point is that everyone will be happier if there is a socially acceptable niche for a great diversity of people. And singlehood is one such niche.

CONCLUSIONS

The life-style of divorced persons is quite varied and depends in part on the economic situation, personality, family composition, and the presence of children in each individual case. It is, therefore, inadvisable to paint a stereotyped picture of what divorced people, men or women, do. There are, indeed, some sectors of the population who believe that the divorced life is either one of constant orgy, or at the other extreme, one of bitter loneliness. As we have seen, either extreme fits only a few cases or fits some cases for only a brief period of time. The life of the divorced, just like the life of everybody else, is not static; it changes according to the situation at hand and alters with time. In fact, though divorced people go through various stages, few of them run the whole gamut, and many go directly from one marriage into another without any intervening stage.

The path of singlehood encompasses a variety of situations and of rationales for making this choice, when it is a choice. It is a stage nearly all divorced people go through before remarrying; it is a state in which many people find a fulfilling, rich, and happy life while others become, or remain, selfish, self-centered and at times exploitative; still others lead lives of frustration. But we find these categories in marriages, first and subsequent, as well; *people* are happy, and selfish, and frustrated. Singlehood, no more nor less than marriage, is a *human* state and a personal choice, and as such partakes of human strengths and human frailties.

The advantages of the single path after divorce are independence, freedom, and mobility as well as the absence of permanent commitment to another adult. The disadvantages result from the fact that our society has not yet fully accepted singlehood as a way of life for people over thirty. Society has not made a constructive place for adult single life, especially among the less affluent segments of society, except in the case of specific vocations such as the religious orders and the priesthood. We saw in this chapter that remarriage also lacks institutional support, in that there are no definite rules to follow and each remarried couple has to invent their own. The same judgment can be applied to society's response to singlehood after divorce and especially to the single state with dependent children. Indeed, the single parent has maximal responsibilities for others, but is offered the fewest alternatives and minimal support by society. The other option after divorce, remarriage, is discussed in Chapter 8.

7   The Children of Divorce

Close to 60% of divorcing couples have children below eighteen years of age: a total of some 30,000 children are involved in divorce each year in Canada and over one million in the United States. In the U.S.A., it is estimated that, of children born in the 1970's, four out of ten will at some point be part of a single-parent family, and that 20-30% of all children will experience the divorce of their parents.[1] Moreover, if children of desertion are taken into consideration, the statistics are even more significant: a study found that approximately 75% of desertion cases involved children.[2] A small-scale survey in Toronto revealed that deserting wives were leaving behind them an average of 2.7 children,[3] which is higher than the national average of children per family unit. It would not be surprising to find that deserting fathers abandon even more children than deserting mothers. In Canada in 1976, there were 559,330 families with only one parent, an increase of 17% over 1971.[4] At any one time, over three and a half million

1. M.J. Bane, "Marital Disruption and the Lives of Children," *Journal of Social Issues*, 32, 1976, pp. 109-110. For additional statistics, see L. Bumpass and R.R. Rindfuss, "Children's Experience of Marital Disruption," *American Journal of Sociology*, 85, July 1979, pp. 49-64.
2. W.M. Kephart and T.P. Monahan, "Desertion and Divorce in Philadelphia," *American Sociological Review*, 17, December 1952, pp. 719-727; W.M. Kephart, *The Family, Society and the Individual*, Boston: Houghton Mifflin, 1966, p. 596.
3. R. Todres, "Runaway Wives: An Increasing North American Phenomenon," *Family Coordinator*, 27, January 1978, p. 18.
4. Statistics Canada, Census of Canada, 1976, *Families, Families by Family Structure and Family Type*, 93-882, Bulletin 4.3.

families in the United States have only one parent and about 85% of these are headed by women.[5] Some of these families result from the death of a parent, but the overall increase over the years stems primarily from divorce and out-of-wedlock births.

Specialists, clergy, and laypersons are often more concerned about the children than about adults when they define divorce as a social problem. They reason that children are more helpless and immature, need the love of both parents, and cannot tolerate a situation of conflict as well as adults can. Moreover, there is a correlation between poverty and single-parent families, especially those headed by women. Children from such families are at a tremendous disadvantage, and, in addition, are an enormous social and financial burden on any society. And, as we will see in the following sections of this chapter, psychological and behavioural disadvantages often stem from divorce for many, although by no means all, children in certain segments of society. Since there is much research still necessary on the subject of the children of divorce, this chapter will not only review the existing literature but will also serve to indicate those areas in which further exploration is necessary.

We will first look at the effect that parental strife, both before and after the divorce, and parental absence may have on children. Custody arrangements are briefly examined. Then we will examine the post-divorce relationship that children have with their parents. We will explore the question as to whether or not children of divorce are themselves more prone to marital instability than others. And then, finally, we will raise some key research questions concerning the effect of unhappy parental marriage and divorce on children.

IMPACT OF MARITAL STRIFE ON CHILDREN

The impact of marital strife on children can be felt in the short term or the long term or in both. The studies we will review here indicate that a negative effect can be seen in both among a

5. R.A. Brandwein et al., "Women and Children Last: The Social Situation of Divorced Mothers and their Families," Journal of Marriage and the Family, 36, August 1974, pp. 498-514.

good proportion of the children concerned. However, the methodological difficulties involved in assessment, especially of the long-term impact, prevent us from forming a clear picture of the situation. In addition, many of these studies do not even allow for the variable of time, in that some of the children in their samples have been in a divorced situation for a few years while others are just entering it.

Another complicating element is that there are two major branches of literature concerned with the impact of marital strife and of divorce on children; one is mainly oriented towards sociological research, while the second is more clinical in its approach and stems from the research of clinicians in a variety of professions.

It is important to note that the *sociological* literature on the effect of divorce on children is more positive than the psychiatric literature. This is related in part to a greater climate of liberalism among academic sociologists who tend to be more positive about certain social problems than about others—and divorce is one such problem with favoured status.[6] Sociologists themselves have fairly high divorce rates, especially if they are married to other sociologists.[7] Their more optimistic stance also stems from the types of samples (more representative samples perhaps) that they study, while much of the psychiatric research takes place within a clinical context. In that context, the type of person studied is necessarily one with problems. There is, therefore, a selective factor involved in *both* types of research and the two should be seen as complementary and corrective rather than as contradictory.

On the positive side, the little we know empirically so far indicates that children of divorce and separation are healthier, happier, less deviant, and better adjusted than children who live in intact but unhappy homes.[8] Nye's comparison of

6. P. Bohannan refers to Tumin's analysis in his Introduction to *Divorce and After*, edited by P. Bohannan, New York: Doubleday, 1970, pp. 9-10.
7. N.D. Glenn and M.S. Keir, "Divorce Among Sociologists Married to Sociologists," *Social Problems*, 19, Summer 1971, pp. 57-67.
8. L.G. Burchinal, "Characteristics of Adolescents from Unbroken, Broken, and Reconstituted Families," *Marriage and Family Living*, 26, February 1964, pp. 45, 51; J. Landis, "The Trauma of Children when Parents Divorce," *Marriage and Family Living*, 1960, 22, pp. 7-13; F.I. Nye, "Child Adjustment in

children in intact and well functioning families, separated/ divorced or reconstituted families, and intact but unhappy families showed a similar ranking in terms of the incidence of affective and behavioural problems. Another study, on university students, found divorce to have had no long-range adverse effects on them.[9] And, as Gardner points out, most children whose parents divorce are not in need of therapy.[10] There is also evidence to suggest that it is not the divorce *per se* which is traumatic for children but the conflicts that preceded it or surround it.[11] In other words, household conflicts which took place before the divorce occurred are probably the greatest stress factor.[12] One important research finding is that there are two variables which have a determining effect on the young child's adjustment after a year of separation; the events that preceded separation and the functioning of the custodial parent.[13] Other evidence indicates that children do not necessarily suffer much from the divorce and are, within one or two years, undistinguishable from other children of their milieu in terms of psychological adjustment. It has also been observed that children who had perceived their home to be happy were the most traumatized by the divorce, perhaps because they did not expect it, and also because such children lose more in divorce, while children who were aware of conflicts and suffered from them may have expected the outcome and may feel a sense of relief: they lose less by the divorce.

On the negative side, Hetherington *et al.* have found that

Broken and in Unhappy Unbroken Homes," *Marriage and Family Living*, 19, November 1957, pp. 356-361.

9. D.A. Luepnitz, "Which Aspects of Divorce Affect Children?" *Family Coordinator*, 28, January 1979, pp. 79-85.

10. R.A. Gardner, "Psychological Aspects of Divorce," in *American Handbook of Psychiatry*, edited by S. Arieti, second edition, vol. 1, New York: Basic Books, 1974, p. 507.

11. J.T. Landis, "A Comparison of Children from Divorced and Nondivorced Unhappy Marriages," *Family Coordinator*, 11, July 1962, pp. 61-65; H. Pannor and S. Child, "Impact of Divorce on Children," *Child Welfare*, 39, February 1960, pp. 6-10.

12. Luepnitz, *op.cit.*

13. J.S. Wallerstein and J.B. Kelly, "Divorce Counselling: A Community Service for Families in the Midst of Divorce," *American Journal of Orthopsychiatry*, 47, January 1977, p. 5.

patterns of child rearing change with divorce as both parents become too caught up in the web of their immediate problems to contribute as much as previously to the growth of their children. Mothers become more restrictive and authoritarian as they try to control their children's behaviour, while fathers tend to indulge the children, probably because they see them less and may fear losing their love. However, after two years of divorce, mothers had again become less restrictive and fathers less indulgent.[14] The same researcher also found households of divorcees more disorganized and susceptible to mental problems than households of intact families.[15] Hunt mentions *in passim* a study in which half of the children of divorce reported having been "used" by their parents against each other.[16]

Still on the negative side, Langner and Michael found that one-third of the respondents of the Midtown Manhattan Study who showed emotional problems were from broken homes, although they also found that the homes broken by separation, desertion, or divorce seemed to show similar mental health risks to those broken by the death of a parent.[17] And, as we saw in Chapter 4, adults who grew up in an unhappy or divorced home have a greater proneness to divorce themselves, a factor we will examine more closely later.

Landis found that the patterns of dating and cross-sexual friendship of college students who perceived their parents' marriage to be unhappy were less favourable than those of other students. Moreover, more students from unhappy homes had at some time desired to be a member of the other sex, and had more doubts about their own chances of having a happy marriage later on.[18] It is unfortunate that this study did not

14. E.M. Hetherington *et al.*, "Divorced Fathers," *Family Coordinator*, 25, 1976, p. 425.
15. E.M. Hetherington *et al.*, "The Aftermath of Divorce," in *Mother-Child, Father-Child Relations*, edited by J.H. Stevens, Jr. and M. Matthews, Washington, D.C.: National Association for the Education of Young Children, 1977.
16. M. Hunt, *The World of the Formerly Married*, New York: McGraw-Hill, 1966, p. 222.
17. T.S. Langner and S.T. Michael, *Life Stress and Mental Health: The Midtown Manhattan Study*, vol. 2, New York: Free Press, 1963, p. 169.
18. J.T. Landis, "Dating Maturation of Children from Happy and Unhappy Marriages," *Marriage and Family Living*, 25, August 1963, pp. 351-353.

also inquire into the attitudes of students from divorced homes.

In *clinical* studies, it has been found that the children of divorced parents seem relatively immune to certain problems while more prone to other problems.[19] For instance, children of divorce show more depressive symptoms,[20] more enuresis,[21] and more delinquency and anti-social behaviour[22] than children from intact homes; however, they also display less anxiety and have fewer sleep-related problems and dietary-related disturbances than children from intact homes.[23] Unfortunately, several of these studies had methodological flaws, one of which was the failure to control for the sex of the children.

Kalter, in his well controlled study, found that in a clinical setting, children of divorce and separation were significantly over-represented in relation to their proportion of the general population.[24] Although he found no other sex differences, he established that living with a step-parent is more stressful for girls than for boys. Boys living in divorced one-parent homes as well as boys living with a step-parent showed more aggressive symptoms. More had problems with the law. However, fewer than in intact families had medical problems. Girls living with one parent or with a step-parent had a wider array of problems at the teenage level, including aggressiveness, unacceptable sexual behaviour, the misuse of drugs, and scholastic difficulties than girls from intact families.[25] Chil-

19. N. Kalter, "Children of Divorce in an Outpatient Psychiatric Population," *American Journal of Orthopsychiatry*, 47, January 1977, pp. 40-51.
20. J. McDermott, "Divorce and its Psychiatric Sequelae in Children," *Archives of General Psychiatry*, 23, 1970, pp. 421-428.
21. J. Morrison, "Parental Divorce as a Factor in Childhood Psychiatric Illness," *Comprehensive Psychiatry*, 15, 1974, pp. 95-102.
22. McDermott, *op.cit.*; J. Tuckman and R. Regan, "Intactness of Home and Behavioral Problems in Children," *Journal of Child Psychological Psychiatry*, 7, 1966, pp. 225-233; B. Schlesinger, "One-Parent Families in Great Britain: The Finer Report," in *The One-Parent Family*, B. Schlesinger, Toronto: University of Toronto Press, third edition revised, 1975, p. 45; D.R. Offord *et al*, "Broken Homes, Parental Psychiatric Illness, and Female Delinquency," *American Journal of Orthopsychiatry*, 49, April 1979, pp. 252-264.
23. Tuckman and Regan, *ibid.*
24. *Kalter, op.cit.*, p. 43.
25. *Ibid.*, p. 47. See also, I. Fast and A. Cain, "The Stepparent Role: Potential for Disturbances in Family Functioning," *American Journal of Orthopsychiatry*, 36, April 1966, pp. 485-491.

dren in single-parent families tended to be more hostile towards their parents than in intact families. Another study also found that children living in one-parent families felt more estranged from their parents than children in two-parent units.[26] However, another study found little difference between people brought up with natural as opposed to stepfathers.[27] Morrison also established that the level of emotional disturbance in *parents* may be an important variable when considering the effect of divorce on children. He found, for instance, that there was greater emotional instability in the divorced parents of children being treated as outpatients.[28]

Kelly and Wallerstein observed a great deal of sadness in seven and eight year-old children of divorce.[29] Among nine and ten year-olds there was a greater attempt to master a situation which they understood better at that age. However, many had had their sense of self badly bruised, felt lonely, and their scholastic performance had suffered. After one year, half of these children were "back to normal," although not without regrets. The other half showed even greater distress.[30]

In spite of the fact that most children tend to come out of divorce in better shape than do children of maladjusted but lasting marriages (with social class as a constant), the fact remains that children of divorce and of unhappy marriages have more problems (often temporary in divorce) and may have more emotional scars than children who have grown up in a happy and stable home, either with two natural parents or with one parent, when the latter does not suffer from poverty or prejudice. Bad marriages, whether they remain intact or

26. L. Weller and E. Luchterhand, "Adolescents' Perceptions of Their Parents by Social Class, Race and Parental Presence," *International Journal of Sociology of the Family*, 6, Spring 1976, pp. 283-290.

27. K.L. Wilson *et al.*, "Stepfathers and Stepchildren: An Exploratory Analysis From Two National Surveys," *Journal of Marriage and the Family*, 37, August 1975, pp. 526-536.

28. Morrison, *op cit.*

29. J.B. Kelly and J.S. Wallerstein, "The Effects of Parental Divorce: Experiences of the Child in Early Latency," *American Journal of Orthopsychiatry*, 46, January 1976, pp. 20-32.

30. J.S. Wallerstein and J.B. Kelly, "The Effects of Parental Divorce: Experiences of the Child in Later Latency," *American Journal of Orthopsychiatry*, 46, April 1976, pp. 256-269.

break up, are detrimental for children, even if only temporarily so.

Personal observation of some fifty children, between five and thirteen years of age, with parents who had separated (many were also divorced) within the past three years, leads me to believe that, if there is a true victim of divorce, it is the child; indeed, I have not met one single child who had not been adversely affected, at least in the short term, by the disintegration of his or her parents' marriage. The symptoms I most commonly observed were sadness or melancholy, a desire for parental reunion (often even after a remarriage or in the context of impending remarriage), a certain discomfort among peers from intact families (the need to explain the situation even if not asked about it, outright lies about parents' marital status and whereabouts or embarrassment when asked), a fear of not being loved by one or both parents, attempts to take as much advantage as possible of each parent, lack of parental guidance, and at times gross permissiveness on the part of parents who felt guilty about their children.

This last point was present in *all* their parents, and is an element in the post-separation parent-child relationship which has not been adequately researched. All the separated/divorced parents I observed were harbouring feelings of guilt vis-à-vis their children, often disproportionate to the harm actually done to the child. This parental guilt, combined with a fear of losing the children's love, leads to various attempts to compensate for the situation that are not healthy for the child; material gifts to a child increase at the risk of passing onto the child the message that material possessions mean love. Another common form of compensation is over-permissiveness. I did not find instances of greater restrictiveness or permissiveness in mothers or in custody fathers, but I found, typically, greater permissiveness in all the fathers, who were the non-custody parent. These fathers allowed their children to do things that they would not previously have accepted: such as drinking alcoholic beverages under age, being drunk, seeing risqué films or shows, eating too much and too many sweets, rudeness to them, their mothers and other adults (including step-mothers and girl friends), lying, minor forms of vandalism, and truancy. I also observed several fathers who were "proud" of their teenage sons' sexual adventures and even exploitation of young girls; these fathers had generally been adulterous themselves. It was as if the sons' behaviour helped to justify the fathers' act: the fathers felt that the sons "understood" them. In these same cases, I observed a distancing between mothers and sons.

These fathers were literally spoiling their children out of a fear of losing their love and, at times, in an attempt to spite the former wife-mother. One can only offer conjectures as to the long-term effects of such parental behaviour. I would suggest that these children are ill prepared to grow into mature and responsible human beings. They are, in essence, being taught to take advantage of others. There was certainly a measurable short-term effect of parental separation in these cases. However, the long-term effect has not yet been measured within this framework and has probably been underestimated.

Children dread parental quarrels and strife unless they can gain something from it by playing each parent against the other. Even in this case the gain is only temporary and outweighed by the long-term harm to the child. And yet, even though they may rationally accept divorce as necessary, as better than an unhappy intact marriage, most children never accept divorce emotionally and hope, often for many years and despite remarriage, that their parents will come together again. This is why many such children reject a remarriage and may even sabotage it after it has taken place. Epstein reports the opinion of an adolescent girl who had gone through a parental divorce.

> If you're going to obligate yourself to marry someone and have children, I think you owe it to those children to stay there. If it's your decision to have them, you ought to stick by them.[31]

The following quote, from a student autobiography, is revealing of a different attitude.

31. J. Epstein, *Divorce in America*, New York: E.P. Dutton, 1974, p. 297.

Looking back, I just wish my parents had divorced. Rather, they stayed together for us kids. But, at night, I used to bury my head under my pillow (I still have the habit: I sleep like that even though I am now married) so I would not hear their yelling and their quarreling. I just wished my father would leave. We would have been so much happier.

The literature, especially the clinical literature, does not present a unified view of the effect of divorce on children. Although there are indications that children of divorce fare better, at least in the short run, than children of unhappy but intact homes, we need more data and especially, more thorough control for socio-economic variables in studies as well as more long-term material. Unfortunately, we know very little about children who live in intact but unhappy homes. It may be that, controlling for socio-economic status, age, and race, such children are in a far more difficult situation than the children of divorce who have at least some respite from parental disharmony. As Morrison has pointed out, there is the untested possibility "that parental divorce and child-hood psychiatric illness may be both related secondarily to a common background factor."[32] However, especially when variables such as poverty are taken into consideration, we see that, in the *short run*, the clinical profile of the children of divorce is not rosy. The following section on parental absence presents additional information.

EFFECT OF PARENTAL ABSENCE

In the past, much of the literature on the effect of divorce on children focused on the single question of the effect of the father's absence on children. Often the question was even more specific: what is the effect of the father's absence on boys? And, more often than not, the focus of such studies was on black male children in the United States since this is a group in which father-absent families are prevalent and also because of its dependence on welfare agencies, this is a group that is readily accessible to researchers. Much was made of

32. Morrison, *op.cit.*, p. 95.

the lack of a proper role model for boys, even though it has been pointed out that mothers teach young boys masculine ways of behaviour that may compensate for the absence of a father.[33] Many of these studies found that boys reared in fatherless homes suffered from lack of masculine identity,[34] had less self-confidence, lower self-esteem, and also exhibited more anti-social behaviour, including problems with the law,[35] and had poorer academic records.[36] More recent studies have been more discriminatory in the selection of their samples, and the variables they control for, and consequently their conclusions are not as unanimous as in the past. For instance, while controlling for race, Hunt and Hunt found the costs of having the father absent to be quite high for white boys but that the same situation actually produced advantages for black boys.[37]

There are many problems in previous studies, and it is interesting to look at them as an indication of how a field of research alters with changes in the social fabric, including ideological shifts[38] such as those experienced in the past few years with regard to sexual equality and the hardships stemming from poverty.

In the first place, these studies often had a sample restricted to families who already had difficulties: families on welfare, families with problem children, and so on. Naturally, researchers using such samples could not avoid finding problems. But these single-parent families were not necessarily representative of all single-parent families: single-parent families (or children) who have no major problems and require little assistance are more difficult to locate and study. There-

33. D.B. Lynn, "The Process of Learning Parental and Sex Role Identification," *Journal of Marriage and Family Living*, 28, November 1966, pp. 466-470.
34. H.B. Biller, "Father Absence and the Personality Development of the Male Child," *Developmental Psychology*, 2, March 1970, pp. 181-201.
35. W.B. Miller, "Lower Class Culture as a Generating Milieu of Gang Delinquency," *Journal of Social Issues*, 14, Summer 1958, pp. 5-19.
36. B. Sutton-Smith et al., "Father-Absence Effects in Families of Different Sibling Composition," *Child Development*, 38, December 1968, pp. 1213-1221.
37. L. Hunt and L.G. Hunt, "Race and the Father-Son Connection: The Conditional Relevance of Father Absence for the Orientations and Identities of Adolescent Boys," *Social Problems*, 23, October 1975, pp. 35-52.
38. L.K. Wilkenson, "The Broken Family and Juvenile Delinquency: Scientific Explanation or Ideology?" *Social Problems*, 21, June 1974, pp. 726-740.

fore, we are less likely to read about the positive accomplishments and victories of successful one-parent units. Second, one important factor that marred several of these studies was their failure to control for economic and racial variables. Indeed, perhaps the most important predictive variable in the success of a single-parent family or of any family is its socioeconomic and racial or ethnic situation.[39] Boys from impoverished backgrounds, with the fathers present, are also known to have higher rates of deliquency, of truancy, of anti-social behaviour, of rejection of their families,[40] less self-esteem and self confidence,[41] and even problems of masculine identity and less satisfactory scholastic achievement. Black boys from intact families have greater difficulty in achieving upward mobility than white boys, but the problems often associated with absent fathers are actually mediated by the economic deprivation which follows on the loss of family resources. Also, Maccoby, in her re-analysis of the Glueck data, points out that the mother's supervision is probably the main variable in terms of delinquency or non-delinquency rather than the presence or absence of a father, or the divorce,[42] or, we will add, the single-parent family.

The third bias in some of these studies is that they focused on boys and on absent fathers, when they could also have focused on girls and on absent mothers. The few studies which examined the effects of father-absence on girls found that lack of a constant adult male presence was related to lack of skills in interaction with men,[43] and may also be related to sexual

39. D.V. Willie, "The Relative Contribution of Family Status and Economic Status to Juvenile Delinquency," *Social Problems*, 14, Winter 1967, pp. 326-335; A.S. Berger and W. Simon, "Black Families and the Moynihan Report: A Research Evaluation," *Social Problems*, 22, August 1975, pp. 145-161.

40. W.H. Sewell and A.O. Haller, "Factors in the Relationship Between Social Status and the Personality Adjustment of the Child," *American Sociological Review*, 24, 1959, pp. 511-520.

41. *Ibid.*

42. S. Glueck and E. Glueck, *Unraveling Juvenile Delinquency*, Cambridge, Mass.: Harvard University Press, 1951; E.E. Maccoby, "Effects upon Children of Their Mothers' Outside Employment," *Work in the Lives of Married Women*, New York: Columbia University Press, 1958.

43. H.B. Biller and S.D. Weiss, "The Father-daughter Relationship and the Personality Development of the Female," *Journal of Genetic Psychology*, 116, March 1970, pp. 79-93.

misconduct and to inappropriate assertiveness with peers.[44] However, mother-absence is often subsumed under the heading of "maternal deprivation" as if the children of both sexes cannot suffer from paternal deprivation as well. Moreover, the Hunts also established that, although father-absence "may have a dampening effect on the achievement of male children, it may work to free female children for stronger attachment to personal achievement goals."[45] Brandwein *et al.* have also pointed out that studies should perhaps focus on how father-absence affects the mother psychologically,[46] and we could add, how the absence of a parent generally affects the custody parent in his/her role.

The fourth bias lay in the way these studies ignored the labelling process involved: in other words, the attitude of society has not been favourable towards single-parent families and it is likely that this prejudice rubbed off on the children involved.[47] Another bias was the fact that the *quality* of fathering present in the control children (those with a father present) was never questioned. For instance, most studies concur that fathers generally participate little in the *daily* routine of child care.[48] If this is the case, how can their absence be so detrimental? Nor was the possible relationship between the quality of fathering and children's personality development studied, as if all fathers had a similarly beneficial effect on their children by the mere fact of their *legal* presence.

As research became more refined, variations in the effect of the father's absence, when any at all were found, were seen to depend on socio-economic situation, race, sex of the child,

44. E.M. Hetherington, "Effects of Father Absence on Personality Development in Adolescent Daughters," *Developmental Psychology*, 7, November 1972, pp. 313-326.
45. L.G. Hunt and L.L. Hunt, "Race, Daughters and Father-Loss: Does Absence Make the Girl Grow Stronger?" *Social Problems*, 25, October 1977, p. 91.
46. R.A. Brandwein *et al.*, "Women and Children Last: The Social Situation of Divorced Mothers and Their Families," *Journal of Marriage and the Family*, 36, August 1974, p. 509.
47. J.K. Burgess, "The Single-Parent Family: A Social and Sociological Problem," *Family Coordinator*, 19, April 1970, pp. 137-144.
48. F. Rebelsky and C. Hanks, "Fathers' Verbal Interaction with Infants in the First Three Months of Life," *Child Development*, 42, 1971, pp. 63-68; M. Kotelchuk, "The Nature of the Child's Tie to his Father," Ph.D. Dissertation, Harvard University, Cambridge, Mass., 1972.

maternal behaviour, discipline, type of paternal absence (desertion, divorce, death, separation, out-of-wedlock births) and the age of the child when the father left. By 1968 researchers were already observing that, when all these variables are taken into consideration, the difference between children with present and absent fathers may be negligible.[49] Hunt and Hunt also point out that, because of the value system of the white society, the white child without a father may *feel* deprived and may attribute his (her) troubles to the family structure rather than to other circumstances such as poverty and lack of resources. Thus, the white boy may exaggerate the importance of the absence of the father, while the black boy may be insulated against its possible negative effect because of the norms and realities of his sub-group.[50]

CUSTODY

In Canada in 1976, the majority of the children of separation and divorce were placed in the custody of their mothers. Table 15 shows us where children go depending on which parent petitions for divorce. First, we see that when the mother is the petitioner, she is almost always likely to obtain custody of the children and she is also likely to do so in half of the cases when the father is the petitioner, so that over 85% of the children have the mother as the custodial parent.

TABLE 15
1975 Divorces with Dependent Children by Parties to Whom Custody was Granted

	HUSBAND AS PETITIONER		WIFE AS PETITIONER	
	F	%	F	%
To the petitioner	3,135	35.81	19,049	88.21
To the respondent	4,473	51.09	1,375	6.37
To other or agency	53	0.61	80	0.37
No award or custody	1,094	12.49	1,090	5.05
	8,755	100.00	21,594	100.00

Source: Statistics Canada, *Vital Statistics, op. cit.*, adaptation of Table 22.

49. E. Herzog and C.E. Sudia, "Fatherless Homes: A Review of Research," *Children*, 15, Sept.-Oct. 1968, pp. 177-182.
50. Hunt and Hunt, 1951, *op.cit.*, p. 50.

In research on court proceedings as well as opinions expressed by specialists in journal articles, there has been a slight shift towards establishing with whom the child has the closest relationship in determining custody awards, even if the psychological parent happens not to be the child's natural parent.[51] Although joint custody is currently emphasized in theory, Stack has found that in practice it carries disadvantages for the children who may feel less secure and stable in such a situation.[52] Greater utilization of child specialists and child's counsel in custody cases is advocated by many, including lawyers.[53] Jenkins lists six maxims that should be followed in determining child custody: choose the most neutral ground available to you; do not divide the child; consult the child; visitation should be in the interest of the child, and not in the interest of the parent; never transplant a child unnecessarily; beware of agreements made between parents under pressure.[54]

RELATIONSHIP WITH PARENTS AFTER DIVORCE

From an even more practical standpoint, and keeping the welfare of the children in mind, we need to know more about the consequences of various custody and visiting rights

51. D. Levine, "Child Custody: Iowa Corn and the Avant Garde," in *The Youngest Minority*, edited by S. Katz, Chicago: American Bar Association Press, 1974; D. Truxillo, "Child Custody: Paternal Authority Versus Welfare of the Child," *Louisiana Law Review*, 35, 1975, pp. 904-913; R. Mnookin, "Child-Custody Adjudication: Judicial Functions in the Face of Indeterminacy," *Law and Contemporary Problems*, 39, 1975, pp, 226-293.
52. C. Stack, "Who Owns the Child: Divorce and Child Custody Decisions in Middle Class Families," *Social Problems*, 23, 1976, pp. 505-515.
53. P. Marschall and M. Gatz, "The Custody-Decision Process: Toward New Roles for Parents and the State," *North Carolina Central Law Journal*, 76, 1975, pp. 50-72; M. Wilcox, "Child's Due Process Right to Counsel in Divorce Custody Procedings," *Hastings Law Journal*, 27, 1976, pp. 917-950; J. Goldstein *et al.*, *Beyond the Best Interests of the Child*, New York: Free Press, 1973; C. Leavell, "Custody Disputes and the Proposed Model Act," *Georgia Law Review*, 2, 1968, pp. 162-192; S.J. Alexander, "Protecting the Child's Rights in Custody Cases," *Family Coordinator*, 26, October 1977, pp. 377-382; A.P. Derdeyn, "A Consideration of Legal Issues in Child Custody Contests," *Archives of General Psychiatry*, 33, February 1976, pp. 165-171.
54. R.L. Jenkins, "Maxims in Child Custody Cases," *Family Coordinator*, 26, October 1977, pp. 385-389.

arrangements.[55] In the United States, the proportion of step-children under twenty-one who are adopted by the new parent has increased, probably because children are now frequently younger than in the past at the time of divorce.[56] From another point of view, it has already been found that children who live in the same city as a parent are happier and feel less rejected when they see that parent often. Infrequent contact with the non-custody parent fosters feelings of abandonment. In fact, the most important factor in children's failure to recover after divorce seems to be the time *lost* with parents; that is to say, if they see one or both parents less after the divorce: "Therefore, the most subtle parameters of the amount of loss of time with a parent need to replace the stereotype of the one-parent or two-parent family."[57] Unfortunately, no research exists concerning the quality of time spent with children.

Of particular interest would be more extensive studies comparing children who live with single mothers and those who live with single fathers. Since the socio-economic situation of the single mother is generally very low, in part because women earn less than men, and have less prestigious positions, or are unemployed, we may expect the self-esteem and scholastic performance of their children to be lower than those of children reared by fathers. We might also hypothesize that children reared by fathers will have fewer clashes with the law because they will accept a father's authority, while many

55. For the role of child psychiatrist in custody cases, see R. Krell, "This Child is Mine! The Battle Cry for Custody," *Canadian Psychiatric Association Journal*, 23, November 1978, pp. 433-439; also, see G.A. Awad, "Basic Principles in Custody Assessment," in same issue, pp. 441-447. For articles on innovative court procedures, see *The Family Coordinator*, 26, October 1977: W.W. Weiss and H.B. Collada, "Conciliation Counselling: The Court's Effective Mechanism for Resolving Visitation and Custody Disputes," pp. 444-446; R.S. Benedek *et al.*, "Michigan's Friends of the Court: Creative Programs for Children of Divorce," pp. 447-450; J.M. Druckman and C.A. Rhodes, "Family Impact Analysis: Application to Child Custody Determination," pp. 451-458; for a comprehensive bibliography, see L. Henley, "The Family and the Law: Selected References," pp. 487-518.
56. A.W. Simon, *Stepchild in the Family. A View of Children in Remarriage*, New York: Cardinal Pocket Books, 1965, p. 232.
57. D.S. Jacobson, "The Impact of Marital Separation/Divorce on Children. 1. Parent-Child Separation and Child Adjustment," *Journal of Divorce*, 1, Summer 1978, p. 357.

studies have shown that discipline is often a problem for single mothers. Women may be perceived by children as less imposing authority figures. We might also expect children reared by women to have superior capabilities for expressiveness, companionship and emotional communication. Finally, it would be interesting to see if single fathers are not more successful than single mothers at enlisting children's cooperation for housework: indeed, children of single mothers may feel that housework is part of their mothers' role as women, while single fathers may be unwilling to spend as great a proportion of their time in housework and may therefore leave more room for initiative in their children.

We also need to know much more about those children who are used as pawns or "trump cards" (one father's expression of how he used his son against his own parents) by their parents, a situation that can last for years. Many divorced couples use their children to complicate each other's lives. They do so in a variety of ways:

> *Not having the children ready on time for their father's visitation, or bringing the children back to their mother's late (or much earlier) than expected, quizzing the children about their mother's life ...; attempting to poison the children's minds on the subject of who broke up the marriage....*[58]

How do such children perceive their parents? Do they play them off against each other? And, if they do, what advantage are they seeking? Do these children develop particular personality profiles, including traits such as manipulativeness? Do such children have a greater chance than other children of divorce of having bad marriages later on? How do they fare generally compared to other children of divorce?

An example of this manipulation carried to an extreme involves those children who are kidnapped by one of the ex-spouses, generally the father, often when the other ex-spouse is the one who actually has legal custody rights. Thus, we read

---

58. J. Epstein, *op.cit.*, p. 225.

the following sentence at the end of an article on "Parents of Kidnapped Children," in *Kinesis*, a Vancouver women's publication (p. 7, October 1978).

> *If you are a parent whose child has been kidnapped, or who lives in constant fear that she or he may be kidnapped by an ex-spouse, or if you are sympathetic to the existing problem that parents of kidnapped children face and wish to push for legal reform and public awareness, contact . . .*

Another area of interest is the effect of socio-economic variables on children of divorce. We need comparisons of children from various backgrounds to see what specific problems they encounter at each of the six phases of separation and the final divorce because of the material difficulties involved in each phase: overcrowding, substandard housing, overworked mothers, lack of recreational facilities, and less adequate school systems. It would be important to know if children from poorer backgrounds see their fathers as often or less often than others. One would surmise that they see them less often because the father has more limited resources and may not be able to reach the children and also because the mother may keep him away from them if he does not support them. Children of desertion certainly see the deserting parent very little, if it all. Therefore, poorer children may suffer more from the absence of the non-custody parent.

At the worst extreme some children of desertion and divorce have to be placed in foster homes and may even eventually be put up for adoption at an age when it is difficult to find adoptive parents and when it is often too late for the scarred children to form new attachments. This means that these children may spend the rest of their youth in foster care. In Canada, this is often the lot of Indian and Metis children. Indeed the "Child of the Day" (in need of adoptive parents) in the *Toronto Star* is too often, not merely one Indian child, but a group of siblings of Indian or mixed ancestry. Studies have also indicated that it is those children who are abandoned and never get to live with either parent who are later themselves most prone to divorce, and to a host of additional problems, when they reach adulthood.[59] It is these children who, because of their situation, have been most stigmatized and have had the fewest opportunities, both material and psychological, in life.

Another area of concern is the effect of the parental life-style after divorce on children. How do they cope with parental dating, sexuality, love affairs? What effect do these have on them and are there crucial ages when the effect is especially marked? Also, how do children fare when they have a sibling or siblings as compared to when they are single children? Does the presence of a sibling give them comfort in the sense that they can share their experience with someone, even if the communication is non-verbal? And are there differences between boys and girls in all of the questions we have asked above?

TRANSMISSION OF MARITAL INSTABILITY

As we saw in Chapter 4, adults who come from unhappy or broken homes have higher divorce rates themselves. In a study of ninety-six married couples in Toronto, Schlesinger found that 45% of previously divorced men and 43% of previously divorced women had had a history of marital separation or divorce in their own families.[60] Moreover, Landis, who studied three generations, found a high incidence of "heredity" in divorce and suggests that youth from divorce-prone families tend to date and marry youth from other divorce-prone families.[61] Many other studies have reported similar results in the U.S.A.,[62] and these results hold even

59. H. Pope and C.W. Mueller, "The Intergenerational Transmission of Marital Instability: Comparisons by Race and Sex," *The Journal of Social Issues*, 32, Winter 1976, p. 58.
60. B. Schlesinger, "Remarriage as Family Reorganization for Divorced Persons," in *The Canadian Family*, edited by K. Ishwaran, Toronto: Holt, Rinehart and Winston of Canada, 1971, p. 383.
61. J.T. Landis, "The Pattern of Divorce in Three Generations," *Social Forces*, 34, March 1956, pp. 213-216.
62. C.W. Mueller and H. Pope, "Marital Instability: A Study of Its Transmission Between Generations," *Journal of Marriage and the Family*, 39, February 1977, pp. 83-92: J. Heiss, "On the Transmission of Marital Instability in Black Families," *American Sociological Review*, 37, February 1972, pp. 89-92; L.L. Bumpass and J.A. Sweet, "Differentials in Marital Instability: 1970," *Ameri-*

when the parents' social class is controlled for.[63] Therefore,
parental divorce is more likely to correlate with children's
divorce than is parental happiness or perhaps even stability.

The role model theory has been presented in an attempt to
explain these results. It postulates that, when a marriage is
broken, children are no longer able to observe normal marital
life at first hand and are deprived of the opportunity to
continue learning proper marital roles. Second, it postulates
that divorcing and divorced parents are less able to teach their
childre⹀ proper familial roles. Until we have more studies
which either prove or disprove that *unbroken* but unhappy
homes have the same problems, role theory is somewhat in
limbo and various researchers have already found results
which are not consistent with it.[64]

An alternative or perhaps complementary explanation has
recently been offered by Mueller and Pope who found that
women from intact families tended on the average to be older,
better educated, and less often pregnant at the time of
marriage and also to marry higher-status, never-married
males than women from divorced families. These results held
for all parental socio-economic strata.[65] The Duncans also
found that men raised in intact families attain superior
occupational achievement more often than those who are the
product of divorce.[66] What these data seem to indicate is that
the social situation of divorce places children at a disadvantage socially, economically and psychologically. These disadvantages may cause them to receive less education, to be
less well adjusted, and to marry too early. These socio-
economic variables serve as links between parental divorce
and divorce among children and could help explain the high

can *Sociological Review*, 37, December 1972, pp. 754-766; H. Pope and C.W.
Mueller, *op.cit.*; G. Gurin *et al.*, *Americans View Their Mental Health*, New
York: Basic Books, 1960, pp. 246-250; T.S. Langner and S.T. Michael, *op.cit.*,
pp. 163-164.
63. Mueller and Pope, *ibid.*
64. Heiss, *op.cit.*, and Pope and Mueller, *op.cit.*
65. Mueller and Pope, *op.cit.*, p. 89.
66. B. Duncan and O.D. Duncan, "Family Stability and Occupational Success," *Social Problems*, 16, Winter 1969, pp. 273-285. A similar finding has
been made in terms of educational attainment: R.M. Hauser and D.L.
Featherman, "Equality of Schooling: Trends and Prospects," *Sociology of
Education*, 49, April 1976, pp. 99-120.

rate of divorce transmission. It may be that divorced families do not provide appropriate forms of social control and opportunity for the future success of their children, both because of a lack of economic resources and because of the disruptions in children's lives that divorce entails.

GENERAL RESEARCH QUESTIONS

Literature on the children of divorce needs to be integrated and research designs streamlined and refined to take account of important or key variables. There are many shortcomings in the current literature; as already indicated by the questions raised in a previous section of this chapter, there are areas of research that are totally unexplored and this prevents us from gaining an overall perspective on the effects of divorce on children. We will, in this section, suggest additional research programmes, especially of the longitudinal type, that may help us to answer many of these questions.

In terms of research on the daily psychological adaptation of children or about the effect of divorce on children, we need to have studies comparing the *same* children longitudinally at various key points of their and their parents' lives. In order to carry out such a study, a sample of the families at risk would have to be followed for a number of years so that, eventually, we would have profiles of families who remain happy and intact, others who are intact but unhappy, and, finally, detailed profiles of the group which is subject to divorce. We would need at the outset a sample adequate for us to cover the following phases;

phase 1	when the parental relationship is normal
phase 2	when the parental relationship is unhappy from the parents' point of view
phase 3	when the parental relationship is perceived as unhappy by the children
phase 4	separation
phase 5	divorce
phase 6	two years or more after divorce comparing children of remarried parents to children of still un-remarried parents

phase 7   when the children have been married for five years

Such an ambitious research programme would allow us to answer many questions of great importance, questions such as:

- how does a child's personality and mental health change over time in a family where divorce takes place, compared to that of a child in an unhappy family which remains intact, and that of a child in a happy, intact family?
- are there specific personality traits or coping mechanisms which appear in these children at each of these phases?
- is the physical or mental health of the children of divorce and of unhappy unions affected at any point (physical or mental illness as a result of stress)?
- is the school life of children of divorce and of unhappy unions any different, at each phase, from that of other children?
- what feelings do the children of divorce and of unhappy unions have about their parents compared to the feelings of other children?
- how do children of divorce and of unhappy unions, compared to other children, perceive their future?
- are these children's relationships with their peers different, at any phase, to those of other children?
- when one parent is happy and the other unhappy, what are the effects on the children? Which parent's unhappiness is more significant; that of the mother or that of the father?
- what is the *relative* importance of phases 2 and 3? Is it parental unhappiness or children's perception of it which affects them?

Two studies found no relationship between the personality adjustment of pre-adolescent children and the independently

assessed marital adjustment of their mothers,[67] or of their
fathers.[68] However, Nye's results pointed to a relationship
between the child's perception of parental happiness and
general personality adjustment.[69] In reviewing these appar-
ently conflicting results, Udry wonders if psychologically
maladjusted children have a tendency to perceive everything,
including their parents' marriages, more negatively.[70] All of
the questions asked above would have to control for variables
such as age of children, sex and socio-economic status.

Studies of adults in their twenties and thirties could be
devised to compare those whose parents divorced with those
whose parents were happy and those whose parents were
unhappy but remained together. Is the first group's own
higher divorce rate related to:

- certain personality configurations?
- inadequate coping mechanisms?
- the choice of a certain type of spouse?
- unrealistic expectations?
- failure in other aspects of their lives, including their
  work?
- a greater acceptance of divorce as an alternative?
- an earlier age at divorce and consequent absence of
  children who might otherwise have prevented divorce?

Another interesting angle from which to approach the topic
of the children of divorce would be to see what happens to
children who are born *after* divorce, that is, in a "reconstituted" family. How are these children affected, if at all, by
their parents' (or one of their parents') previous marriage? We
would expect that such children would be very similar to
children raised in a first marriage: in both cases, the home is

67. A.L. Stroup, "Marital Adjustment of the Mother and the Personality of the
Child," *Marriage and Family Living*, 8, 1956. pp. 109-113.
68. L.G. Burchinal *et al.*, "Marriage Adjustment Personality Characteristics
of Parents and the Personality Adjustment of their Children," *Marriage and
Family Living*, 19, 1957, pp. 366-372.
69. Nye, *op.cit.*
70. J.R. Udry, *The Social Context of Marriage*, Philadelphia: Lippincott, 1971,
second edition, pp. 441-442.

legally intact. However, in this case, parental background is different, and there may be half-brothers and sisters who have another parent elsewhere. Does such a situation give a different life perspective to these children? Will they grow up more tolerant of divorce because they have not experienced its bad aspects but only its aftermath? They may, in fact, be more tolerant of divorce than their half-siblings, who *lived* through both the traumas that preceded divorce and those that occurred within it.

These research questions, and others not formulated herein, would allow us to gather information about the children involved in a *real* social problem, namely unhappy unions or bad marriages, whether they end in divorce or not. Intact unhappy unions are the least amenable to research for the simple reason that we cannot easily locate them unless they come to the attention of agencies or treatment facilities. However, it is almost certain that those families who do come to such attention are a very specific group, perhaps a more disorganized group, a poorer group, or a multi-problem group. As such, these families cannot be taken as a representative sample of *all* intact but unhappy homes, and research results stemming from a study of them may not be applicable to the majority of intact unhappy unions.

CONCLUSIONS

Were we living in a world of equality, one where women were equal to men, and where material needs were met without regard to class and race, we could probably conclude here that the gloomiest predictions of social thinkers of the past have not materialized with respect to the children of divorce. Indeed, such children are not generally the social problem they were heralded to be. However, we have also seen that unhappy parental marriages and divorces do affect children adversely in the short term and perhaps also in the long term.

The available literature, however unsatisfactory, does seem to make certain points quite clear: unhappy marriages, including the ones which end in divorce, are never a blessing for children; many children are hurt in the short run while others never seem to recover from a detrimental family atmosphere.

The fact that most children of divorce and desertion live with their mothers and that women are both undervalued by society and unable to give their children as many social advantages as most two-parent families can, gives rise to a vast number of problems. Related to this, racial discrimination and poverty probably hit children of divorce harder than other children as the detrimental effects of these variables compound each other in the context of divorce. If divorce is a social problem, it is especially so for underprivileged children and their mothers.

The literature is for the most part too sketchy to allow for a great many generalizations. In reality we know very little about the children of divorce and even less about the children of intact but unhappy marriages. We have few longitudinal studies and such data as we do possess are too contaminated by variables that the research design, generally an *ex post facto* one, did not control for. It is too soon to say that divorce does not adversely affect children in the long run as some studies have already done on the basis of a few indicators. And if it does, we need to know which types of children are most affected and which situations are most deleterious, for even simple observation tells us that not all children are equally affected.

8   Remarriage

Four-fifths of divorced men and two-thirds of divorced women remarry.[1] Remarriage is by far the path most often followed after divorce. Remarriage rates are at their peak in the first eighteen months after divorce and decline gradually thereafter. Moreover, for women especially, age and number of children are barriers to remarriage; the older a woman is at divorce, the less her chance of remarriage. The same may hold true for women with a greater number of children,[2] although at least one study has shown that, if we hold age constant, the difference between women with none or only one child and women with many children disappears. Age is the important variable, and since women who have had many children are generally older, these two variables tend to become confused.[3] Another important variable in remarriage is economics. From studies done in the U.S.A., it appears that "divorced women who are weak in ability to support themselves are the most likely to remarry,"[4] and women who are more independent financially are less likely to remarry, perhaps because they

1. See, for instance, L. Riley and C.E. Spreitzer, "A Model for the Analysis of Lifetime Marriage Patterns," *Journal of Marriage and the Family*, 36, February 1974, pp. 66-67. Since cohabitation is a life-style alternative following separation and divorce, we should devote a chapter to this topic. However, it appears that, for a majority of the persons involved, cohabitation is merely a stage towards remarriage. Moreover, we have no data on its frequency and little on its processes.
2. J. Sweet, "Differentials in Remarriage Probabilities," Working Paper #73-29, Madison, Wis.: University of Wisconsin, September 1973.
3. P.C. Glick, *American Families*, New York: John Wiley, 1957, p. 138.
4. H. Carter and P.C. Glick, *Marriage and Divorce: A Social and Economic Study*, revised edition, Cambridge, Mass.: Harvard University Press, 1976, p. 269; also L. Benson, *The Family Bond*, New York: Random House, 1971, p. 313.

need marriage less.[5] The reverse seems to hold for men: recently divorced men have a higher income than men who have been divorced for years (and will presumably remain divorced) while remarried men's income profiles are similar to those of the married and the recently divorced.[6] A woman with a low income and education may be helped by remarriage, as she may not be otherwise well equipped to support herself[7] while the low-income divorced man may find it difficult to remarry because his means are not sufficient to support a new or perhaps an additional household.

It is interesting to follow the statistical progression of remarriages throughout the years. Starting in 1941, the first year for which these data are available in Canada, only 1.0% of marriages for both men and women were remarriages of previously divorced persons. This rate then climbs very slowly to 3.8% and 3.4% for men and women respectively in 1950, and to 3.9% in 1960; the figure jumps to 6.9% and 6.4% for men and women in 1969, just after the reform of divorce laws. Thereafter, percentages increase steadily each year as more people divorce and remarry. In 1975, 10.8% of women who married had been divorced while 12.1% of men who married had been divorced.[8] As the percentage of remarriages moved above 8% of all marriages, the differential in remarriages in favour of men began to increase, a natural consequence of the fact that men remarry more than women and sooner after divorce.[9] In the United States, at least 20% of all existing marriages are second marriages and over 6% are third marriages; and in 1975, 25% of all brides had previously been divorced.[10]

5. J.N. Edwards, "The Future of the Family Revisited," *Journal of Marriage and the Family*, 29, August 1967, pp. 505-511.

6. Carter and Glick, *op.cit.*, p. 268.

7. K.S. Renne, "Health and Marital Experience in an Urban Population," *Journal of Marriage and the Family*, 33, May 1971, p. 347.

8. Widowed men also remarry more than widowed women: W.P. Cleveland and D.T. Gianturco, "Remarriage Probability After Widowhood: A Retrospective Method," *Journal of Gerontology*, 31, 1976, pp. 99-103.

9. Statistics Canada, *Vital Statistics, Vol. II, Marriages and Divorces, 1975*, Ottawa, July 1977, Table 7, p. 18.

10. U.S. National Center for Health Statistics, 1977. *Vital Statistics Report. Advance Report. Final Marriage Statistics, 1975*, Washington, D.C.: Government Printing Office.

TABLE 16
Percentages of 1975 Bridegrooms and Brides Who
Had Been Previously Divorced by Province

PROVINCES	MEN	WOMEN
Newfoundland	3.5	2.9
Prince Edward Island	5.2	5.9
Nova Scotia	11.3	10.5
New Brunswick	7.3	6.9
Quebec	7.7	5.8
Ontario	13.6	12.0
Manitoba	11.0	10.6
Saskatchewan	8.1	7.3
Alberta	16.1	15.7
British Columbia	19.6	18.4
Yukon*	20.4	18.9
Northwest Territories*	13.6	12.3
CANADA	12.1	10.8

Source: Statistics Canada, *Vital Statistics, op. cit.*, Table 7, pp. 19-24.
*These had only 201 and 220 marriages (including remarriages) in 1975.

In terms of geographic distribution (see Table 16), British Columbia has the highest percentage of remarriages, 19.6% for men and 18.4% for women, while Quebec still has a very low rate with 7.7% for men and 5.8% for women,[11] perhaps reflective of the difficulties entailed in remarriage for Roman Catholic couples as well as of the relative recency of the escalation of divorce in Quebec. Lenski also found a lower remarriage rate among Catholics in the U.S.A.[12] It is my impression, however, that there may be a high rate of cohabitation in Quebec to compensate for this low rate of remarriage. Overall, provincial rates of remarriages are closely tied to divorce rates, with Quebec, for the present, an exception to this rule.

In 1975, of the divorced women who remarried, 9,942 married a single man and 9,775 married a divorced man. Only 1,595 married a widower. However, if we look at the statistics for divorced men, we see that they show a marked preference

11. Statistics Canada, *op.cit.*, Table 7, pp. 18-24.
12. G. Lenski, *The Religious Factor*, Garden City, N.Y.: Doubleday, 1961.

for single women in terms of remarriage: 12,126 married single women, while 9,775 married divorced women and 2,047 married widowed women.[13] This, again, is a reflection of the fact that divorced men remarry more than divorced women and in so doing often choose women who are not only much younger than they are but who are also younger than their first wives: in order to do this they have to seek partners in the ranks of single women who are, on average, younger than previously married women.[14]

Women who had been divorced were on the average 34.9 years old when they remarried in 1975, while men were 38.3 years old. These figures can be contrasted with 22.5 years for women getting married for the first time and 24.9 for men. Widows and widowers who remarried were on the average 53.1 and 58.8 years old.[15] A total of 21,312 divorced women remarried in 1975 and 23,948 divorced men did so. The most common age of remarriage for divorced women was in the 25-29 bracket (5,983 remarriages) followed by the 30-34 bracket (4,385 remarriages). For men, the most common age for remarriage was in the 30-34 bracket (5,450) and then the 25-29 bracket (4,937). There were also 2,506 remarriages among divorced women younger than 24 years of age and 899 for men of similar ages. Therefore, 60% of divorced women and 47% of divorced men who remarry do so before they are thirty.

If we return to the average ages at remarriage and at divorce for 1975, an interesting comparison can be made. We saw in Table 6 that the average ages at divorce in 1975 were 35.4 and 38.3 for men and women respectively (median ages: 32.9 and 35.9) while the average ages at remarriage were 34.9 years for women and 38.3 years for men. This statistic indicates that people who remarry do so *on the average* fairly soon after divorce. The high percentage of people who remarry when they are still below thirty years of age contributes to this

13. Statistics Canada, *Marriages and Divorces, op.cit.*, Table 9, p. 25.
14. C.E. Bowerman, "Age Relationships at Marriage, by Marital Status, and Age at Marriage," *Marriage and Family Living,* 18, 1956, pp. 231-233; B. Schlesinger "Remarriage—An Inventory of Findings." *Family Coordinator,* 17, 1968, pp. 248-250.
15. Statistics Canada, *Marriages and Divorces, op.cit.*, Table 8, p. 25.

phenomenon. People who do remarry tend to be found among those who divorce *young*. Those who divorce later may take a longer time to remarry. It is probably those persons who remarry only much later or who do not remarry at all who raise the median age of the overall divorced population to 41.5 years for women and 44.4 years for men.

Another important factor in remarriages is that they have been found, in the United States, to be more vulnerable to divorce than first marriages; approximately 40% of second marriages end in divorce (as compared to the current 33-36% of first marriages). We do not, however, have the data necessary to make such a comparison in Canada. The only statistic available (Table 5) is that about 5.6% of all divorces in 1975 were redivorces.

In the following sections of this chapter, we will first look at how divorced people remarry, then at what differences and similarities there are between remarriages and first marriages, and at what the specific problems and advantages of remarriage are. We will also look at the extent to which remarriage is successful.

PATH TO REMARRIAGE

In any age bracket, divorced people have a higher rate of marriage than single people. Perhaps it is because they already have had the experience of a deep relationship and find it easier to relate to marriage than people who have never been married do. Or, perhaps, divorced people are considered more attractive partners than single persons, especially in the older age brackets. In fact, the popular literature seems to support the latter point as many women say that they would rather marry and risk divorce than remain single because a divorcée has more prestige than a single woman beyond a certain age, presumably after thirty.

The choice of a mate in a remarriage is perhaps less random and more specific than in a first marriage, in the sense that divorced persons have been through it all once, know what they like and do not like, and may be more practical in their considerations than they had been earlier. There is some evidence, although it is mainly journalistic at this time, that divorced persons tend to choose a mate who is different from their previous one, and who can fulfill needs that the first one did not fulfill.[16] One study also found that women who remarry are more dissimilar to their spouses than women who marry for the first time. "Twice-wed women experience low homogamy in both their current and first marriage."[17] The implication here is that lack of similarity is a factor in marital failure. Whatever the case is, the remarried are generally as romantic about marriage as younger people or people marrying for the first time. In fact, the element of excitement, of the sense of discovery of another person, and of romanticism is an important variable in the personality renewal that often accompanies remarriage.

We know little about remarriage, especially about specific questions such as whether there are typical patterns of first encounters between divorced people. One factor that seems fairly typical is that they become involved sexually more rapidly and that they live with their future spouse before marriage more often than was the case prior to their first marriage or even than is the case for people their age who are marrying for the first time. Often this is out of necessity, as in cases when the divorce takes a long time to be obtained. Divorced people probably have a somewhat more matter-of-fact attitude towards non-marital sex and living together than their contemporaries, in part because they have already acquired the habit within marriage itself.

In a 1952 study, Hollingshead found that the shortest period of dating and engagement in various categories of married couples was for those who had both been previously married. The entire period was shorter for them by at least eleven months than for couples who were in their first marriage.[18] Divorced persons may re-enter unions more rapidly after acquaintanceship because they have a greater need for marriage, because it is easier for them to decide to settle down the

16. L.A. Westoff, *The Second Time Around. Remarriage in America,* New York: Viking Press, pp. 33-34.
17. G. Dean and D.T. Gurak, "Marital Homogamy the Second Time Around," *Journal of Marriage and the Family,* 40, August 1978, pp. 559-570.
18. A.B. Hollingshead, "Marital Status and Wedding Behavior," *Marriage and Family Living,"* 14, November 1952, p. 310.

second time around, and because rules of social etiquette are less well established for them. Courtship is simpler, more to the point, and more overtly goal-oriented. In the same study Hollingshead even found that the wedding ceremony, and all the formalities generally surrounding and following it, were simpler by far than in first marriages.

Another matter to consider is that of those divorced persons who would like to remarry but cannot, generally because they have no way of meeting suitable persons of the other sex. The higher remarriage rate of males would seem to indicate that this lack of opportunity occurs more often among women than men, and perhaps even more among women of certain groups, such as educated black women in the U.S.A., who suffer from a scarcity of educated men at their own level, and Jewish women of a certain age and social class, because a great proportion of divorced Jewish males remarry outside their faith. However, women in general have fewer opportunities than men to meet suitable people, especially if they are not employed, are home bound, and do not have enough money either to go out or to pay for a baby sitter.

DIFFERENCES FROM FIRST MARRIAGES

In retrospect, many of the couples saw their first marriage as a kind of training school, somewhat similar to the college they had left with academic degrees but little knowledge of themselves. Divorces were their diplomas. All agreed that a second marriage was the "real thing" at last. They had entered it with much clearer ideas regarding the things that really mattered, whether those things were love, friendship, understanding, or sex.[19]

First marriages, needless to say, precede remarriages chronologically, and still make up the majority of all marriages. They are, therefore, the rule while subsequent marriages are still an exception, albeit an exception which is on the way to becoming a rule. It is, therefore, interesting to look at the similarities and differences that exist between the two.

19. Westoff, *op.cit.*, p. 40.

We must also indicate those areas where more information is needed, for there are actually no large-scale studies comparing first marriages with remarriages in terms of psycho-sociological variables. Much of what we know is simply common sense or is derived *ex-post facto* from studies on related topics.

Remarriages take place, on the average, between people who are older than the average age at first marriage. The main consequence of this is that the personalities involved are more complete, have had the time to mature and to crystallize. On the one hand, this is an advantage because the partners, or at least one of them, will change less over time. When one marries at twenty-one, it is difficult to predict how the other will be at forty. But at forty it is less difficult to predict how the other will be at sixty. Young adults (18-28) experience much pressure to change: they are just out of the family nest, out of school, beginning a new job, or working hard at building a career. These factors demand adjustments which in turn can substantially alter a personality and disrupt a marriage. In remarriages, there are fewer chances of this occurring. However, age also carries a disadvantage, as we will see in the following paragraphs.

Many remarriages involve children, whether they are in the custody of one of the remarrying partners (especially the mother) or else visiting. Although a number of first marriages also involve a pregnancy and premature parenthood, remarriages have to deal with children who have formed attachments to another parent, are older, are not necessarily cooperative and may present specific problems.

The influence and advice of the spouses' parents are probably minimal in remarriage since divorced adults have usually been on their own for a great length of time. Parents may oppose a remarriage, as they may a first marriage, for very similar reasons, but their opposition carries less weight and can do less damage unless they are playing an important role in the life of their grandchildren, or when they contribute important financial resources.

Financially, although divorced persons generally have higher paying jobs than at first marriage, some may not be richer since they may actually have to support two households. This can be a strain, as they may have been used to a certain life-style and may have to start practically from scratch again at an age at which one should start harvesting financial rewards. But remarriages often involve two adults who are both employed and a double income at a more advanced age will likely compensate during the period of time in which the other household has to be supported. Child support (and ex-spouse's maintenance) are tax-deductible and this helps to offset much of a disadvantage which is, at any rate, usually only temporary.

Another important difference in remarriage is the fact that one or both of the new partners may have suffered in the previous marriage and may either carry harmful scars or may be the wiser for it and, therefore, have more realistic expectations. The individuals in remarriage are more experienced but there is a certain edge to their experience: they have been through it before, while it is new for the couple at first marriage. Not having any basis for direct comparison, young couples may find themselves freer to experiment with various arrangements until they find the one most suitable to them, while it is possible that some divorced people have been rendered less flexible by their previous experience. On the other hand, some may have learned the virtue of flexibility. Nevertheless, it is often with a great deal of uncertainty that couples enter on remarriage, as they are often doubtful of their capacity to undertake and maintain a healthy and stable relationship.[20] Therefore, the first task of the new partners often consists of keeping the past at bay and rebuilding their self-confidence in the realm of their new relationship.[21]

Remarried couples have to find a new niche within well-established patterns of friendship, while people marrying for the first time, being younger, may have more flexibility in that they can simply make friends as their marriage develops. Each partner in remarriage brings with him or her a set of friends

20. H. Goldstein, "Reconstituted Families: The Second Marriage and Its Children," *Psychiatric Quarterly*, 48, 1974, pp. 433-440.
21. J.W. Ransom *et al.*, "A Stepfamily in Formation," *American Journal of Orthopsychiatry*, 49, January 1979, p. 38.

who may find it more difficult to accept the new partner than the old one. On the other hand, divorce often provides the opportunity to break old ties and remarriage may simply signal the beginning of the formation of a new social circle more compatible to the needs of the couple.

Another difference that seems to emerge in remarriages involves sexuality. Divorced people are more experienced, have had more partners, and have had more time to learn about their own needs and the needs of the other sex. They may have become more flexible and their repertoire is probably more varied than that of couples in first marriages. At least one study has found that, age held constant, women have intercourse more frequently in remarriages than in their first marriages.[22] After the final tense months or years of a failing marriage, in which one partner was often blamed for the lack of pleasure of the other, a new and successful sex life is a great boost to divorced persons and they are likely to place more emphasis on sexuality in their second marriage than in their first. There is generally less searching and more certainty about what one wants in remarriages and this pertains to the domain of sex as well.

However, remarriages may also pay the price of a long period of sexual inactivity imposed by a first marriage. Indeed, there are many couples who have little sexual contact in the last year or so of a failing marriage, with a spouse becoming sexually dysfunctional and at times temporarily impotent. It often takes a long time for them to re-establish their sexual needs, and the extended period of imposed abstinence may have permanently lowered their sexual capability and rendered them less adequate partners.

There are a great many questions concerning remarriage for which we have no data. For instance:

- are the partners more or less similar in terms of general background than in first marriages?

---

22. The National Fertility Study of 1970, referred to by Westoff, *op.cit.*, p. 126.

- are divorced persons influenced by the personality of their previous spouse in their choice of a second one? For instance, do they tend to look for someone different when the first spouse was especially wanting in certain areas?
- does their greater experience make them sexually more compatible or less so?
- what are the immediate causes of failure or of divorce in remarriages as compared to first marriages?
- holding constant the age of the spouses, what is the fertility rate in remarriages?
- are women in remarriages more or less likely to be employed outside their homes?
- are remarried persons more or less religious than in first marriages?
- what is the health configuration in remarriages compared to that in first marriages?
- what are the differences in life-style between couples in first marriages and remarriages?
- what are the differences in inter-action between spouses in first marriages and remarriages?
- how do sex roles and the division of labour in remarriages compare to those in first marriages?
- does the pattern of decision making differ in remarriages?

SPECIFIC PROBLEMS

We have already broached a few of the problems specific to remarriages. The first one mentioned was age: remarriages take place when individuals (or at least one of them) are older and more mature, and their personalities are more crystallized. The potential danger is that older people are more set in their ways than younger ones and may find it difficult to readjust to the habits and peculiarities of a new spouse and, at times, of a new set of children. This may be especially difficult for persons who have been divorced for a long period. Strain and tension may follow and may place a heavy burden on the relationship. It may also be that, at a certain age, if things go wrong, people are more ready to think, "I have only one life to live and, at my age, why should I put up with this?"

Children are a significant factor in a remarriage. Children who live with a new step-parent adjust better when younger and have a better chance of forming an attachment to the new person. However, teenagers and pre-teens can cause acute problems because they are older and therefore better able to create problems for the step-parent specifically and for the relationship in general. In fact, step-children may deliberately try to break up a new marriage.[23] Children may resent the new relationship for many reasons:

- the new partner seems to be taking the place of the loved natural parent;
- the new partner may take away much of the time and attention that was previously directed to the children themselves;
- the children of the woman who lives with the father of other children may be seen as direct rivals by those natural children who do not live with their father;
- the new relationship often means the establishment of new rules and the children may resent this;
- the presence of a second adult may mean that the children receive closer supervision and, again, they may resent it;
- the children may be encouraged by their other natural parent to make life miserable for the step-parent and to create guilt feelings in the mind of the parent who remarried;
- the children may even be goaded by grandparents or other close relatives who do not approve of the re-marriage and may never have accepted the divorce in the first place;
- when the children have personality or school problems, these may be blamed on the remarriage (while actually the first marriage is the culprit).

23. See Chapter 3 of C.B. Reingold, *Remarriage,* New York: Harper & Row, 1976.

These are only a few of the main reasons; there are many others, individual ones, too numerous to be enumerated here.

There are indications that the role of step-mother is a more difficult one than that of step-father, not because of the pejorative archetype, but because it is the woman who takes care of the children and therefore bears the brunt of any conflicts which arise,[24] and also because the role of step-father is socially more acceptable than that of step-mother.[25] And if children can cause strain in the new relationship, the parent and step-parent may, in turn, contribute to the problem in the following ways:

- by criticizing the natural parent who is the former spouse in front of the children;
- by disagreeing with the natural parent who lives elsewhere, thereby creating a conflict that may be reflected in the children themselves;
- by overindulging the step-children to win them over;
- by trying to reshape their lives too abruptly and in a way that is not acceptable to them, especially at the teen level;
- by favouring their own children over the step-children;
- by disagreeing with each other about child rearing, discipline, household responsibilities, curfews, etc.;
- by allowing the children to interfere with their private lives;
- by rejecting step-children because of guilt feelings about natural children living with the ex-spouse;
- by allowing children to be critical of and to disrespect the step-parent;
- by not sufficiently preparing children for the new situation.

There are specific problems depending on the structure of the household as well. For, as we saw in Chapter 4, the "reconsti-

24. J. Bernard, *Remarriage*, New York: Russell and Russell, 1971, pp. 222-223, 319.
25. C.E. Bowerman and D.P. Irish, "Some Relationships of Stepchildren to Their Parents," *Marriage and Family Living*, 24, May 1962, p. 118.

tuted family" can take any one of five different forms each with potential dangers and benefits. Apart from the last one, in which a child is born into the new family, it has been found that the combination which works out best is when both parents have children with them: parents have to structure the situation more carefully; children can find companions or complements within their groups and leave their parents alone to build up their relationship; parents do not have as many guilt feelings about absent children or about caring for step-children while feeling guilty about their own natural children whom they cannot take care of on a regular basis; spouses may receive more support and help from parents, relatives, and friends; there is less time to pay attention to the nagging of *two* ex-spouses and, in this situation, both spouses are in the same boat: they both have to tolerate ex-spouses.

It has also been found that lower-class children adjust more readily to such a reconstituted family than middle- and upper-class children. There may be several reasons for this. Lower-class children may be less selfish because they have few material possessions, are used to living in more crowded conditions, and may be more ready to share with another set of children. Lower-class persons may also have a stronger sense of family than others. It has also been found that a baby born of the reconstituted family almost always contributes to unite such a family,[26] perhaps because the baby is perceived as a symbol of the fact that the relationship is something serious and lasting; it is a child that they can all share, whereas previously the family was divided into "us" and "them." The birth of another child is also a new experience; one which creates a common culture for the family.

Children of remarriage generally do better than children who remain in an intact but unhappy first marriage and better than children who remain in a divorced situation. Remarriage ought not to be considered the problem it has been made out to be for children. It is, generally, a healthy solution, offering stability, a new sense of belonging, and additional sources of love; it is also a learning experience and this may be the reason

26. reference lost.

why children in remarriages have been found to be more self reliant than others. Parents should enter remarriage with confidence, and lay aside guilt feelings; nor should they leave room for their children to intrude into the relationship between spouses or to manipulate it.[27] Parents, relatives and ex-spouses who are non-cooperative should be kept at arm's length until their attitude mellows (and it generally does, over time). Nevertheless, the fact remains that in remarriages with children, the very presence of these children prevents the establishment of the exclusive spouse-to-spouse relationship which is the norm in our society and which generally predates parenthood.[28] In remarriages the cart is placed before the horse, so to speak, as the new spouses often become either instant parents or parents of instant, additional children.

Of the eight remarried persons I interviewed in 1979 for the purpose of gathering illustrative material, six had step-children and five of the six were very unenthusiastic, to say the least, about these children. The one person who was a happy and fulfilled step-parent had remarried a woman with a baby boy born of a casual affair after her divorce. The baby had no legal father and the man was on the way to becoming the real father. He was obviously proud of the infant and took care of him as much as the mother did as they were both employed. However, the following case is more typical.

Jane remarried, to a man called Peter, two years ago. She has a three-year-old boy from her previous marriage and her former husband has since moved back to the U.S.A. (he was a draft dodger) so that he has not maintained his relationship with his son. The boy has easily become attached to Peter who treats him as his own son. Jane is very apprecia-tive of this. Peter has two daughters from a previous marriage, aged eight and ten. While they both live with their un-remarried mother, they visit Peter each weekend. At first Jane looked forward very much to having the girls. But now, after two years, she sees the girls as a real burden to her and a threat to her remarriage. She feels that Peter spoils

27. Reingold, *op.cit.*, p. 33.
28. Ransom *et al.*, *op.cit.*, p. 37.

204 Divorce in Canada

them and gives them the run of the house. Jane feels that she is their servant. She has to pick up after them, put up with their rude behaviour, and her workload is considerably increased by their presence. Moreover, they rarely go out during weekends since Peter does not feel it is right to leave the girls alone for the few days he has them. She can never plan their weekends ahead because Peter always waits to find out what the girls will choose to do. Jane also resents the fact that the incidental budget allocated to the girls by Peter is far greater than the amount she has to spend for herself. It was obvious throughout our interview that Jane resented the children, and her husband's lack of thoughtfulness towards her in this respect, and that she welcomed the opportunity to get all of this off her chest once and for all in a context that was non-punitive.

The financial responsibility of one spouse to the ex-spouse and children may create difficulties in remarriage. First, it is a financial drain and may prevent the new couple from achieving many of the material goals they have set for themselves. Second, the new spouse may resent these payments, especially if she herself is gainfully employed and contributes to a common pool of resources: she may feel she is paying for the ex-spouse who, in turn, usually does not like her very much and may create many unpleasant situations for her through the children.

> The way I feel about it, I'm subsidizing my husband's first wife. What with alimony payments and child support, I'll never be able to stop working. And we'll never be able to afford a child of our own.[29]

This leads us to a problem typical of remarriages: the exspouse or spouses with whom one or both partners may have had children and may be supporting, in part or totally. Unless the ex-spouse is remarried, he/she is unlikely to be very enthusiastic about the remarriage, especially when children are involved. Many ex-spouses try to get back at their former

29. Reingold, op.cit., p. 92.

mates by using their children to create guilt feelings and tension in the new marriage. They may escalate their financial demands, or may restrict access to children. They may ignore the new spouse or find excuses to phone her or him and either nag that person or attack the ex-mate. The ideal situation in remarriage is probably when there are no children (or, to be quite cynical, no living ex-spouse) and no financial obligations. In these circumstances, if the ex-spouse creates difficulties for the new couple, he or she may be advised to leave the scene.

As Westoff puts it, "when one remarries, one is never alone with a new mate."

One lives with vibrations of other people who were part of one's old life and the new partner's former life. There are constant reminders of the past spent with others—portraits, photographs, monograms, laundry marks, furniture, tastes, habits—living ghosts that go along with every remarriage.[30]

The previous spouse is present in other ways as well, especially at the very beginning of a remarriage. Open comparisons are at times made, regrets are expressed about the demise of the previous relationship, attempts may be made to mold the current spouse's behaviour to those good traits of the previous one. The current spouse may even sympathize with the previous one and, in the heat of a quarrel, may exclaim, "No wonder he-she couldn't live with you!"[31] On the other hand, the previous spouse can also be an advantage to the remarriage if the comparison between the first relationship and the current one is so overwhelmingly in favour of the current one.

At the outset of a remarriage, the former spouse can exert still another type of influence by inducing, willingly or not, guilt feelings in the remarried ex-spouse. The latter may feel guilty about his/her happiness and may even consciously downplay certain aspects of the new marital life in order to

30. Westoff, *op.cit.*, p. 46.
31. Bernard, *op.cit.*, p. 5.

soothe the guilt feelings. The new partner, caught in this web of conflicting emotions, may not know how to cope, may feel rejected, and may resent the previous spouse, an act that can only aggravate an already difficult situation.

POSITIVE ASPECTS OF REMARRIAGES

One of the advantages of remarriage after divorce is that one has a basis of comparison and may therefore be more likely to appreciate the good aspects of the present relationship, especially those which were painfully lacking in the previous one. The new spouses can marvel at their "good luck" in having found each other after so many years of active unhappiness or simple emotional barrenness.

> Such is the case for John and Rita who had both been previously married for six years, were childless, and have been together for two years; he, after a three-year period of singlehood, she, after a four-year period. Being more extroverted and open, John is the one who so often marvels out loud, "All those wasted years! I wish I had met you twelve years ago!" And Rita says that he hugs her and kisses her, to her great delight, as these gestures increase her feelings of being important in his life, which is the essence of her feelings about their relationship.

However, this advantage generally tends to be a short-term one in that the new partners inevitably get used to each other and forget about the "bad old life," while also forgetting about their new blessings, and begin to take things for granted. A certain degree of routine sets in and the initial advantage disappears. Nevertheless, even if this advantage exists only temporarily, it can contribute immensely to the new relationship and boost it toward greater stability.

Another advantage of remarriage already alluded to is that generally both partners are more experienced sexually as well as maritally. Sexually, they have been able to discover many of the practices they especially enjoy and are also more willing to experiment. There may be greater variety and fewer inhibitions in their sex lives. For some, sex may have been practically non-existent in the previous marriage or else shrouded in inhibitions. These inhibitions may lead to difficulties at the outset of the remarriage. However, it is as likely that the new union will offer a loving base from which the person whose sexuality has been distorted can rebuild it with confidence. Maritally, the new partners are generally more aware of a wider range of sexual and conjugal roles and this may render them more flexible and more willing to compromise. A remarriage can be more successful because the new partners can work from experience and are aware of the potential pitfalls in such relationships. They may consciously work at avoiding those mistakes that had been detrimental to the first union. They may be more committed to the new relationship and invest more in it because they know that they cannot afford a second (or third) failure, not only for themselves but also because of family and community reaction.

When there is neither an ex-spouse nor non-resident children to support, the partners in a remarriage are usually in a better financial situation than they were in their first marriages, because they are older and are generally more established in their employment. The wife probably worked, at least between her two marriages in order to support herself, and she may be reluctant to relinquish her employment. The combination of two stable salaries raises the life-style of the pair and continues to enhance their satisfaction with each other.

Because of greater life-expectancy and the fact that first marriages are often of short duration, remarriages last longer than first marriages. In the long run, they may become *the* marriage in the spouses' lives. Bernard points out that in remarriages which are of long duration and are stable, people tend to forget that they are remarried.[32] In fact, where remarriages are stable and/or successful, a greater proportion of them will become the most common form of marriage, at least in terms of duration, because of the average age at divorce and at remarriage of the Canadian population.

32. Bernard, *ibid.*, p. 14.

Remarriages can also serve a very beneficial cathartic function for the personalities involved, especially when they have been badly hurt and egos have been deflated in the previous relationship. Many individuals come out of divorce with diminished self-esteem, a sense of being unlovable, a fear of not being able to love again, and a long list of faults they have discovered in themselves with the "help" of their previous spouse. In a remarriage, they find that they *can* love and be loved again and that they are appreciated, at times for the very same traits that had made them "unbearable" in the previous relationship. They may rebuild their self-confidence and become able to assess their own personalities more realistically, to lower their defence mechanisms, to relax, and to allow their vulnerable points to show without fear of being taken advantage of.

SUCCESS OF REMARRIAGES

In Canada, in 1975, 5.6% of all the persons who were divorcing were going through at least their second divorce. American statistics indicate a higher divorce rate for second marriages than for first marriages,[33] although not all studies are unanimous.[34] There is also evidence that the probability of divorce increases after each subsequent divorce.[35] A study carried out over twenty-five years ago found that, while first marriages had the lowest rate of divorce, they were followed by marriages in which only one partner was remarrying, while marriages in which both spouses were remarrying were the least stable.[36] More recent results would be highly desirable,

33. A. Cherlin, "The Effects of Children on Marital Dissolution," *Demography*, 14, August 1977, pp. 265-272; H. Carter and P.C. Glick, *Marriage and Divorce: A Social and Economic Study*, Cambridge, Mass.: Harvard University Press, 1976, revised edition, p. 396; L.L. Bumpass and J.A. Sweet, "Differentials in Marital Instability: 1970," *American Sociological Review*, 37, December 1972, pp. 754-766; T.P. Monahan, "How Stable are Remarriages?" *American Journal of Sociology*, 58, November 1952, pp. 280-288; "The Changing Nature and Instability of Remarriages," *Eugenics Quarterly*, 5, June 1958, pp. 73-85, and "The Duration of Marriage to Divorce: Second Marriages and Migratory Types," *Marriage and Family Living*, 21, May 1959, pp. 134-138.
34. For one study which did not find any greater probability of divorce among the remarried, see Riley and Spreitzer, *op.cit.*, pp. 66-67.
35. Cherlin, *op.cit.*
36. Monahan, 1952, *op.cit.*

since public attitudes about divorce have changed so much. Moreover, these rates of stability or instability do not tell us a great deal about the *quality* of second marriages since many first marriages which are very unhappy are never terminated for various religious and socio-economic reasons and the same may apply to second marriages. Moreover, it has been found that second marriages now last longer than they used to, compared to the first marriages of divorced people. In the U.S.A. in 1967, the average duration of second marriages was on the average four-fifths that of first marriages, among men, and of about an equal span of time for women, a substantial improvement over 1955.[37] This in part reflects the often brief duration of first marriages and increased longevity; it may also reflect the fact that remarriage is now easier for spouses because public opinion is more accepting of remarriage and because there are more divorces: hence people have a better chance of having a more durable remarriage.

In a recent study of public opinion polls carried out in the U.S.A. in 1973, 1974 and 1975, Glenn and Weaver found that, in second marriages, men were somewhat more satisfied with the marriage than remarried women were. This is also the impression I gathered in the interviews I carried out, and the major cause of unhappiness for the remarried women was their husbands' children from a previous marriage. Even in the two cases where the women felt that they liked their step-children very much, they were uneasy about the increased workload the children entailed. The husbands, even when they had step-children, were not similarly encumbered: their masculine role shielded them from these difficulties. It was also my impression that they saw their wives' situation as perfectly "normal" and had little notion of the problems the wives often faced.

However, the results of the Glenn and Weaver study were not very conclusive, and little information could be derived from them. More conclusive were results showing that women in their first marriages were more satisfied than women in subsequent marriages.[38] In a large sample of 4,452 homes in

37. J. Bernard reporting statistics in *Remarriage, op.cit.,* p. 1 of new Preface.
38. N.D. Glenn and C.N. Weaver, "The Marital Happiness of Remarried Divorced Persons," *Journal of Marriage and the Family,* 39, May 1977, p. 335.

California, Renne reported that previously divorced, remarried persons were less happy with their marriages than those who were in their first marriages.[39] Goode, however, reported a different finding, but in the context of a question designed to have the respondents *compare* their own two marriages.

What these studies indicate is that remarriage, in spite of problems and failures, offers an opportunity for many persons to rebuild a happy and satisfactory marital life. Although we have seen that there are some very specific difficulties attached to remarriage, many couples are able to circumvent them. Moreover, many couples who remarry are in a good financial situation, do not have problems with ex-spouses or children who might complicate the situation, or else have cooperative children. Their problems are fewer and, for them, the advantages or rewards of remarriage far outweigh the costs.

Cherlin has hypothesized that, by contrast with first marriages, remarriages after divorce lack institutionalized guidelines for solving problems peculiar to this type of marriage. Remarriages have a less adequate basis for family unity,[40] familial roles are less well defined and step-parents experience a great deal of uncertainty about their roles with regard to their spouse's children.[41] Nor are there rules as to "proper" conduct regarding a former spouse. In view of this lack of social support, it is surprising that remarriages are as successful as they are. We can expect, for the future, that as remarriages become more common and public reaction more favourable, remarriages will have an even better chance of being happy and durable.

CONCLUSIONS

Again, as we remarked for divorce *per se*, there are many patterns of remarriage, dependent on the socio-economic

39. K.S. Renne, "Health and Marital Experience in an Urban Population," *Journal of Marriage and the Family*, 33, May 1971, pp. 338-350.

40. A. Cherlin, "Remarriage as an Incomplete Institution," *American Journal of Sociology*, 84, November 1978, pp. 634-650.

41. I. Fast and A.C. Cain, "The Stepparent Role: Potential for Disturbances in Family Functioning," *American Journal of Orthopsychiatry*, 36, April 1966, pp. 485-491.

status of the persons involved, their age, previous marital experience, the presence of children, the relationship with former spouses, relatives and friends, the financial responsibility for another household, and the needs and personalities of the individuals involved.

Remarriage is not as problematic as in the past we were led to believe it is; this attitude was perhaps related to a general disapproval of divorce and of persons who divorce, even if they remarry. It was thought that children especially would be hurt and we have seen that this is not necessarily the case, and that sometimes the contrary is true.

In fact, a second marriage in one's middle years may be compared to a breath of fresh air in an environment that was becoming stale. Remarriage is, for many people, an opportunity for renewal, a new lease on life, a chance to rediscover the best in themselves, and the possibility of making another adult and perhaps some children happy. Remarriage is often accompanied by a general reassessment of life-style as the persons involved may regard it as a crossroad in their lives. They may wish for a change in their work environment or may adopt a less frantic and more relaxed approach to work; they may reorder their priorities and, after one marriage, may decide that this new one should be given more time so that more enjoyment will result from it. Divorce may have led some individuals into a search for themselves and this search may be brought to fruition through the new relationship.

However, there are individuals who enter remarriage defensively, mainly because they have not worked out the personal problems created by their previous union, and are ready for the worst and prepared to see in their new spouse the image of former ones. Such remarriages may never have a chance, because one of the partners remains aloof from the relationship and fears immersing himself or herself in it. As one partner strives for love and intimacy, the defensive one withdraws into a shell. Then there are those individuals who enter a remarriage just because they find it too difficult to live by themselves or because they want to spite their previous spouse or because they want to "get away from it all." Such a remarriage is given very little thought and the choice of partner may be erratic and unsatisfactory. Finally, there are those persons who have divorced once and who feel very ready, too ready, to divorce again. Such persons will never sit down and tackle their problems; they will walk out without even trying.

Just as there is a degree of pathology involved in certain first marriages, divorces, and intact but unhappy marriages, so too there is, unavoidably, pathology involved in some remarriages. However, remarriage is a rewarding experience for at least half of those who contract it. It is certainly *not* a social problem: it is a healthy reconstruction, both at the individual and at the social level. But remarriage is not the only healthy outcome of divorce: remaining single can be as rewarding a life for many persons.

9 Conclusion

What we have seen throughout this text is that individuals, whether adults or children, would be better off without unhappy marriages. It is quite clear that bad marriages are a major problem in our society, and should be labelled as such. Not only do they involve many people but the harm they inflict can be felt both at the individual and at the social level.

At the individual level, we have seen that both men and women can suffer from a vast array of problems when they are involved in detrimental marriages. These problems reduce people's personal happiness and their potential as individuals, parents, citizens, workers, and tax-payers. Children suffer immensely in such situations and their school activities, play, and social activities are affected. Health professionals, social workers, and counsellors of various kinds are called in to help the situation, but often can do little to improve the relationship that is the source of the problem. Bad marriages are therefore costly socially. And they are also costly when open marital strife, separation or divorce follow, especially under adverse socio-economic conditions. In such cases, the problems of divorce are directly related to the problem of social inequality, whether economic or sexual.

However, while we can conclude that, ideally, unhappy marriages should not exist because they constitute a real problem, we cannot conclude that divorce should not exist— because divorce is often the only way to solve the problem of a bad marriage, by ending it. While it has been observed that divorce brings many sorrows and difficulties, it has also been observed that divorce would not be necessary were bad marriages non-existent. Divorce is a mixed blessing: it involves problems but, in the long run, solves more of them than it creates. Divorce destroys only the legal marriage: the psychological and social destruction of the conjugal unit has already taken place. In fact, divorce allows for reconstruction, while, by contrast, remaining in a hopelessly unhappy marriage does not allow for anything beyond the perpetuation of a destructive liaison.

Hence the conclusions of this book; that divorce is a solution to the social problem of bad marriages. This should not be taken as a glorification of divorce. All that can be said is that divorce is a rational and logical solution to a problem, and should be viewed and studied as such.

As far as unhappy marriages themselves are concerned, there are probably few other viable solutions besides divorce once a relationship has reached a point of no return. But bad marriages are a disease that can sometimes be prevented, and such prescriptions as we could pass on can be read between the lines of the chapters on the causes of divorce. However, human nature being what it is, the occurrence of a certain number of unhappy marriages in a large society is unavoidable even in the healthiest and most enlightened of social circumstances. There will always be mismatches, couples who grow in different directions, and external influences that place a heavy strain on a relationship.

It may also be that our type of society, as implied in Chapter 3, unavoidably exacts a heavy toll in this respect. A high incidence of unhappy marriages may be unavoidable for the time being. If this is the case, high divorce rates are also unavoidable. But remarriage rates are also high and rising steadily. As Morton Hunt points out, this is not a "sign of dissatisfaction with marriage but only with unsatisfying marriage."[1] It is also an indicator that the fabric of Canadian family life is not tearing apart but that it is now made up of

1. M. Hunt, *The Affair*, New York: World Publishing Co., 1969, p. 288.

more diverse materials than it used to be.[2] Temporary instability of family units in no way correlates with the instability of the family as an institution.[3] Divorce does not represent a radical change in the institution of marriage because it is thoroughly supportive of most of its conventions.[4] We are far from the death of the family. Rather, divorce signals a possible reconstitution of matrimony, perhaps at a different level of organization.

2. For an elaboration of this and other points, see W.J. Goode, "Marital Satisfaction and Instability: A Cross-Cultural Class Analysis of Divorce Rates," *International Social Science Journal*, 14, 1962, pp. 507-526.
3. F.I. Nye and F.M. Berardo, *The Family, Its Structure and Interaction*, New York: Macmillan, 1973, p. 463.
4. M. Hunt, "The Future of Marriage," in *Choice and Challenge, Contemporary Readings in Marriage*, edited by C.E. Williams and J.F. Crosby, Dubuque, Iowa: Wm. C. Brown, 1974, p. 8.

Canadian References

Abernathy, T.J. Jr. and M.E. Arcus, "The Law and Divorce in Canada," *Family Coordinator,* 26, October 1977, pp. 409-413.

Ambert, A.-M., *Sex Structure,* Don Mills, Ont.: Longman, second edition, revised and expanded, 1976.

Awad, G.A., "Basic Principles in Custody Assessment," *Canadian Psychiatric Association Journal,* 23, November 1978, pp. 441-447.

Bracher, M.D. and P. Krishnan, "Family and Demography: A Selected Canadian Bibliography," *Journal of Comparative Family Studies,* 7, Summer 1976, pp., 367-372.

Canadian Welfare Council, *A Study of Family Desertion in Canada,* Ottawa, 1968.

Elkin, F., *The Family in Canada,* Ottawa: The Vanier Institute of the Family, 1964

Gillis, A.R., "High-Rise Housing and Psychological Strain," *Journal of Health and Social Behavior,* 18, December, 1977, pp. 418-431.

Gregory, I., "Factors Influencing First Admission Rates to Canadian Mental Hospitals III. An Analysis by Education, Marital Status, Country of Birth, Religion and Urban-rural Residence, 1950-52," *Canadian Psychiatric Association Journal,* 4, April 1959, pp. 133-151.

Grills, C.C., *Parents Without Partners,* Master's Thesis, School of Social Work, University of Toronto, 1963, unpublished.

Guyatt, D.E., *One-Parent Family in Canada,* Ottawa: The Vanier Institute of the Family, 1971.

Hansen, F.C., *Parents Without Partners,* Master's Thesis, School of Social Work, University of Toronto, 1963, unpublished.

Henshel, (Ambert) A.-M., "Swinging, The Sociology of Decision Making," in *Marriage, Family and Society,* edited by S.P. Wakil, Toronto: Butterworth, 1975.

Henshel (Ambert), A.-M., "Swinging: A Study of Decision Making in Marriage," *American Journal of Sociology*, 78, January 1973, pp. 885-891.

Henshel, R.L. and A.-M. Henshel (Ambert), *Perspectives on Social Problems*, Don Mills, Ont.: Longman of Canada, 1973.

Katz, S., in *The Toronto Star*, March 10, 1979, p. C5.

Kinesis (Vancouver, B.C.), October 1978, p. 7.

Krell, R., "This Child is Mine! The Battle Cry for Custody," *Canadian Psychiatric Association Journal*, 23, November 1978, pp. 433-439.

Llewellyn-Thomas, E., "The Prevalence of Psychiatric Symptoms Within an Island Fishing Village," *Canadian Medical Association Journal*, 83, 1960, pp. 197-204.

Meissner, M. *et al.*, "No Exit for Wives: Sexual Division of Labour and the Cumulation of Household Demands," *Canadian Review of Sociology and Anthropology*, 12, November 1976, pp. 424-439.

Offord, D.R. *et al.*, "Broken Homes, Parental Psychiatric Illness, and Female Delinquency," *American Journal of Orthopsychiatry*, 49, April 1979, pp. 252-264.

Palmer, S.E., "Reasons for Marriage Breakdown: A Case Study in Southwestern Ontario," *Journal of Comparative Family Studies*, 2, 1971, pp. 251-262.

Peters, J.F., "Divorce in Canada: A Demographic Profile," *Journal of Comparative Family Studies*, 7, 1976, pp. 335-349.

Pike, R., "Legal Access and the Incidence of Divorce in Canada: A Sociohistorical Analysis," *Canadian Review of Sociology and Anthropology*, 12, 1975, pp. 115-133.

Podoluck, J.R., *Incomes of Canadians*, Ottawa: Dominion Bureau of Statistics, 1968.

Report of the Royal Commission on *The Status of Women in Canada*, Ottawa, 1970.

Reed, P., "A Preliminary Analysis of Divorce Actions in Canada, 1969-1972," Paper presented at the Annual Meeting of the Canadian Sociology and Anthropology Association, Edmonton, May, 1975.

Robson, B., *My Parents Are Divorced, Too*, Toronto: Dorset, 1979.

Roy, L., *Le Divorce au Québec: Evolution Lente*, Gouvernement du Québec, Mars 1978.

Schlesinger, B., *The One Parent Family*, Toronto: University of Toronto Press, 1975, third edition revised.

Schlesinger, B., "Remarriage as Family Reorganization for Divorced Persons," in *The Canadian Family*, edited by K. Ishwaran, Toronto: Holt, Rinehart and Winston of Canada, 1971.

Schlesinger, B., "Remarriage—An Inventory of Findings," *Family Coordinator*, 17, 1968, pp. 248-250.

Skarsten, S., "Family Desertion in Canada," *Family Coordinator*, 23, January 1974, pp. 19-25.

Statistics Canada, Advanced Information Sheets, December 4, 1978 and September 4, 1979.

Statistics Canada, 1976 Census of Canada, *Families. Families by Number of Children*, Ottawa, 1978, Cat. no. 93-823.

Statistics Canada, 1976 Census of Canada, *Families. Families by Family Structure and Family Type*, Ottawa, 1978, Cat. no. 93-882.

Statistics Canada, 1976 Census of Canada, *Labour Force Activity, Labour Force Activity by Marital Status, Age and Sex*, Ottawa, September 1978, Cat. no. 94-805.

Statistics Canada, 1976 Census of Canada, *Population. Demographic Characteristics, Marital Status*, Ottawa, 1978, Cat. no. 92-824.

Statistics Canada, 1976 Census of Canada, *Population: Demographic Characteristics, Marital Status by Age Groups*, Ottawa, April 1978, Cat. no. 92-825.

Statistics Canada, *Vital Statistics*, volume II. *Marriages and Divorces, 1975*, Ottawa, July 1977, Cat. 84-205.

Statistics Canada, *Canada Year Book 1975*, Ottawa, December 1975.

Todres, R., "Runaway Wives: An Increasing North American Phenomenon," *Family Coordinator*, 27, January 1978, pp. 17-21.

Topp, J.L., *Parents Without Partners*, Master's Thesis, School of Social Work, University of Toronto, 1963, unpublished.

United Community Services, Vancouver, The Area Development Project, n.d.

Weissleder, W., "No-Illusion Marriage and No-Fault Divorce," *Canadian Review of Sociology and Anthropology*, 11, 1974, pp. 214-229.

Wright, E.N., *Student's Background and Its Relationship to Class and Programme in School*, Toronto: The Board of Education, 1970.

Non-Canadian References

Ackerman, C., "Affiliations: Structural Determinants of Differential Divorce Rates," *American Journal of Sociology*, 69, July 1963, pp. 13-20.

Adams, M., *Single Blessedness*, New York: Basic Books, 1976.

Adams, M., "The Single Woman in Today's Society: A Reappraisal," in *The Women's Movement*, edited by H. Wortis and C. Rabinovitz, New York: John Wiley, 1972.

Alexander, S.J., "Protecting the Child's Rights in Custody Cases," *Family Coordinator*, 26, October 1977, pp. 377-382.

Atkin, E. and E. Rubin, *Part-Time Father*, New York: The Vanguard Press, 1976.

Baber, R.E., *Marriage and the Family*, New York: McGraw-Hill, 1953.

Bacon, L., "Early Motherhood, Accelerated Role Transition, and Social Pathology," *Social Forces*, 52, March 1974, pp. 333-341.

Baguedor, E., *Separation. Journal of a Marriage*, New York: Simon and Schuster, 1972.

Balswick, J.O. and C.W. Peek, "The Inexpressive Male: A Tragedy of American Society," *Family Coordinator*, 20, October 1971, pp. 363-368.

Bane, M.J., "Marital Disruption and the Lives of Children," *Journal of Social Issues*, 1976, 32, pp. 109-110.

Bauman, K.E., "The Relationship Between Age at First Marriage, School Dropout, and Marital Instability: An Analysis of the Glick Effect," *Journal of Marriage and the Family*, 29, November 1967, pp. 672-680.

Bell, R.R., *Marriage and Family Interaction*, Homewood, Ill.: Dorsey, 1971, third edition.

Bell, R.R., "A Multivariate Analysis of Female Extramarital Coitus," *Journal of Marriage and the Family*, 37, May 1975, pp. 375-384.

Benedek, R.S. *et al.,* "Michigan's Friends of the Court: Creative Programs for Children of Divorce," *Family Coordinator,* 26, October 1977, pp. 447-450.

Benson, L., *The Family Bond,* New York: Random House, 1971.

Berger, A.S. and W. Simon, "Black Families and the Moynihan Report: A Research Evaluation," *Social Problems,* 22, August 1975, pp. 145-161.

Bernard, J., "The Paradox of the Happy Marriage," in *Women in Sexist Society,* edited by V. Gornick and B.K. Moran, New York: Basic Books, 1971.

Bernard, J., *Remarriage. A Study of Marriage,* New York: Russell & Russell, 1971 re-issue.

Biller, H.B. and S.D. Weiss, "The Father-daughter Relationship and the Personality Development of the Female," *Journal of Genetic Psychology,* 116, March 1970, pp. 79-93.

Biller, H.B., "Father Absence and the Personality Development of the Male Child," *Developmental Psychology,* 2, March 1970, pp. 181-201.

Blau, P.M., *Exchange and Power in Social Life,* New York: Wiley, 1964.

Block, J.L., *Back in Circulation,* New York: Macmillan, 1969.

Blood, R.O., Jr. and D.M. Wolfe, *Husbands and Wives,* New York: Free Press, 1960

Bloom, B.L. *et al.,* "Marital Disruption as a Stressful Life Event," in *Divorce and Separation,* edited by G. Levinger and O.C. Moles, New York: Basic Books, 1979.

Bloom, B.L. *et al.,* "Marital Separation: A Community Survey," *Journal of Divorce,* 1977, 1, Fall, pp. 7-19.

Bohannan, P., "Introduction" and "The Six Stations of Divorce," in *Divorce and After,* edited by P. Bohannan, New York: Doubleday, 1970.

Bowerman, C.E. and D.P. Irish, "Some Relationships of Stepchildren to Their Parents," *Marriage and Family Living,* 24, 1962, pp. 113-121.

Bowerman, C.E., "Age Relationships at Marriage, by Marital Status, and Age at Marriage," *Marriage and Family Living,* 18, August 1956, pp. 231-233.

Bradburn, N.M., *The Structure of Psychological Well-Being,* Chicago: Aldine, 1969.

Bralowe, M., "Runaway Wives," *Wall Street Journal,* October 1, 1975, p. 5.

Brandwein, R.A. *et al.*, "Women and Children Last: The Social Situation of Divorced Mothers and Their Families," *Journal of Marriage and the Family*, 36, August 1974, pp. 498-514.

Briscoe, W.C. and J.C. Smith, "Psychiatric Illness, Marital Units and Divorce," *Journal of Nervous and Mental Disease*, 158, 1974, pp. 440-445.

Briscoe, W., "Divorce and Psychiatric Disease," *Archives of General Psychiatry*, 29, July 1973, pp. 119-125.

Brown, P. and R. Manela, "Changing Family Roles: Women and Divorce," *Journal of Divorce*, 1, Summer 1978, pp. 315-328.

Brown, P. *et al.*, "Sex Role Attitudes and Psychological Outcomes for Black and White Women Experiencing Marital Dissolution," *Journal of Marriage and the Family*, 39, August 1977, pp. 549-561.

Bumpass, L.L. and R.R. Rindfuss, "Children's Experience of Marital Disruption," *American Journal of Sociology*, 85, July 1979, pp. 49-64.

Bumpass, L.L. and J.A. Sweet, "Differentials in Marital Instability: 1970," *American Sociological Review*, 37, December 1972, pp. 754-766.

Burchinal, L.G., "Trends and Prospects for Young Marriage in the United Sates," *Journal of Marriage and the Family*, 27, May 1965, pp. 243-254.

Burchinal, L.G., "Characteristics of Adolescents from Unbroken, Broken, and Reconstituted Families," *Marriage and Family Living*, 26, February 1964, pp. 44-52.

Burchinal, L.G. and L.E. Chancellor, "Social Status, Religious Affiliation, and Ages at Marriage," *Marriage and Family Living*, 25, May 1963, pp. 219-221.

Burchinal, L.G. *et al.*, "Marriage Adjustment Personality Characteristics of Parents and the Personality Adjustment of Their Children," *Marriage and Family Living*, 19, 1957, pp. 366-372.

Burgess, E.W. and P. Wallin, *Engagement and Marriage*, Philadelphia: Lippincott, 1953.

Burgess, E.W. and H.J. Locke, *The Family*, New York: American Book Co., 1945.

Burgess, J.K., "The Single-Parent Family: A Social and Sociological Problem," *Family Coordinator*, 19, April 1970, pp. 137-144.

Burr, W.R., "Satisfaction with Various Aspects of Marriage Over the Life Cycle: A Random Middle Class Sample," *Journal of Marriage and the Family*, 32, 1970, pp. 28-37.

Carter, H. and P.C. Glick, *Marriage and Divorce: A Social and Economic Study*, Cambridge, Mass.: Harvard University Press, 1976, revised edition.

Cassady, M., "Runaway Wives," *Psychology Today*, 42, 1975.

Cherlin, A., "Remarriage as an Incomplete Institution," *American Journal of Sociology*, 84, November 1978, pp. 634-650.

Cherlin, A., "The Effects of Children on Marital Dissolution," *Demography*, 14, August 1977, pp. 265-272.

Chiriboga, D.A. and L. Cutler, "Stress Responses Among Divorcing Men and Women," *Journal of Divorce*, 1, Winter 1977, pp. 95-106.

Christensen, H.T. and K.E. Barber, "Interfaith Versus Intrafaith Marriages in Indiana," *Journal of Marriage and the Family*, 29, August 1967, pp. 461-469.

Christensen, H.T. and H.H. Meissner, "Studies in Child Spacing: Premarital Pregnancy as a Factor in Divorce," *American Sociological Review*, 18, 1953, pp. 641-644.

Clark, R.A. *et al.*, "Husbands' Work Involvement and Marital Role Performance," *Journal of Marriage and the Family*, 40, February 1978, pp. 9-21.

Cleveland, W.P. and D.T. Gianturco, "Remarriage Probability After Widowhood: A Retrospective Method," *Journal of Gerontology*, 31, 1976, pp. 99-103.

Collins, J. *et al.*, "Neurosis and Marital Interaction: III. Family Roles and Functions," *British Journal of Psychiatry*, 119, 1971, pp. 232-242.

Coombs, L.C. and Z. Zumeta, "Correlates of Marital Dissolution in a Prospective Fertility Study: A Research Note," *Social Problems*, 18, Summer 1970, pp. 92-102.

Cutler, B.R. and W.G. Dyer, "Initial Adjustment Processes in Young Married Couples," *Social Forces*, 44, 1965, pp. 195-201.

Dean, G. and D.T. Gurak, "Marital Homogamy the Second Time Around," *Journal of Marriage and the Family*, 40, August 1978, pp. 559-570.

Derdeyn, A.P., "A Consideration of Legal Issues in Child Custody Contests," *Archives of General Psychiatry*, 33, February 1976, pp. 165-171.

Deutscher, I., "The Quality of Postparental Life: Definitions of the Situation," *Journal of Marriage and the Family*, 26, 1964, pp. 52-59.

Druckman, J.M. and C.A. Rhodes, "Family Impact Analysis: Application to Child Custody Determination," *Family Coordinator*, 26, October 1977, pp. 451-458.

Duncan, B. and O.D. Duncan, "Family Stability and Occupational Success," *Social Problems,* 16, Winter 1969, pp. 273-285.

Duselberg, R.M., "Marriage Problems and Satisfaction in High School Marriages," *Marriage and Family Living,* 24, February 1962, pp. 74-77.

Dyer, E.D., "Parenthood as a Crisis: A Re-Study," *Marriage and Family Living,* 25, May 1963, pp. 196-201.

Edwards, J.N., "The Future of the Family Revisited," *Journal of Marriage and the Family,* 29, August 1967, pp. 505-511.

Elder, G.H. and R.C. Rockwell, "Marital Timing in Women's Life Patterns," *Journal of Family History,* 1, 1976, pp. 34-55.

England, J.L. and P.R. Kunz, "The Application of Age-Specific Rates to Divorce," *Journal of Marriage and the Family,* 37, February 1975, pp. 40-46.

Epstein, J., *Divorced in America,* New York: E.P. Dutton, 1974.

Fast, I. and A.C. Cain, "The Stepparent Role: Potential for Disturbances in Family Functioning," *American Journal of Orthopsychiatry,* 36, April 1966, pp. 485-491.

Feldman, H., "The Effects of Children on the Family," in *Family Issues of Employed Women in Europe and America,* edited by A. Michel, Lieden: E.F. Brills, 1971.

Figley, C.R., "Child Density and the Marital Relationship," *Journal of Marriage and the Family,* 35, May 1973, pp. 272-282.

Fischer, A. *et al.,* "The Occurrence of the Extended Family at the Origin of the Family of Procreation: A Developmental Approach to Negro Family Structure," *Journal of Marriage and the Family,* 30, 1968, pp. 290-300.

Foote, N., "Matching of Husband and Wife in Phases of Development," *Transactions of the Third World Congress of Sociology,* 4, 1956, pp. 24-34.

Frank, S., *The Sexually Active Man Past Forty,* New York: Macmillan, 1968.

Fullerton, G.P., *Survival in Marriage,* New York: Holt, Rinehart and Winston, 1972.

Furstenberg, F.F. Jr., "Premarital Pregnancy and Marital Instability," *Journal of Social Issues,* 32, 1976, pp. 67-86.

Gardner, R.A., "Psychological Aspects of Divorce," in *American Handbook of Psychiatry,* edited by S. Arieti, vol. 1, second edition, New York: Basic Books, 1974.

Gebhard, P.H., "Postmarital Coitus Among Widows and Divorcees," in *Divorce and After,* edited by P. Bohannan, New York: Doubleday, 1970.

Gershon, E.S. *et al.*, "Assortative Mating in the Affective Disorders," *Biological Psychiatry*, 7, 1973, pp. 63-73.

Gibson, C., "The Association Between Divorce and Social Class in England and Wales," *The British Journal of Sociology*, 25, March 1974, pp. 79-93.

Ginsberg, G.L. *et al.*, "The New Impotence," *Archives of General Psychiatry*, 26, 1972, pp. 218-220.

Glass, S.P. and T.L. Wright, "The Relationship of Extramarital Sex, Length of Marriage, and Sex Differences on Marital Satisfaction and Romanticism: Athanasiou's Data Reanalyzed," *Journal of Marriage and the Family*, 39, November 1977, pp. 691-703.

Glasser, L.N. and P.H. Glasser, "Hedonism and the Family: Conflict in Values?" *Journal of Marriage and Family Counselling*, October 1977, pp. 11-18.

Glenn, N.D. and C.N. Weaver, "The Marital Happiness of Remarried Divorced Persons," *Journal of Marriage and the Family*, 39, May, 1977, pp. 331-337.

Glenn, N.D. and M.S. Keir, "Divorce Among Sociologists Married to Sociologists," *Social Problems*, 19, Summer 1971, pp. 57-67.

Glick, P.C., *American Families*, New York: John Wiley, 1957.

Glick, P.C. and A.J. Norton, "Perspectives on the Recent Upturn in Divorce and Remarriage," *Demography*, 10, August 1973, pp. 301-314.

Glueck, S. and E. Glueck, "*Unraveling Juvenile Delinquency*," Cambridge, Mass.: Harvard University Press, 1951.

Goldscheider, C. and S. Goldstein, "Generational Changes in Jewish Family Structure," *Journal of Marriage and the Family*, 29, May 1967, pp. 267-276.

Goldstein, H., "Reconstituted Families: The Second Marriage and its Children," *Psychiatric Quarterly*, 48, 1974, pp. 433-440.

Goldstein, J. *et al.*, *Beyond the Best Interests of the Child*, New York: Free Press, 1973.

Goode, W.J., "Family Disorganization," in *Contemporary Social Problems*, edited by R.K. Merton and R. Nisbet, New York: Harcourt, Brace, Jovanovich, third edition, 1971.

Goode, W.J., "Marital Satisfaction and Instability: A Cross-Cultural Class Analysis of Divorce Rates," *International Social Science Journal*, 14, 1962, pp. 507-526.

Goode, W.J., *Women in Divorce*, New York: Free Press, 1956.

Gove, W.R., "The Relationship Between Sex Roles, Marital Status, and Mental Illness," *Social Forces*, 51, September 1972, pp. 34-44.

Gove, W.R. and J.F. Tudor, "Adult Sex Roles and Mental Illness," in *Changing Women in Changing Society*, edited by J. Huber, Chicago: Chicago University Press, 1973.

Gunter, B.G., "Notes on Divorce Filing as Role Behavior," *Journal of Marriage and the Family*, 39, February 1977, pp. 95-97.

Gurin, G. *et al.*, *Americans View Their Mental Health*, New York: Basic Books, 1960.

Hagnell, O. *et al.*, "Mental Illness in Married Pairs in a Total Population," *British Journal of Psychiatry*, 125, 1974, pp. 293-302.

Hauser, R.M. and D.L. Featherman, "Equality of Schooling: Trends and Prospects," *Sociology of Education*, 49, April 1976, pp. 99-120.

Havens, E.M., "Women, Work and Wedlock: A Note on Female Marital Patterns in the United States," *American Journal of Sociology*, 78, January 1973, pp. 213-219.

Hawke, S. and D. Knox, *One Child by Choice*, Englewood Cliffs, N.J.: Prentice-Hall, 1977.

Heiss, J., "On the Transmission of Marital Instability in Black Families," *American Sociological Review*, 37, February 1972, pp. 89-92.

Heiss, J.S., "Interfaith Marriage and Marital Outcome," *Marriage and Family Living*, 23, August 1961, pp. 228-232.

Henley, L., "The Family and the Law: Selected References," *Family Coordinator*, 26, October 1977, pp. 487-518.

Herzog, E. and C.E. Sudia, "Fatherless Homes: A Review of Research," *Children*, 15, Sept.-Oct. 1968, pp. 177-182.

Hetherington, E.M., "Effects of Father Absence on Personality Development in Adolescent Daughters," *Developmental Psychology*, 7, November 1972, pp. 313-326.

Hetherington, E.M. *et al.*, "The Aftermath of Divorce," in *Mother-child, Father-child Relations*, edited by J.H. Stevens Jr. and M. Matthews, Washington, D.C.: National Association for the Education of Young Children, 1977.

Hetherington, E.M. *et al.*, "Divorced Fathers," *Family Coordinator*, 25, 1976, pp. 417-428.

Hill, C.T. *et al.*, "Breakups Before Marriage: The End of 103 Affairs," *Journal of Social Issues*, 32, 1976, pp. 147-168.

Hobbs, D.F., Jr., "Parenthood as a Crisis: A Third Study," *Journal of Marriage and the Family*, 27, August 1965, pp. 367-372.

Hobbs, D.F., Jr. and S.P. Cole, "Transition to Parenthood: A Decade Replication," *Journal of Marriage and the Family*, 38, November 1976, pp. 723-731.

Hollingshead, A.B., "Marital Status and Wedding Behavior," *Marriage and Family Living,* 14, November 1952, pp. 308-311.

Hong, L.K., "The Instability of Teenage Marriage in the United States; An Evaluation of the Socio-Economic Status Hypothesis," *International Journal of Sociology of the Family,* 4, Autumn 1974, pp. 201-212.

Horton, P.B. and G.R. Leslie, *The Sociology of Social Problems,* New York: Appleton-Century-Crofts, fourth edition, 1970.

Hunt, L.G. and L.L. Hunt, "Race, Daughters and Father-Loss: Does Absence Make the Girl Grow Stronger?" *Social Problems,* 25, October 1977, pp. 90-102.

Hunt, L.L. and L.G. Hunt, "Race and the Father-Son Connection: The Conditional Relevance of Father Absence for the Orientations and Identities of Adolescent Boys," *Social Problems,* 23, October 1975, pp. 35-52.

Hunt, M., "The Future of Marriage," in *Choice and Challenge, Contemporary Readings in Marriage,* edited by C.E. Williams and J.F. Crosby, Dubuque, Iowa: Wm. C. Brown, 1974.

Hunt, M., *Sexual Behavior in the 70's,* Chicago: Playboy Press, 1974.

Hunt, M., *The Affair,* New York: World Publishing Co., 1969.

Hunt, M., *The World of the Formerly Married,* New York: McGraw-Hill, 1966

Inselberg, R.M., "Marriage Problems and Satisfaction in High School Marriages," *Marriage and Family Living,* 24, February 1962, pp. 74-77.

Jacobson, A., "Conflict of Attitudes Toward the Roles of the Husband and Wife in Marriage," *American Sociological Review,* 17, 1952, pp. 146-150.

Jacobson, D.S., "The Impact of Marital Separation/Divorce on Children: 1. Parent-Child Separation and Child Adjustment," *Journal of Divorce,* 1, Summer 1978, pp. 341-360.

Jacobson, P.H., *American Marriage and Divorce,* New York: Rinehart, 1959.

Janov, A., *The Primal Scream,* New York: Dell, 1970.

Jenkins, R.L., "Maxims in Child Custody Cases," *Family Coordinator* 26, October 1977, pp. 385-389.

Kalter, N., "Children of Divorce in an Outpatient Psychiatric Population," *American Journal of Orthopsychiatry,* 47, January 1977, pp. 40-51.

Kelly, J.B. and J.S. Wallerstein, "The Effects of Parental Divorce: Experiences of the Child in Early Latency," *American Journal of Orthopsychiatry*, 46, January 1976, pp. 20-32.

Keniston, K., *All Our Children*, New York: Harcourt, Brace, Jovanovich, 1977.

Kephart, W.M., *The Family, Society and the Individual*, Boston: Houghton, Mifflin, 1966.

Kephart, W.M., "Occupational Level and Marital Disruption," *American Sociological Review*, 20, August 1955, pp. 456-465.

Kephart, W.M., The Duration of Marriage," *American Sociological Review*, 19, June 1954, pp. 287-295

Kephart, W.M. and T.P. Monahan, "Desertion and Divorce in Philadelphia," *American Sociological Review*, 17, December 1952, pp. 719-727.

Kerckhoff, A.C. and A.A. Parrow, "The Effect of Early Marriage on the Educational Attainment of Young Men," *Journal of Marriage and the Family*, 41, February 1979, pp. 97-107.

Kirkpatrick, C., *The Family as Process and Institution*, New York: Ronald Press, 1953.

Knox, D. and K. Wilson, "The Differences Between Having One and Two Children" *Family Coordinator*, 27, January 1978, pp. 23-25.

Komarovsky, M., *Blue Collar Marriages*, New York: Random House, 1964.

Kotelchuk, M., *The Nature of the Child's Tie to his Father*, Ph.D. Dissertation, Cambridge, Mass.: Harvard University, 1972.

Kreitman, N. *et al.*, "Neurosis and Marital Interaction: I. Personality and Symptoms," *British Journal of Psychiatry*, 117, 1970, pp. 33-46.

Kunz, P.R. and S.L. Albrecht, "Religion, Marital Happiness, and Divorce," *International Journal of Sociology of the Family*, 7, July-December, 1977, pp. 227-232.

Landis, J.T., "Social Correlates of Divorce and Nondivorce Among the Unhappily Married," *Marriage and Family Living*, 25, May 1963, pp. 178-180.

Landis, J.T., "Dating Maturation of Children from Happy and Unhappy Marriages," *Marriage and Family Living*, 25, August 1963, pp. 351-353.

Landis, J.T., "A Comparison of Children from Divorced and Nondivorced Unhappy Marriages," *Family Coordinator*, 11, July 1960, pp. 61-65.

Landis, J.T., "The Trauma of Children when Parents Divorce," *Marriage and Family Living*, 22, 1960, pp. 7-12.

Landis, J.T., "The Pattern of Divorce in Three Generations," *Social Forces*, 34, March 1956, pp. 213-216.

Langner, T.S. and S.T. Michael, *Life Stress and Mental Health: The Midtown Manhattan Study*, vol. 2, New York: Free Press, 1963.

Leavell, C., "Custody Disputes and the Proposed Model Act," *Georgia Law Review*, 2, 1968, pp. 162-192.

Lee, G.R., "Age at Marriage and Marital Satisfaction: A Multivariate Analysis with Implications for Marital Stability," *Journal of Marriage and the Family*, 39, August 1977, pp. 493-504.

Lee, R. and M. Casebier, *The Spouse Gap*, New York: Abingdon Press, 1971.

LeMasters, E.E., "Parenthood as a Crisis," *Marriage and Family Living*, 19, November 1957, pp. 352-355.

Lenski, G., *The Religious Factor*, Garden City, N.Y.: Doubleday, 1961.

Lerner, S.H., "Effects of Desertion on Family Life," *Social Casework*, 35, January 1954. pp. 3-8.

Levine, D., "Child Custody: Iowa Corn and the Avant Garde," in *The Youngest Minority*, edited by S. Katz, Chicago: American Bar Association Press, 1974.

Levinger, G., "A Social Psychological Perspective on Marital Dissolution," *Journal of Social Issues*, 32, 1976, pp. 21-47.

Levinger, G., "Marital Cohesiveness and Dissolution: An Integrative Review," *Journal of Marriage and the Family*, 27, February 1965, pp. 19-28.

Liem, R. and J. Liem, "Social Class and Mental Illness Reconsidered: The Role of Economic Stress and Social Support," *Journal of Health and Social Behavior*, 19, June 1978, pp. 139-156.

Locke, H.J., *Predicting Adjustment in Marriage*, New York: Holt, 1951.

Lowrie, S.H., "Early Marriage: Premarital Pregnancy and Associated Factors," *Journal of Marriage and the Family*, 27, February 1965, pp. 48-56.

Luckey, E.B. and J.K. Bain, "Children: A Factor in Marital Satisfaction," *Journal of Marriage and the Family*, 32, February 1970, pp. 43-44.

Luepnitz, D.A., "Which Aspects of Divorce Affect Children?" *Family Coordinator*, 28, January 1979, pp. 79-85.

Lynn, D.B., "The Process of Learning Parental and Sex Role Identification," *Journal of Marriage and Family Living*, 28, November 1966, pp. 466-470.

Maccoby, E.E., "Effects upon Children of Their Mothers' Outside Employment," in *Work in the Lives of Married Women*, New York: Columbia University Press, 1958.

Manville, W.H., "The Locker Room Boys," *Cosmopolitan*, 166, 11, 1969, pp. 110-115.

Marschall, P. and M. Gatz, "The Custody-Decision Process: Toward New Roles for Parents and the State," *North Carolina Central Law Journal*, 76, 1975, pp. 50-72.

Martindale, D., "Social Disorganization: The Conflict of Normative and Empirical Approaches," in *Modern Sociological Theory*, edited by H. Becker and A. Boskoff, New York: Dryden, 1957.

Martinson, F.M., "Ego Deficiency as a Factory in Marriage," *American Sociological Review*, 20, 1955, pp. 161-164.

McDermott, J., "Divorce and its Psychiatric Sequelae in Children," *Archives of General Psychiatry*, 23, 1970, pp. 421-428.

Mendes, H.A., "Single Fatherhood," *Social Work*, 21, July 1976, pp. 308-312.

Meyerowitz, J.H. and H. Feldman, "Transition to Parenthood," *Psychiatric Research Report*, 20, 1966, pp. 78-84.

Miller, A.A., "Reactions of Friends to Divorce," in *Divorce and After*, edited by P. Bohannan, New York: Doubleday, 1970.

Miller, B.C., "A Multivariate Developmental Model of Marital Satisfaction," *Journal of Marriage and the Family*, 38, November 1976, pp. 643-657.

Miller, W.B., "Lower Class Culture as a Generating Milieu of Gang Delinquency," *Journal of Social Issues*, 14, Summer 1958, pp. 5-19.

Mnookin, R., "Child-Custody Adjudication: Judicial Functions in the Face of Indeterminacy," *Law and Contemporary Problems*, 39, 1975, pp. 226-293.

Monahan, T.P., "When Married Couples Part: Statistical Trends and Relationships in Divorce," *American Sociological Review*, 27, 1962, pp. 625-634.

Monahan, T.P., "The Duration of Marriage to Divorce: Second Marriages and Migratory Types," *Marriage and Family Living*, 21, May 1959, pp. 134-138.

Monahan, T.P., "The Changing Nature and Instability of Remarriages," *Eugenics Quarterly*, 5, June 1958, pp. 73-85.

Monahan, T.P., "How Stable are Remarriages?" *American Journal of Sociology*, 58, November 1952, pp. 280-288.

Monahan, T.P. and W.M. Kephart, "Divorce and Desertion by Religious and Mixed-Religious Groups," *American Journal of Sociology*, 59, March 1954, pp. 462-465.

Moore, P., "Enjoying the Eccentric Family," *The Single Parent*, 15, July-August, 1972, pp. 5-7.

Morrison, J., "Parental Divorce as a Factor in Childhood Psychiatric Illness," *Comprehensive Psychiatry*, 15, 1974, pp. 95-102.

Moss, J.J., "Teenage Marriage: Cross National Trends and Sociological Factors in the Decision of When to Marry," *Journal of Marriage and the Family*, 27, May 1965, pp. 230-242.

Moss, J.J. and R. Gingles, "The Relationship of Personality to the Incidence of Early Marriage," *Marriage and Family Living*, 21, 1959, pp. 373-377.

Motz, A.B., "Conceptions of Marital Roles by Status Groups," *Marriage and Family Living*, 20, 1950, pp. 136-162.

Mowrer, H.R., *Personality Adjustment and Domestic Discord*, New York: American Book Co., 1935.

Mueller, C.W. and H. Pope, "Marital Instability: A Study of Its Transmission Between Generations," *Journal of Marriage and the Family*, 39, February 1977, pp. 83-92.

Napolitane, C. and V. Pellegrino, *Living and Loving After Divorce*, New York: Rawson Associates, 1977.

Nelson, B. *et al.*, "Neurosis and Marital Interaction: II. Time Sharing and Social Activity," *British Journal of Psychiatry*, 117, 1970, pp. 47-58.

Nock, S.L., "The Family Life Cycle: Empirical or Conceptual Tool?" *Journal of Marriage and the Family*, 41, February 1979, pp. 15-26.

Nye, F.I., "Child Adjustment in Broken and in Unhappy Unbroken Homes," *Marriage and Family Living*, 19, November 1957, pp. 356-361.

Nye, F.I. and F.M. Berardo, *The Family, Its Structure and Interaction*, New York: Macmillan, 1973.

Nye, F.I. *et al.*,"A Preliminary Theory of Marital Stability: Two Models," *International Journal of Sociology of the Family*, 3, March 1973, pp. 102-122.

O'Higgins, K., *Marital Desertion in Dublin*, Dublin: The Economic and Social Research Institute, 1974.

Orthner, D.K. *et al.*, "Single-parent Fatherhood: An Emerging Family Life Style," *Family Coordinator*, 25, October 1976, pp. 429-437.

Ovenstone, I.M., "The Development of Neurosis in the Wives of Neurotic Men," *British Journal of Psychiatry*, 122, 1973, pp. 35-45.

Pahl, R. and J. Pahl, *Managers and their Wives*, Baltimore: Penguin Books, 1971.

Pannor, H.P. and S. Child, "Impact of Divorce on Children," *Child Welfare*, 39, February 1960, pp. 6-10.

Parke, R., Jr., and P.C. Glick, "Prospective Changes in Marriage and the Family," *Journal of Marriage and the Family,* 29, May 1967, pp. 249-256.

Pearlin, L.I. and J.S. Johnson, "Marital Status, Life-Strains and Depression," *American Sociological Review,* 42, October 1977, pp. 704-715.

Pearlin, L.I. and C. Schooler, "The Structure of Coping," *Journal of Health and Social Behavior,* 19, March 1978, pp. 2-21.

Pope, H. and C.W. Mueller, "The Intergenerational Transmission of Marital Instability: Comparisons by Race and Sex," *Journal of Social Issues,* 32, Winter 1976, pp. 49-66.

Pospishill, V.J., *Divorce and Marriage: Towards a New Catholic Teaching,* New York: Herder and Herder, 1967.

Pratt, L., *Family Structure and Effective Health Behavior, The Energized Family,* Boston: Houghton Mifflin, 1976.

Preston, S. and J. McDonald, "The Incidence of Divorce Within Cohorts of American Marriages Contracted Since the Civil War," *Demography,* 16, 1979, pp. 1-25.

Rainwater, L. and K.K. Weinstein, *And the Poor Get Children,* Chicago: Quadrangle, 1960.

Ransom, J.W. *et al.,* "A Stepfamily in Formation," *American Journal of Orthopsychiatry,* 49, January 1979, pp. 36-43.

Raschke, H.J., "The Role of Social Participation in Post Separation and Post Divorce Adjustment," *Journal of Divorce,* 1, Winter 1977, pp. 129-140.

Rebelsky, F. and C. Hanks, "Fathers' Verbal Interaction with Infants in the First Three Months of Life," *Child Development,* 42, 1971. pp. 63-68.

Reed, A., *The Woman on the Verge of Divorce,* London: Nelson, 1970.

Reingold, C.B., *Remarriage,* New York: Harper & Row, 1976.

Renne, K.S., "Health and Marital Experience in an Urban Population," *Journal of Marriage and the Family,* 33, May 1971, pp. 338-350.

Renne, K.S., "Correlates of Dissatisfaction in Marriage," *Journal of Marriage and the Family,* 32, February 1970, pp. 54-62.

Riley, L. and C.E. Spreitzer, "A Model for the Analysis of Lifetime Marriage Patterns," *Journal of Marriage and the Family,* 36, February 1974, pp. 64-70.

Rindfuss, B.R. and L.L. Bumpass, "Fertility During Marital Disruption," *Journal of Marriage and the Family,* 39, August 1977, pp. 517-528.

Rollins, B.C. and H. Feldman, "Marital Satisfaction over the Family Life Cycle," *Journal of Marriage and the Family*, 32, February 1970, pp. 20-28.

Rosenblatt, P.C., "Behavior in Public Places: Comparison of Couples Accompanied and Unaccompanied by Children," *Journal of Marriage and the Family*, 36, November 1974, pp. 750-755.

Rosenthal, E., "Divorce and Religious Intermarriage: The Effects of Previous Marital Status Upon Subsequent Marital Behavior," *Journal of Marriage and the Family*, 32, August 1970, pp. 435-440.

Rosenthal, E., "Jewish Intermarriage in Indiana," *Eugenics Quarterly*, 5, December 1968, pp. 277-287.

Ross, H.L. and I.V. Sawhill, *Time of Transition: The Growth of Families Headed by Women*, Washington, D.C.: The Urban Institute, 1975.

Roth, J. and R.F. Peck, "Social Class and Social Mobility Factors Related to Marital Adjustment," *American Sociological Review*, 16, August 1951, pp. 478-487.

Rubin, L.B., *Worlds of Pain: Life in the Working-Class Family*, New York: Basic Books, 1976.

Russell, C.S., "Transition to Parenthood, Problems and Gratifications," *Journal of Marriage and the Family*, 36, 1974, pp. 294-302.

Russell, C.S., "Transition to Parenthood: A Restudy," M.A. Thesis, University of Minnesota, 1972.

Ryder, N.B. and C.F. Westoff, *The Contraceptive Revolution*, Princeton, N.J.: Princeton University Press, 1977.

Ryder, N.B. and C.F. Westoff, *Reproduction in the United States, 1965*, Princeton, N.J.: Princeton University Press, 1971.

Ryder, R.G., "Longitudinal Data Relating Marriage Satisfaction to Having a Child," *Journal of Marriage and the Family*, 35, November 1973, pp. 604-606.

Safilios-Rothschild, C., "Family Sociology or Wives' Sociology? A Cross-Cultural Examination of Decision-Making," *Journal of Marriage and the Family*, 31, 1969, pp. 290-301.

Scanzoni, L. and J. Scanzoni, *Men, Women and Change*, New York: McGraw-Hill, 1976.

Schoen, R., "California Divorce Rates by Age at First Marriage and Duration of First Marriage," *Journal of Marriage and the Family*, 37, August 1975, pp. 548-555.

Sewell, W.H. and A.O. Haller, "Factors in the Relationship Between Social Status and the Personality Adjustment of the Child," *American Sociological Review*, 24, 1959, pp. 511-520.

Shipman, G., "In My Opinion: The Role of Counseling in the Reform of Marriage and Divorce Procedures," *Family Coordinator*, 26, October 1977, pp. 395-407.

Simon, A.W., *Stepchild in the Family. A View of Children in Remarriage*, New York: Cardinal Pocket Books, 1965.

Singleton, M.A., *Life After Marriage: Divorce As a New Beginning*, New York: Stein and Day, 1974.

Spicer, J.W. and G.D. Hampe, "Kinship Interaction After Divorce," *Journal of Marriage and the Family*, 37, February 1975, pp. 113-119.

Sprey, J., "Family Disorganization: Toward a Conceptual Clarification," *Journal of Marriage and the Family*, 28, November 1966, pp. 398-406.

Srole, L. et al., *Mental Health in the Metropolis*, New York: McGraw-Hill, 1962.

Stack, C., "Who Owns the Child: Divorce and Child Custody Decisions in Middle Class Families," *Social Problems*, 23, 1976, pp. 505-515.

Steigman, J.E., "The Deserted Family," *Social Casework*, 38, 1957, p. 168.

Steigman, J.E., "Effects of Desertion on Family Life," *Social Casework*, 35, January 1954, pp. 3-8.

Stein, P.J., *Single*, Englewood Cliffs, N.J.: Prentice-Hall, 1976.

Stein, P.J., "Singlehood: An Alternative to Marriage," *Family Coordinator*, 24, October 1975, pp. 489-503.

Stetson, D.M. and G.C. Wright, Jr., "The Effects of Laws on Divorce in American States," *Journal of Marriage and the Family*, 37, August 1975, pp. 537-547.

Strauss, R., "Alcohol and the Homeless Man," *Quarterly Journal of Studies on Alcohol*, 7, December 1946, pp. 360-404.

Strauss, R. and R.G. McCarthy, "Nonaddictive Pathological Drinking Patterns of Homeless Men," *Quarterly Journal of Studies on Alcohol*, 12, December 1951, pp. 601-611.

Stroup, A.L., "Marital Adjustment of the Mother and the Personality of the Child," *Marriage and Family Living*, 18, May 1956, pp. 109-113.

Sutton-Smith, B. et al., "Father-absence Effects in Families of Different Sibling Composition," *Child Development*, 38, December 1968, pp. 1213-1221.

Sweet, J., "Differentials in Remarriage Probabilities," Working Paper # 73-29, Madison, Wis.: The University of Wisconsin, September, 1973.

Tallman, I. and R. McGee, "Definition of a Social Problem," in *Handbook on the Study of Social Problems*, edited by E.O. Smigel, Chicago: Rand McNally, 1971.

Terman, L.M., *Psychological Factors in Marital Happiness*, New York: McGraw-Hill, 1938.

Thibaut, J.W. and H.H. Kelley, *The Social Psychology of Groups*, New York: John Wiley, 1959.

Thornton, A., "Children and Marital Stability," *Journal of Marriage and the Family*, 39, August 1977, pp. 531-540.

Truxillo, D., "Child Custody: Paternal Authority Versus Welfare of the Child," *Louisiana Law Review*, 35, 1975, pp. 904-913.

Tuckman, J. and R. Regan, "Intactness of Home and Behavioral Problems in Children," *Journal of Child Psychological Psychiatry*, 7, 1966, pp. 225-233.

Udry, J.R., *The Social Context of Marriage*, Philadelphia: Lippincott, second edition, 1971.

Udry, J.R. *et al.*, "An Empirical Investigation of Some Widely Held Beliefs About Marital Interaction," *Marriage and Family Living*, 25, 1963, pp. 388-390.

U.S. Bureau of the Census, Current Population Reports, Series P-20 No. 297, "Number, Timing and Duration of Marriages and Divorces in the United States: June 1975," U.S. Government Printing Office, Washington, D.C., 1976.

U.S. Department of Health, Education and Welfare, *Divorces, Analysis of Changes, United States, 1969*, Vital and Health Statistics, series 21, no. 22, April 1973.

U.S. National Centre for Health Statistics, 1977. *Vital Statistics Report, Advance Report, Final Marriage Statistics, 1975*, Washington, D.C.: Government Printing Office.

Waller, W.W. and R. Hill, *The Family*, New York: Holt, Rinehart & Winston, revised edition, 1951.

Wallerstein, J.S. and J.B. Kelly, "Divorce Counselling: A Community Service for Families in the Midst of Divorce," *American Journal of Orthopsychiatry*, 47, January 1977, pp. 4-22.

Wallerstein, J.S. and J.B. Kelly, "The Effects of Parental Divorce: Experiences of the Child in Later Latency," *American Journal of Orthopsychiatry*, 46, April 1975, pp. 256-269.

Weed, J.A., "Age at Marriage as a Factor in State Divorce Rate Differentials," *Demography*, 11, August 1974, pp. 361-375.

Weiss, R.S., "The Emotional Impact of Marital Separation," *Journal of Social Issues*, 32, 1976, pp. 135-145.

Weiss, W.W. and H.B. Collada, "Conciliation Counselling: The Court's Effective Mechanism for Resolving Visitation and Custody Disputes," *Family Coordinator*, 26, October 1977, pp. 444-446.

Weller, L. and E. Luchterhand, "Adolescents' Perceptions of Their Parents by Social Class, Race and Parental Presence," *International Journal of Sociology of the Family*, 6, Spring 1976, pp. 283-290.

Westoff, L.A., *The Second Time Around. Remarriage in America*, New York: Viking Press, 1977.

Wilcox, M., "Child's Due Process Right to Counsel in Divorce Custody Proceedings," *Hastings Law Journal*, 27, 1976, pp. 917-950.

Wilkenson, L.K., "The Broken Family and Juvenile Delinquency: Scientific Explanation or Ideology?" *Social Problems*, 21, June 1974, pp. 726-740.

Williams, R.M., Jr., *American Society*, New York: Alfred A. Knopf, 1965, second edition, revised.

Willie, D.V., "The Relative Contribution of Family Status and Economic Status to Juvenile Delinquency," *Social Problems*, 14, Winter 1967, pp. 326-335.

Wilson, K.L. *et al.*, "Stepfathers and Stepchildren: An Exploratory Analysis From Two National Surveys," *Journal of Marriage and the Family*, 37, August 1975, pp. 526-536.

Wiseman, R., "Crisis Theory and the Process of Divorce," *Social Casework*, 56, 1975, pp. 205-212.

Woodruff, R.A., "Divorce Among Psychiatric Outpatients," *British Journal of Psychiatry*, 121, 1972, pp. 289-292.

Young, M. and P. Willmott, *The Symmetrical Family*, New York: Pantheon, 1973.

INDEX